Dedicated to all those across the planet whose visible and invisible motherhood dance
is one of courage, determination, pain, and joy in this rapidly changing world.
In celebration of the frontiers you redefine.
In solidarity with the struggles you face.
With the hope that sharing these stories brings greater clarity and connection in your journey.

MOTHERS, MOTHERING, AND GLOBALIZATION

Funded by the Government of Canada
Financé par la gouvernement du Canada

Demeter Press
140 Holland Street West
P. O. Box 13022
Bradford, ON L3Z 2Y5
Tel: (905) 775-9089
Email: info@demeterpress.org
Website: www.demeterpress.org

Demeter Press logo based on the sculpture "Demeter" by Maria-Luise Bodirsky
www.keramik-atelier.bodirsky.de

Printed and Bound in Canada

Library and Archives Canada Cataloguing in Publication

Mothers, mothering, and globalization / edited by Dorsía Smith Silva, Laila Malik and Abigail L. Palko.

Includes bibliographical references.
ISBN 978-1-77258-132-4 (softcover)

1. Mothers. 2. Motherhood. 3. Globalization.
I. Smith Silva, Dorsía, editor II. Malik, Laila, editor
III. Palko, Abigail L., editor

HQ759.M897 2017 306.874'3 C2017-906352-9

MOTHERS, MOTHERING, AND GLOBALIZATION

EDITED BY

Dorsía Smith Silva, Laila Malik, and Abigail L. Palko

DEMETER PRESS

Table of Contents

Acknowledgements

The first glimmer of this book flickered into being in October 2011 when Dorsía and Abby met each other at the annual MIRCI Conference in Toronto. Mutual scholarly interests and the kind of interesting life parallels and interconnections that can occur in a globalized world led to first a friendship and then collaboration on this volume. We are grateful to Andrea O'Reilly for nurturing a global community of matrifocal scholars, introducing us to our co-editor Laila Malik, and supporting our work on *Mothers, Mothering, and Globalization.*

We would also like to thank the contributors for their dedication and diligent commitment to the revision process and final stages of preparing the book for publication. We greatly appreciate the time that they have given to making the book a success. The stories and insights that they share here offer a multi-faceted perspective on the realities of mothering in the age of globalization.

We would also like to thank our families for cheering us on while we were working on this book, especially Antonio and Antonio Alejandro, Dunya and Alya, and John and Nora. We are grateful for your endless support and thank you from the depths of our hearts and souls.

As we were copyediting this volume in late summer 2017, a number of natural disasters caused suffering around the globe. There were landslides in the Democratic Republic of the Congo and Sierra Leone; a series of earthquakes struck Mexico; monsoons caused extreme flooding in Bangladesh, India, and Nepal; and hurricanes Harvey, Irma, and Maria made landfall in Texas,

Florida, and the Caribbean, devastating communities and entire islands. We think in particular of those mothering in the face of Mother Nature's challenges. With globalization comes increased awareness of the impact of disasters such as these upon those with the least resources, and a moral obligation to respond. If we listen carefully, maternal voices will direct our response.

Introduction

Formulating Mothers, Mothering, and Globalization

DORSÍA SMITH SILVA, LAILA MALIK, AND ABIGAIL L. PALKO

ACCORDING TO JOCELYN FENTON STITT in "Globalization and Mothering," globalization "is commonly used to refer to the rise of interdependent national economies that created a global flow of capital, people, goods, and services during the second half of the 20th century" (457). It encourages, among many aspects, "the increased movement of people for trade and work, the rise of transnational corporations and of the involvement of supranational actors and economic institutions (International Monetary Fund, World Bank, World Trade Organization, etc.) in national social policy formation" (Chavkin 6). This process has greatly affected mothers' economic, social, and political power. Although it has allowed more mothers to subvert patriarchy by entering the workforce, earning an income working outside of the home, and forming international feminist and mothering networks, globalization has also produced several tensions: "unsafe working conditions, women's labor made cheap through national and international policies, environmental damage, women's transnational migration, and a global care crisis" (Stitt 458). This complexity, we argue, is the result of the intersection of globalization and mothering, and calls for a critical conceptualization of motherhood that investigates the rich nuances of women's diverse maternal experiences. In doing so, it is our intention to further Stitt's definition of globalization by incorporating a discussion of the changing and multidimensional process of globalization as it affects mothers, mothering practices, and the feminist political economy. We hope to acknowledge and deepen understanding of the complex experiences of motherhood within a globalized social context, especially as they branch into new worlds and perspectives.

TRANSNATIONAL MOTHERHOOD

Within the narrative of mothering and globalization, one salient aspect is "transnational motherhood." Pierette Hondagneu-Sotelo and Ernestine Avila coined the term to refer primarily to "Latina immigrant women who work and reside in the United States while their children remain in their countries of origin [and who] constitute one variation in the organizational arrangements, meanings, and priorities of motherhood" (548). As an extension, transnational motherhood is now commonly associated with "mothering at a distance": "an arrangement of motherhood that has evolved in direct response to a situation where a large number of immigrant others find themselves geographically separated from their children over long periods of time" (Firth and Lavery 89). This arrangement is largely due to the demands that increased labour needs place upon the recruitment of women, especially in the sectors of childcare, domestic work, and other low-wage industries. Feminist critiques of transnational motherhood point to the inequality of entrapping women into low-wage employment, separating mothers from their children, and forcing migrant women to confront political, social, economic, sexual, and racial discrimination. Migrant women are, as a result, mistreated, devalued, and, ultimately, pitted in a global process that contributes to the larger tensions between mothering and globalization. Yet others note that transnational mothers have the opportunity to provide financially for their families and provide them with greater resources. As Hondagneu-Sotelo and Avila state, "Milk, shoes, and schooling—these are major activities of transnational motherhood. Providing for children's sustenance, protecting their current well-being, and preparing them for the future are the widely shared concerns of motherhood" (256).

Transnational motherhood, by definition, requires a conceptualization that weighs the benefits and challenges encountered by transnational mothers. Explorations of the experiences of transnational mothers must include the wider contradictions and transformations, especially as they relate to definitive claims about the sociocultural norms of maternal roles and the politics of gendered economics. Hondagneu-Sotelo and Avila illustrate this problematic framework reverberating in transnational motherhood by stating that "the idea of biological mothers raising their own children is widely held but it also widely broken at both ends of the class spectrum. Wealthy elites have always relied on others—nannies, governesses, and boarding schools—to raise their children, while poor families often rely on kin and 'other mothers'" (557). As Heather Millman notes, contemporary notions of motherhood are shaped for transnational mothers by globalization, the feminization of migrant caregiving work, and the interplay between traditional and new gender roles (80). Transnational motherhood has myriad implications, and we must widen our critical examination to incorporate gender, migration, labour, mothering, and social, economic, racial, and political conditions to address the complexities of transnational motherhood.

One significant and well-examined result of globalization and transnational motherhood has been the globalization of care work. At the turn of the century, Arlie Hochschild, concerned about the impact of transfers of care work from poorer women to richer women, understood the global care chain as "personal links between people across the globe based on the paid or unpaid work of caring" (131). Describing the interplay between care work and social policy, Nicola Yeates adds that "As a key dimension of reproductive labour, care occupies an important position in social policy because of what its social organization reveals about the nature of social relations and practices as well as of welfare formations more widely" (136). As families are split by the migration inherent in the global care chain, social problems manifest themselves in new ways.

The interaction of mothering practices, globalization forces, and social problems is influenced by the realities of the global care chain, as women are forced to earn money by seeking employment performing care work for other women's families. The collective acquiescence to this economic structure reflects a global lack of commitment to mothers and children. This less than wholehearted support for the needs of those mothering, in turn, becomes tacit approval of the social policing that posits mothers and their behaviour as a social problem. Furthermore, national emphasis on women's literal reproductive work in service of the metaphorical reproduction of the nation continues unabated in the era of globalization (and in fact, takes on new resonance). These factors coalesce to shape the ways that women experience mothering in the face of social problems—most notably in the ways their mothering practices are perceived as social problems.

WRITINGS ABOUT MOTHERING AND GLOBALIZATION

Texts on mothering and globalization predominantly consider the effects of globalization upon mothers, especially regarding migration, technology, employment, reproduction, childcare, childrearing, education, health care, social and political concerns. *Mothers, Mothering, and Globalization* extends this tradition by not only examining the institution of motherhood but confronting the complexities and intersectionalities of mothers in the contemporary era of globalization. We acknowledge the overlapping perspectives and representations of motherhood and their interrelationships with globalization. We call for new models to understand the transformative and agentic potential of motherhood in a globalized world.

MOTHERING, GLOBALIZATION, AND IDENTITY

In Section I of *Mothers, Mothering, and Globalization*, writers explore how mothering and motherhood are shaped by the factors of globalization, and how this ultimately influences the changing landscape of identity. Writers here expose the intersections of multiple identities and identify ways that mothers, mothering, and motherhood form bridges across globalization. Examining cinematic portrayals of the recent explosion of female migrant workers and global care chains, Dwayne Avery's opening chapter aims to point out the importance of cinema as an important vehicle for disseminating and reflecting changes in the way that motherhood, mothering practices, and domestic femininity are perceived and practiced by societies. Through an exploration of Hollywood as well as independent films on the subject, Avery asks how cinema has adapted to a new transnational breed of mothers—whether representations of transnational mothers complicate the traditional good-bad mother duality and whether these representations depict gendered, ethnic, and racial differences in the image of transnational motherhood. His findings point to what he describes as a new climate of ambivalence facing transnational mothers who participate in global care chains, wherein the narrative desire to blame transnational mothers for perceived transgression remains firmly in place, despite an ongoing redefinition of what makes a good mother.

Elizabeth Cummins Muñoz's chapter offers a poignant examination of the narratives of two immigrant women who work as nannies in Houston, Texas. Cummins Muñoz explicates the experiences of these women as workers and mothers in a transnational economy. The chapter exemplifies the connections between motherhood and the economic worth of immigrant care work in a transnational context, and presents a theoretical framework entrenched in cultural narratives of motherhood, women's transnational domestic labour, and transnational motherhood.

In her chapter, Roxana Cazan situates her reading of Michele Coomber's documentary *Trial of a Child Denied* (2011) within the context of nationalistic rhetoric about Roma identity and Roma women's reproductive activities. Through a rhetorical reading of the documentary, Cazan explores the question of who has the power to decide which women should bear children. As Cazan points out, this policing of an ethnic group's reproduction is not limited to the Czech response to Roma women. Across the globe, ethnic minorities face efforts, both rhetorical and legislative, to suppress their childbearing—suppression permitted and even encouraged by the homogenizing forces of globalization.

Focused on the discursive and practical outcomes of sharing mothering stories from beyond the physical boundaries of a homeland, Sucharita Sarkar is interested in how online spaces are used by middle-class, diasporic Indian mothers to grapple with hegemonic narratives of good Indian motherhood and articulate the challenges of mothering in globalized situations. In her chapter, she examines two diasporic Indian mothering community blogs—with contributors based in Canada, the United States, Australia, Europe, and India—through the lens of maternal resource, resistance, and recreation. She also compares and contrasts the complex ways writers reproduce and disrupt the dominant narrative, which move beyond the silent and subjugated Indian mother for the emergence of and connection between a multiplicity of new diasporic maternal voices, meanings, and practices across geographically dispersed Indian communities.

Just as it does for Sarkar, online platforms provide Gavaza Maluleke a fertile site for exploring the dynamic construction, disruption, and reformulation of diasporic and transnational mothering practice and performance in the context of globalized movement. In her chapter, she reflects on the experiences of mothering and motherhood by African migrant women living in Europe in the online platform called *African Women in Europe* (AWE). Maluleke uses a transnational feminist perspective to look at the various strategies that migrant women share, question, and rebuild to mother in dramatically new and different geographical contexts. The forum discussions of AWE network members showcase their diverse perspectives and experiences as mothers from different African countries, all currently situated in various countries in Europe. Maluleke highlights various points of their intersectionality—women, African, residents of Europe—and examines how they build solidarity through a shared experience of marginalization.

In her chapter, Aimee Tiu Wu describes herself as a "tigerish mom" who formulates her life as a second-generation Chinese woman, mother, academic, wife, and daughter-in-law through her ambivalences about Western models of parenting and considerations of her different cultures. Tiu Wu argues that her perspective as a bicultural academic woman contributes to the discussion on mothering dynamics, and lays the groundwork for illustrating the everyday realities of the feminist practices of mothering and parenting, especially in a multigenerational Chinese household. In her narrative, she provides an in-depth perspective on redefining motherwork and emphasizes her personal journey as an Asian immigrant educated in North America and as a young mother raising her children in the West.

The section concludes with Michelle Hughes Miller's chapter in which she uses content analysis to explain the context of women's empowerment across international development efforts enacted by the United Nations and its affiliates since 2000. Miller articulates an inherent paradox in the formation of Western feminist messages for equality, which often negate transnational feminist arguments and approaches that place mothers, mothering, and motherhood in a place of central importance within the global community. In addition, she stresses that maternal theory and transnational feminisms should assess transnational platforms, particularly in light of women's empowerment and global transformation.

INTERLUDE

Jessica Adams's personal essay provides an interlude between the two sections of this volume. In "At Sea," Adams reflects on her experience mothering while living on a boat, and notices how moving beyond national borders stripped mothering down to its bare essentials. Not only did Adams locate herself outside the privileges associated with mothering in a Western context, but she was also, in her words, "scrubbed of the markers that separated myself from a perceived other." It is, of course, never possible to completely eliminate privilege: as much as Adams and her family live with and among the people whose lands they sail to, they sail with the knowledge that they come from somewhere else. "At Sea" serves as a bridge between this volume's interrogations of the ways globalization affects maternal identities and the ways national identity intersects with globalization to shape maternal work. Adams's efforts to strip away nation and cultural identity illustrate poignantly their profound impact on mothers and their mothering work.

MOTHERING, GLOBALIZATION, AND NATION

On a more physical and functional level, the nation-state poses enduring physical constraints and possibilities to mothering practice and performance within this era of accelerated globalization. At the same time, as contributor Jocelyn Celero points out, motherhood has also been historically and culturally defined as women's role in building nation-states and societies. The chapters in Section Two grapple with the changing, reciprocal relationship between mothering and the nation-state in the context of globalization through examining both the impact of external factors and mothers' actions. They identify ways that external factors like socioeconomic class and national legislation around citizenship, denizenship, and permanent residence create constraints and opportunities for individual mothering practices, as well as ways in which mothers are creating, reproducing, and disrupting the nation-state itself through individual choices and collective action.

Abigail L. Palko's chapter discusses the entrenched complexities of abortion politics in Edna O'Brien's *Down by the River* (1997). Irish policies surrounding childbearing create state-sanctioned and state-enforced reproduction, at times shaping women's sexuality, mothering, and their relationship to the Irish Republic. Palko explains how geopolitical and economic global events foreground O'Brien's text, especially regarding the novel's exploration of the impact of globalization upon reproductive labour. These ramifications, as Palko argues, are an important area of inquiry in feminist analyses of the globalization of motherhood and its effects on women's mothering practices and understandings of mothering.

Jocelyn Celero's chapter explores the dynamic reciprocity of constructions of nation-building and mothering. Starting with the premise that motherhood is a crucial practice through which women activate membership to society, Celero examines the intersection between motherhood, citizenship, and migration in the life narratives of Filipina women leading transnational Japanese-Filipino families. Understanding Filipina migrant women as "transborder citizens whose lives are influenced by legal pluralisms," she highlights a mixed picture through which these mothers (re)configure Japanese and Filipino citizenship, denizenship, and transmigrant identity in family life. Along with mothering their own children and as a result of the network of legalistic constraints imposed by the nation-state, Celero argues that Filipinas mothers in Japan are mothering two nations, with complex implications for both.

Catherine Marsh Kennerley explores another form of tension within maternal activities in "A Motherhood Manifesto: Ivy Queen's Vendetta." In her chapter, Kennerley details the backlash experienced by reggaetón star Ivy Queen when she announced her pregnancy and analyzes her response. Shut out of the music scene because she was pregnant, Ivy Queen chose to embrace this new facet of her identity and integrate it into her music; she refused to surrender her professional identity to the performance of patriarchal, institutionalized motherhood.

Although this manifestation of positioning mothering as a social problem may seem different than the one explored by other writers in this section, a careful reading of these chapters reveal underlying commonalities that offer important insights into the ways that maternal work is affected by globalization. For instance, Ivy Queen explained the emotions driving the title track of her album *Vendetta* as follows: "I was venting about the fact that because one is a woman, it doesn't mean that by becoming a mother one dies, it doesn't mean that when one is a mother one has to leave behind one's dreams because now the kids are there ... I wanted to vent about attacks that were being made against me, for being pregnant and wearing heels." Likewise, other chapters in this section identify a pervasive concern that globalization positions mother and citizen as incompatible identities, which may then lead to the policing of mothers' actions to ensure they do not cause social problems. The end result is not only the lack of autonomy for women and mothers, but also false perceptions of compatibility of motherhood and citizenship.

The extent to which class realities inform such autonomy is one of Kezia Batisai's preoccupations. Batisai maps the maternal choices of Zimbabwean migrant women in South Africa, and looks at the impact of class on the mothering choices of three categories of Zimbabwean migrant women in Johannesburg. With the rise of South Africa as a major transnational destination for migrants from different African countries, Batisai points out that earlier, male-centric migration patterns have been disrupted and replaced by the influx of Zimbabweans of all genders, marital statuses, age groups, and diverse professional backgrounds. Drawing on six months of fieldwork with Zimbabwean migrant women in Johannesburg, Batisai examines the experiences of mothers who migrated with their children, those who left their children in Zimbabwe, and those who have deferred the choice to become mothers altogether in favour of pursuing their careers. What emerges is a complex picture of sharply contrasting experiences, opportunities, and choices that are profoundly shaped by the class realities of the groups in question.

Crystal Whetstone shifts the focus from the impact of the nation on globalized mothering experience and practice to the ways in which mothers are collectively making use of new methods and old ideas about motherhood to disrupt the traditional construct of nation and gain access to male-dominated political decision-making spaces. Building upon the model of Sara Ruddick's *Maternal Thinking: Toward a Politics of Peace* (1995), Whetstone examines the transnational maternal activism of the Mano River Women's Peace Network (MARWOPNET) and the West African Women in Peacebuilding (WIPNET) Network. In addition, she examines how globalization—specifically, the rise of transnational advocacy networks (TANs) of mothers in Western Africa—opens up new spaces for asserting collective maternal power to challenge and participate in national processes. She also traces how women from different countries in the Mano River region came together with different religious communities in Liberia as TANs at different moments of state conflict and used evocative symbolic and practical tools (such as public shaming, sex strikes, and collective weeping) to be heard and secure a seat at the conflict resolution table. As Whetstone demonstrates, the power of maternal framing in TANs can be significant, and experimentation with this approach warrants much further investigation.

The concluding chapter returns the focus to care work and the impact of globalization and migration on mothering practices. Dorsía Silva Smith's reading of Edwidge Danticat's *Breath, Eyes, Memory* (1994) serves to illustrate the difficulties faced by transnational mothers who have migrated in search of higher paying employment and have left their children behind in their home countries in the care of female relatives. She argues that there is an inherently contradictory process in transnational mothering, which forces these mothers and their children to address the realities of transnational experiences and navigate the trauma within the transnational process. As Smith demonstrates, the transnational nature of Martine and Sophie's mother-daughter relationship in *Breathe, Eyes, Memory* is the vehicle by which Martine's trauma is transposed onto Sophie, perpetuating it across generations.

Smith highlights one of the challenges posed by mothering and globalization, breaking a cycle of trauma. This is an incredibly difficult undertaking: the negative secondary repercussions can be minimized if the actual primary impact can also be minimized, as we see in Sophie's ability to protect her daughter from the trauma. Her effort is only made possible because she herself has gained currency in the realm of globalized mothering.

CONCLUSION

The chapters of *Mothers, Mothering, and Globalization* examine the diverse and complex experiences of motherhood and mothering from a broad interdisciplinary perspective. The collective analysis of how globalization influences the lives of mothers—especially regarding cultural, political, historical, social, and economic factors—reveals both the pressures exerted on mothering practices by the forces of globalization as well as the ways women assert their needs, desires, and own perceptions of good mothering in the face of these pressures. The collection also surveys multiple approaches to mothers, mothering, and globalization, and contributes to a nascent dialogue through its interrogation of the impact of globalization on mothers and mothering practices through the lenses of feminist ideologies, literary criticism, and cultural, social, and economic analyses.

As we compiled the chapters of this manuscript, we have had to contend with the recent political and geopolitical events throughout North America and Europe which suggest several changes in globalization and a turn toward nationalization ("Is This the End?"). Whether or not this prognostication holds true, the impact of the past few decades of globalization on mothers and mothering will not disappear. The most notable of these are the ways the concentration of capital and employment in the north has marginalized families in the south, who in turn have radically restructured their living arrangements in response, as many migrated for paid care work (Millman 72). Although scholarship tends to describe changes to migration as the "feminization of migrant labour," this obscures the ways migrant labour has been "maternalized" and the subsequent effects on mothers and their children. The chapters that follow give voice to the multiple constructions of their varied experiences and probe the tensions associated with global situations and motherhood.

WORKS CITED

Chavkin, Wendy. "The Globalization of Motherhood." *The Globalization of Motherhood: Deconstructions and Reconstructions of Biology and Care*, edited by JaneMaree Maher and Wendy Chavkin, Routledge, 2010, pp. 3-15.

Firth, Claire H., and Jane E. Lavery. "Transnational Motherhood in Brazilian Community in South-eastern Massachusetts." *Immigration: Views and Reflections—Histories, Identities and Keys of Social Intervention*, edited by Rosa Santibáñez and Concepción Maiztegui Oñate, University of Deusto, 2006, pp. 89-119.

Hochschild, Arlie R. "Global Care Chains and Emotional Surplus Value." *On the Edge: Living with Global Capitalism,* edited by Will Hutton et al., 2000, pp. 130-146.

Hondagneu-Sotelo, Pierrette, and Ernestine Avila. "'I'm Here, but I'm There': The Meanings of Latina Transnational Motherhood." *Gender and Society*, vol. 11, no. 5, 1997, pp. 548-71.

"Is This the End of Globalization." *Marsh*, 2017, https://www.marsh.com/content/dam/marsh/Documents/PDF/US-en/Political%20Risk%20Map%202017%20Globalization-02-2017.pdf. Accessed 20 Apr. 2017.

Millman, Heather L. "Mothering from Afar: Conceptualizing Transnational Motherhood." *Totem: The University of Western Ontario Journal of Anthropology*, vol. 21, no. 1, 2013, pp. 72-82.

Ruddick, Sara. *Maternal Thinking: Toward a Politics of Peace.* Beacon, 1995.

Stitt, Jocelyn Fenton. "Globalization and Mothering." *Encyclopedia of Motherhood,* edited by Andrea O'Reilly, Sage, 2010, pp. 457-61.

Yeates, Nicola. "Global Care Chains: A State-of-the-Art Review and Future Directions in Care TransnationalizationRresearch." *Global Networks*, vol. 12, no. 2, 2012, pp. 135-54.

I.
MOTHERING, GLOBALIZATION, AND IDENTITY

1. Mothering from Afar

Cinema and the Ambivalence of Transnational Motherhood

DWAYNE AVERY

DOMESTIC CARE IN AN AGE OF TRANSNATIONALISM

IN THE OPENING OF HER ESSAY, "America's Dirty Work: Migrant Maids and Modern-Day Slavery," Joy M. Zarembka provides this unsettling observation about the harsh realities facing domestic workers in America: "Tucked behind the manicured lawns and closed doors of our wealthiest residents live some of the most vulnerable people in the United States: abused migrant domestic workers, who are sometimes the victims of slavery and human trafficking" (142). Similarly, in her study of the global city, Saskia Sassen notes a dramatic increase in the creation and facilitation of an unjust global care industry, as cheap domestic labour is sold to what she calls the "professional household without a wife"—a group of busy, urban professionals, who are unable to take care of household duties on their own. "As a consequence," Sassen writes, "we see the return of the so-called serving classes ... and these classes are largely made up of immigrant and migrant women" (376).

Over the past few decades, a burgeoning literature has emerged around the claim that postindustrial societies are experiencing a "care crisis"—a shortage of workers to perform intimate and affective modes of work, from caring for small children to assisting with the elderly. In response to this so-called crisis, countries, such as the U.S., Canada, Denmark, Sweden, and the UK, have come to rely on the import of female migrant care workers, usually from the Global South, to meet their care needs. Undoubtedly, transnational domestic labour represents one of the most pressing issues of globalization, as women now make up over half of all global migrant workers. Moreover, although increases in transnational care workers create many benefits for families, especially as more women are given the opportunity to enter the labour market, the globalization of care workers fosters new, complex terrains of power that leave many workers hopeless and vulnerable (Eckenwiler 7-9). One figure that exemplifies the global precarity involved in this "care crisis" is the transnational mother. As Arlie Hochschild makes clear in her work on global care chains, the transnational provision of motherly care—whether in the form of hired nannies or daycare workers—has created a commodified care industry that reinforces geopolitical inequalities: whereas those on top of the global care chain benefit directly from the sale of domestic labour, those on the bottom are, all too often, treated poorly and suffer from their role as "emotional labourers." As Nicola Yeates, professor of social policy, writes,

> Global care chains reflect a basic inequality of access to material resources arising from unequal development globally but they also reinforce global inequalities by redistributing care resources, particularly emotional care labour, from those in poorer countries for consumption by those in richer ones. Thus, the emotional labour involved in caring for children of parents further down the chain is displaced onto children of parents living further up it. Global care chains, then, are a mechanism for extracting "emotional surplus value." (373)

Although the rise in transnational care workers has been the source of much recent theorization, little has been written about the role popular culture, especially cinema, plays in narrating the shift to a global care society. This is unfortunate, since cinema, with its long history of visualizing the home's gender inequalities, has been instrumental in registering and reacting to changes in the perception and practice of female domesticity. In this chapter, I wish to fill this void by looking at how recent cinema represents domestic care workers, especially the figure of the transnational mother. Historically, popular cinema has relied on the good-bad mother dichotomy to promote a hegemonic view of domesticity, which limits the subjectivity of mothers: mothers are either heroically praised for their self-sacrifice or they are demonized for their pursuit of individual desire, as if the search for female pleasure posed a direct threat to the welfare of the family. Within many contemporary narratives, however, this dichotomy no longer holds, as the transnational mother provides an ambivalent and, at times, liberating model of mothering that straddles multiple locations, mothering practices, and emotions. Both here and there, both liberated and subjugated, both a hard-working breadwinner and a self-sacrificing, emotional caretaker—the transnational mother embodies the hope and despair bound up with global care industries. Yet, as I hope to show, while the transnational mother provides new representational terrain for cinema by redefining what makes a good mother, the old dichotomy blaming mothers for society's problems remains firmly intact. In her search for a better life, the transitional mother may enjoy the economic freedoms from working abroad, but she does so at a major cost: relegated to the new serving classes, she must face a care industry intent on exploiting her affective labour.

IN NEED OF HELP: CINEMA AND THE RISE OF THE DOMESTIC CARE WORKER

Given the recent increase in domestic care workers, it is not surprising that popular culture has capitalized on the figure of the domestic labourer. The popularity of films and television shows—such as *Downton Abbey* (2011-2015), *The Help* (2011), *The Nanny Diaries* (2007), *Nanny McPhee* (2006), *Spanglish* (2004), and *Maid in Manhattan* (2002)—have helped shed light on a domestic figure that traditionally lurks in the background. Domestic maids and nannies are rarely perceived as characters worthy of the Hollywood limelight. As Suzanne Leonard writes:

> The figure of the domestic worker has long existed at the margins of American cinema: the glimpses viewers catch of her are fleeting at best, as she traipses through rooms,

> carrying trays of food ... caring for children outside the central activity of the home, and, indeed, the narrative. While this tendency to acknowledge elliptically the labour of the domestic all the while denying her a full subjectivity has surely not abated, American mass culture has witnessed an unprecedented rise in popular representations of maids and nannies, figures who remain paradoxically visible and invisible at the same time. (107)

As Leonard makes clear, popular culture provides a double reading of the domestic care worker. On the one hand, by shedding light on the hidden and neglected lives of domestic workers, popular culture creates new narrative possibilities for representing the inequalities facing working women, especially the social injustices associated with global care chains. Indeed, by bringing labour to the forefront, cinema recasts the domestic worker as an affective instance of alienated capitalistic labour: she is someone who, by being consumed by the task of caring for others, finds herself not only alienated from herself but from the loved ones around her. On the other hand, by treating the domestic labourer as a sentimental, even glamourous figure, popular narratives tend to obfuscate the tangible, everyday realities facing the new serving classes, as Hollywood provides a mythic and fantastical image of the female pleasures involved in domestic work.

An excellent example of cinema's double role in coding domestic care workers involves the Hollywood film *Spanglish*. Released in 2004, *Spanglish* is not only one of the few "nanny films" focusing on the widespread immigration of Latino care workers to America, but it gives an unprecedented voice to the figure of the transnational mother. Whereas most "nanny films" depict white, middle-class care workers, who use their pleasurable and fleeting experiences in domestic labour to rise to bigger and better things, *Spanglish* differs in its apposite use of a transnational perspective to contrast the mothering practises of different nationalities and cultures. Ernestine Avila and Pierrette Hondagneu-Sotelo's seminal essay on the transnational mother (1997)—a global, mothering identity that provides an alternative model of caretaking—offers a clear lens through which to consider *Spanglish's* treatment of domestic labour. Whereas the dominant U.S., white, middle-class model of the good mother is aligned with the nurturing prowess of the domestic housewife, the transnational mother, who finds work abroad to care for her family, is entrusted with two competing parental responsibilities: the financial pursuits of breadwinning and the emotional task of caring and nurturing her children. As we will see, while this combination of traditionally displaced labour activities provides the transnational mother with a series of overwhelming challenges, it is also the principal way in which she exercises her radical subjectivity. For by merging the bread-winning labour traditionally reserved for men with the affective labour of maternal caretaking, the transnational mother offers a hybrid model of mothering that bypasses the hegemony of earlier gendered dichotomies.

Undoubtedly, *Spanglish* foregrounds the financial dreams of the transnational mother. Flor, the film's main character, is represented as a hard-working, self-sacrificing mother, who hopes to give her daughter a better future by moving to America. Both moral guardian and financial gatekeeper, Flor encapsulates the mothering practises of the transnational mother, as she is forced to conjoin the responsibilities of breadwinning with the emotional care of her daughter. The problem with this representational strategy, however, is that aside from this rudimentary narrative device (the immigrant's pursuit of the American Dream), the film does little to tackle the real-world image of the suffering transnational mother, who must endure the emotional, mental, and physical hardships of being separated from her children. Indeed, as with many popular portraits of the domestic care worker, *Spanglish* offers a guilt-free, aseptic image of the migrant worker, whose desire for a new life in a foreign country is ripe with excessively romanticized plot lines and melodramatic spectacle. Everything about Flor's life as a nanny, for example, exudes with sensual romance and senseless frivolity. While the film tries to convince the viewer that Flor's greatest struggle entails instilling in her daughter a love of working-class values, this is merely the cover for something far more conservative: Flor's real challenge involves resisting the heterosexual communion typical of the romantic comedy, as she desperately fights to avoid falling in love with Adam Sandler's character (a sensitive father who shares Flor's sentiments on parenting). Here, Flor's experiences inside America's "manicured lawns" appear more like the kitschy dream-world of the van Trapp family than the gloomy world of alienated affective labour associated with the commodification of care.

In "Ready-Maid Postfeminism?," Susanne Leonard acutely observes that what is at stake in many films about domestic labour is the way in which anxiety over the migrant worker is evaded by coding the nanny as young and desirable. Equally important is attending to the neoconservative way white, upper-class women are represented through a backlash sensibility, whereby it is the affluent career woman who represents the largest threat to the family's cosmic order. In *Spanglish*, for example, Flor's moral superiority over her employer, Deborah, is demonstrated not only through her working-class, self-sacrificial attitude but, more importantly, her maternal plenitude. Unlike Flor, whose motherly goodness and warmth is immeasurable, Deborah is depicted as a parental degenerate, a hysterical career woman who is only concerned with herself. According to Leonard, Deborah is the "insufferable, upper-class, white woman"—a stock character found in many romantic comedies, whose sole purpose is to draw the viewer's attention to the domestic help's caring and nurturing sensibilities. As Leonard writes, Deborah's individual and parental subjectivity coalesces around her vanity:

> As it pertains to the body, she exercises obsessively. In her sexual relationships, she oozes self-absorption: she worries over petty love affairs or stalled romances, she steals other people's lovers and/or she overinvests in her sexual pleasure while forgetting her partner's. She routinely neglects her family, rarely knows her children's whereabouts and fails to support or even care about their emotional wellbeing. Consumed by her own life, she also treats her help badly, ignoring them, and calling them by the wrong names. (116)

Leonard's analysis of domestic help in the romantic comedy

rightly demonstrates the ways in which the figure of the nanny reinforces the hegemonic dichotomy of the good-bad mother. In *Spanglish*, however, an interesting reversal takes place, a repositioning of the migrant worker that only appears to take her plight seriously. Whereas the good mother is traditionally depicted as a white woman of privilege—the familiar mythic image of suburban domesticity—in *Spanglish* it is the migrant "other" who must come to the rescue and educate the ambitious career woman about her parental misgivings. However, this heroic role should not be misconstrued as a moment of victory for the domestic underclasses. Her rise to prominence does not serve to document or critique the injustices endured by domestic care workers; rather her purpose is far more insidious: the domestic worker is there to enforce the conservative traits of domestic femininity. As Leonard writes, the function of the "nanny" is to ensure that viewers recognize that the emotionally healthy woman is always domestically inclined.

Near the end of her essay, Leonard mentions briefly that not all "nanny films" subscribe to this hegemonic narrative structure. Other films, like the documentary *Maid in America*, give credence to the real woes and tensions facing migrant care workers. In the next part of this chapter, I consider some of these other, more promising films and look to see if the backlash sensibilities found in the romantic comedy are present in other film styles and genres. For example, in the past decade, a wide range of foreign and independent films—such as *Ilo Ilo* (2014), *Mammoth* (2009), *Babel* (2006), and *Mother Nanny* (2006)—have emerged that provide a much more nuanced and critical account of the trials and tribulations experienced by migrant mothers.

Whereas the romantic comedy sidesteps the everyday realities facing domestic workers by codifying the help as young and desirable, films such as *Babel* and *Ilo Ilo* explore the ambivalent subjectivities sustained by transnational mothers, who must leave their children behind to find work abroad. As such, many of the questions avoided by the romantic comedy (power, race, class) hold more weight in these films, as they examine both the humiliations and hopeful possibilities that come from mothering from afar.

AWAY FROM HOME: TRANSNATIONAL MOBILITY FROM A MOTHER'S PERSPECTIVE

Border crossings, transnational migration, speed, and flows—these are some of the common characteristics defining life in postindustrial global societies. For the transnational mother, who must cross various national, legal, political, and cultural boundaries to provide for her family, the ubiquity of movement and flows is, without doubt, a prominent feature of her role as emotional labourer. Like other transnational workers, from the international jetsetter to the migrant farmer, the transnational mother participates in a fragmented and disorderly geopolitical environment, wherein home entails the dispersion of intimate and affective spaces across multiple locations. Indeed, not only does the life of a transnational mother entail various physical movements across space, but she is equally bound up with the global circulation of "emotional commodities," which allow her to foster and sustain bonds with family members left behind. Remittances—whether in the form of gifts or currency—represent one of the most important ways transnational mothers contribute to a system of global mobility centered on the creation, maintenance, and distribution of systems of care.

Undoubtedly, understanding the hardships and hopes facing transnational mothers requires tracing the complex spatial and affective circuits created by global care chains. This preoccupation with global mobility and flows, however, runs the risk of concealing another vital part of the migrant's experience that has little to do with the dematerialized and frictionless flows commonly attributed to global networks. Indeed, in a post 9/11 world, where national security in many countries, especially the U.S., entails the heightened militarization and surveillance of national borders, border crossings have become a restrictive and perilous experience for many migrant workers. Thus, in addition to documenting the migrant worker's participation in global care circuits, we must equally attend to globalization's creation of forms of immobility, especially the boundaries (national, legal, spatial, political) that exist to monitor and impede the movements of those deemed undesirable. As anthropologist Sarah Horton writes,

> In this era of heightened border militarization ... we may speak less of an unhindered mobility of people and things ... and more of the ironies of migrants' immobility in an era of cross-border flows.... The coincidence of these two changes—the increasing inflow of women and the heightened militarization of the border—has served to increasingly separate immigrant mothers from their children. (24)

Indeed, for many migrant mothers, who are unable to gain legal status in their host country, the restrictions placed on migrant bodies has lead to the normalization of domestic and familial separation. Since many transnational mothers refuse to visit their children for fear of being deported (Menjivar 314-15), the prospect of reuniting with their families is considered highly unlikely, a fate that proves destructive for all parties involved. Subsequently, many migrant mothers not only feel "trapped" and "imprisoned" by their immobility, and come to live in a state of constant fear, but their movement abroad comes with another equally alienating prospect: the permanent disconnection and emotional separation from their families.

Interestingly, *Spanglish* makes no reference to this new culture of global restriction and immobility. Quite the contrary, Flor's experiences as a transnational mother entails a steady path of upward mobility, as she moves easefully from her impoverished home in Mexico to the posh world of Deborah's upper-class home in L.A. In the border crossing scene, for example, Flor's transportation to the U.S. is visualized as a non-event: after entering a forest at the border, Flor magically reappears, delightfully transposed to her new home in Los Angeles. As in most Hollywood narratives, Flor's destiny does not entail any hint or possibility of denial, but revolves solely around how she will get what she ultimately deserves. In films, such as *Babel* and *Ilo Ilo*, however, things are never this optimistic or rosy; rather, spatial restrictions and the constant threat of surveillance are presented as an everyday part of life for migrant workers. Even worse, the films show how the authorities treat the surveillance of migrant mothers as the result of either their own deficiencies as caretakers or, worse, their criminality.

For example, in *Babel*, Amelia, an undocumented nanny who has been living in the U.S. for over twenty years, finds herself in trouble when she decides to take the children in her care across the Mexican border. Upon reentering the U.S., border police detain her when they discover that she illegally transported the children into Mexico without receiving consent from her employers. Even though the film presents Amelia as the children's primary caretaker (like Flor, Amelia exudes a warm maternal presence), in this scene the viewer is forcefully reminded of her ambivalent position as a migrant worker, whose role as mother is reduced to the abstract world of commodified labour. Things then go from bad to worse: when Amelia's nephew, who has been driving the car, decides to flee the authorities and illegally reenter the U.S., Amelia's precariousness is amplified. Abandoned by her nephew in the hot desert, Amelia is left to care for the children in a harsh and inhospitable environment. In one scene, Amelia decides to leave the children behind to find help. Disoriented and unhinged, Amelia frantically runs through the desert—a desperate and lost mother, whose chaotic movements symbolize her perilous place in the global care chain. Indeed, although Amelia and the children are rescued eventually, she is nonetheless punished severely for her supposed recklessness: not only is she reprimanded severely by her employers, but she is forced to return Mexico, a fate that permanently severs her from her "other" children.

In *Ilo Ilo* surveillance of the transnational mother is the product, not of the strong arm of the state, but the meddlesome, controlling tendencies of her employer. Like *Babel*, *Ilo Ilo* documents the everyday life of a migrant worker, Terry—a Filipina mother who moves to Singapore to help the Lim family. Immediately, Terry's subservient position in the home is established though the spatial restrictions placed on her body. For example, rather than being given her own room, Terry's employer forces her to sleep on the floor. Along with her confined space in the home, Terry's movements throughout the city are constantly monitored. In one scene, the mother, Hwee Leng, severely chastises Terry for wandering around the city at night, and threatens to fire her if she veers away from the home, even on her days off. As with many migrant women who face the contradictory experience of having their movements curtailed at the very moment they are given access to work opportunities abroad, the film depicts Terry as an unfortunate member of the new serving classes, whose motherly services grant her the financial power to assist her family, but only at the cost of her personal subjugation. Indeed, like Amelia, who at the end of *Babel* is shown being deported, *Ilo Ilo* concludes with Terry being forced to return home. When the Lim family is financially ruined by an economic crisis, Terry is sent packing, as if she were a depersonalized commodity that could be seamlessly repositioned within the global care chain.

THE AMBIVALENCE OF DOMESTIC CONNECTIVITY

The transnational family structure presented in *Spanglish* is exceptional: taking her entire family with her to America, and maintaining little to no contact with relatives back in Mexico, Flor envisions the home as a blank slate that requires little transnational connectivity. As with many films centered on the immigrant's search for the American Dream, the narrative trajectory of *Spanglish* heads in only one direction: the hopeful promise of the future. For most transnational mothers, however, maintaining a transnational family involves a far more disjointed and negotiated sense of time and space. Since for the migrant worker home is not dependent on co-presence but is spread across multiple destinations, experiences, and relationships, the possibility of miscommunication, confusion and emotional disconnection is ever-present (Boccagni). It is this geographical division, or absence-presence, that acts as the catalyst for so many of the ambivalent experiences felt by migrating mothers. As media and communications scholar Mirca Madianou writes:

> For mothers with left-behind children, migration can exacerbate their maternal ambivalence due to the deterritorialization of mothering. While ambivalence is a normal state for many mothers ... most negotiate their contradictory roles as workers and mothers and the related feeling of

> ambivalence in the context of everyday life. For migrant mothers such negotiation is more challenging because work and mothering are spread across different countries and continents. (285-86)

Although uncertainty is a common experience of many mothers, the ambivalence arising from the transnational mother's geographic distance may not be so easily overcome, as the emotional proximity between mother and child is constantly thwarted by the working mother's need to remain physically distant.

In the film *Mammoth*, the deterritorialization of mothering is visualized as an unending, tumultuous, and complicated labour activity that consumes Gloria, a Filipina nanny who works in Thailand and New York. As with *Babel*—which mimics globalization's complex, circuitous transnational flows by employing a disjointed and non-linear narrative structure—*Mammoth* moves back and forth between three predominant narrative settings: New York (the migrant home of Gloria), the Philippines (the home of Gloria's children), and Thailand (the business destination of Gloria's employer, Leo). Fluctuating between these international locations, the film creates the overwhelming sensation of perpetual flux, a discordant experience of travel that reflects the emotional uncertainties Gloria faces as she tries to cope with the constant negotiations associated with transnational motherhood. Although advancements in communication technologies allow her to maintain regular contact with her children, Gloria's virtual connectivity does little to assuage the guilt she feels over leaving her children. In one scene, an emotionally distraught Gloria speaks to her mother about returning home, since she no longer feels that moving away was the right decision. Using her religious faith as a source of clarity, Gloria pleads, "What God wants is for me to be with my children." Her mom interjects, providing a counter-argument that focuses on the financial benefits that come from working abroad: "You need to be there so that you can give your children a better future." In these scenes, the film's exploration of maternal ambivalence is doubly accentuated, as the narrative conflict entails not only Gloria's battles with her employer, but the intergenerational disagreements she has with her mother. Whereas Gloria's mother sees transnational motherhood as a liberating act, wherein moving abroad offers legitimate financial opportunities, Gloria no longer perceives her prowess in breadwinning as an acceptable justification for abandoning her children.

In her article on non-normative transnational mothers, Ann Phoenix uses Hallden's ideas about the "child as project" to discuss the strategies transnational mothers use to justify their decisions to leave their children (345-46). According to Phoenix, the "child as project" metaphor, which envisions mothering as an ongoing project that focuses solely on what the child will become in the future, represents a common justification many transnational mothers evoke to explain their desire to move abroad. In other words, while many transnational mothers are deeply troubled by the loss of their children, their suffering is considered worthwhile, since leaving is the only way they can secure a bright future for their children. In all the films I analyze the "child as project" metaphor is used to reimagine the transnational mother as the ultimate good mother, who combines breadwinning with intensive mothering to create a hybrid form of mothering from a distance. For example, even though Gloria laments her separation from her children, she acknowledges that her job is a necessary evil that will provide her children with a promising future—a desire aptly symbolized through the new house Gloria's family has begun to build back in the Philippines. As Gloria is reminded by her mother, without her courageous act of self-sacrifice, their life in the Philippines would be hopeless and dire.

By depicting its heroines as hard-working mothers who combine breadwinning with emotional care from a distance, films such as *Ilo Ilo*, *Babel,* and *Mammoth* contribute to a significant cultural reworking of the cinematic mother. Traditionally, the predominant, white, Western model of mothering has celebrated the domesticated exploits of the suburban housewife, whose intensive mothering is at odds with the working pursuits of the career woman. This model of mothering, however, is far from the norm. Historically, working-class women and women of colour have never enjoyed the luxury of full-time motherhood, having to struggle to find strategies to balance the demands of work and parenting. By drawing attention to the ways in which many women must combine breadwinning with emotional caretaking, the transnational mother revives an image of motherhood that has all too often been cast aside, submerged under the mythic weight and authority of the stay-at-home mom. This revived image of motherhood is not the fantastical image of blissful domesticity conjured up by *Leave It to Beaver*; nor is it the image of the feisty career mom, as depicted by *Murphy Brown*. It is a common image of motherhood as experienced by many working women all over the world. Above all it is a model of mothering that demonstrates that the choice between intensive mothering and work has been a rare privilege few mothers ever get to consider.

The transnational mother's ability to provide financially for her family represents one of the greatest benefits of long-distance mothering; however, as an ambivalent experience, mothering from afar can just as easily result in emotional distress, conflict, and tragedy. "Any impulse to romanticize transnational motherhood," write Hondagneu-Sotelo and Avila, "is tempered by the ... problems they sometimes encounter with their children and caregivers. A primary worry among transnational mothers is that their children are being neglected or abused in their absence" (560). In *Mammoth*, the possibility of abuse is understood as a by-product of the unreliable nature of long-distance relationships, especially the lack of trust created through the absence of face-to-face communication. Although Gloria uses the latest information technologies to remain emotionally available to her family, her lack of physical presence in the home creates a host of new vulnerabilities that accentuate her feeling of maternal inadequacy. As Atsushi Takeda writes,

> While advanced communication technology allows migrants and their kin to engage in transnational contact, the ongoing and constant communications also heighten and reinforce migrants' sense of their long-distance family responsibilities and obligations ... and engender more expectations of the migrant. With increased expectations, the failure to perform family roles from a distance often causes greater disappointment. (25)

While advanced information technologies allow some transnational mothers to ease the emotional strain created from mothering from afar, the virtual presence created by new technologies cannot overcome the communicative limitations created by physical distance. At the end of *Mammoth*, these difficulties are tragically displayed when Gloria learns that her eldest son has been the victim of a horrible sex crime. Hoping to find a job so that Gloria can return home, the young boy inadvertently falls prey to a pedophile, who offers the boy money in exchange for a variety of sexual favours. The boy is found later, nearly beaten to death, and is rushed to hospital. Upon hearing the grave news, Gloria packs her things, jumps in a cab, and heads back home. Even though Gloria is not responsible for the crime, the film creates the dreadful feeling that the boy's tragedy could have been avoided if his mother were living at home. As the film concludes and we watch Gloria huddle close to her sick child, viewers are left with this severe message about migrant mothers: a disembodied voice should never be considered a substitute for the guidance of a mother's active presence.

Mammoth's tragic ending calls into the question the maternal goodness associated with the transnational mother. Whereas in the romantic comedy the nanny is championed as a restorative figure whose maternal plenitude returns the home to its proper cosmic order, in such films as *Babel* and *Mammoth*, the transnational mother precariously straddles the good-bad mother dichotomy: she is a figure who is both celebrated for her industriousness and harshly stigmatized for her reckless abandonment of children. By the end of *Babel*, Amelia's warm and caring personality is tainted by the image of her as a neglectful and irresponsible caretaker, who almost caused the deaths of two innocent children. In *Mammoth*, a similar narrative conclusion is reached. Even though Gloria is initially painted as a caring and self-sacrificing mother, the tragic events surrounding her son transform her into a fallen mother, who, despite her good intentions, must be held accountable for her son's neglect. Subsequently, while these films escape Hollywood's mythic image of the migrant care worker, they nonetheless do little to shed the stigmatizing framework that often blames mothers for society's ills.

THE OTHER MOTHERS: BACKLASH OR CRITIQUE?

For Leonard, the function of the domestic care worker is to enforce a conservative, backlash image of domestic femininity; through her infectious prowess in care-taking, the nanny slowly brings the misinformed and selfish career woman back to the domestic fold. Even more, the romantic comedy serves to naturalize the neoliberal belief in the social powers of privatization, whereby all parenting problems can be solved through the combination of self-determination and laissez-faire capitalism. In the independent films I analyze a different approach is taken. While many of the films depict career-oriented moms as versions of the "insufferable upper-class woman," their parental imperfections do not enforce the backlash sensibilities featured in many romantic comedies. Indeed, whereas Leonard complains that many romantic comedies trivialize the plight of the domestic help, films like *Babel, Ilo Ilo,* and *Mammoth* uncover the structural inequalities and precarious work conditions that underpin global care chains, even for those women working at the top. For example, while Gloria's employer, Ellen, has little time for her daughter and is constantly overshadowed by the nanny, she is far from the selfish and egomaniacal mothers described by Leonard. Quite the contrary, when she is not working, Ellen desperately tries to engage with her daughter; what prevents her from being an active parent is not a question of her lack of motherly care but her complicated work life, as she is unable to balance her hectic job as a surgeon with the responsibilities of domestic care. Here, the film suggests that the decline of the family stems not from the self-aggrandizing pursuits of the career woman, but a socioeconomic system requiring workers to toil around the clock, with little time provided for the maintenance of social bonds. Likewise, in *Ilo Ilo*, the Asian economic crisis of 1997 is featured as the contextual framework for the film and the principal reasons Terry is dismissed from her job (the family loses everything when the market crashes). Here, the Lim's domestic woes have more to do with a widespread fear of job insecurity than the selfish pursuits of individual pleasures or unbridled consumption.

By attending to the structural inequalities bound up with global care industries, films such as *Ilo Ilo*, *Babel*, and *Mammoth* avoid the neo-conservative rhetoric witnessed in many Hollywood films about domestic care workers. Even more, what differentiates these films from the aseptic films analyzed by Leonard is the way they map out a new climate of maternal ambivalence: from the surveillance techniques used to curtail the movements of migrant women to the conflicts arising from mothers' use of communication technologies to connect with their families, the work of migrant mothers involves negotiating with a precarious labour market that can make life unbelievably harsh and cruel. At the same time, at the heart of the transnational mother is a recognition of the hopeful opportunities stemming from a model of mothering that sees migrant workers as capable of being both emotional caretakers and breadwinners. This can be seen in the way the transnational mother is depicted as the ultimate good mother, whose hard work, self-sacrifice, and intensive parenting from afar provides her family with a better future. Nonetheless, although these films give some credence to the transnational mother's new skills at parenting from a distance, all too often this celebratory image is mired by a narrative desire to punish mothers for some kind of transgression. Thus, while the transnational mother may escape momentarily the old dichotomy of good-bad mother, she is still cast as that age-old scapegoat for society's problems.

WORKS CITED

Boccagni, Paolo. "Practicing Motherhood at a Distance: Retention and Loss in Ecuadorian Transnational Families." *Journal of Ethnic and Migration Studies*, vol. 38, no. 2, 2012, pp. 261-77.

Eckenwiler, Lisa A. *Long-term Care, Globalization, and Justice.* Johns Hopkins UP, 2012.

Halldén, Gullina. "The Child as Project and the Child as Being: Parents' Ideas as Frames of Reference." *Children & Society*, vol. 5, no. 4, 1991, pp. 334-46.

Hochschild, Arlie, A. "Global Care Chains and Emotional Surplus Value." *On the Edge: Globalization and the New Millennium*, edited by Will Hutton and Anthony Giddens , Sage, 2012, pp. 130-46.

Hondagneu-Sotelo, Pierrette, and Ernestine Avila. "'I'm Here but

I'm There': The Meanings of Latina Transnational Motherhood." *Gender & Society*, vol. 11, no. 5, 1997, pp. 548-71.

Horton, Sarah. "A Mother's Heart is Weighed Down with Stones: A Phenomenological Approach to the Experience of Transnational Motherhood." *Culture, Medicine, and Psychiatry*, vol. 33 no. 1, 2009, pp. 21-40.

Leonard, Suzanne. "Ready-Maid Postfeminism? The American Domestic in Popular Culture." *Feminism, Domesticity and Popular Culture*, edited by Stacey Gillis and Joanne Hollows, Routledge, 2009, pp. 107-22.

Madianou, Mirca. "Migration and the Accentuated Ambivalence of Motherhood: The Role of ICTs in Filipino Transnational Families." *Global Networks* vol. 12, no. 3, 2012, pp. 277-95.

Menjivar, Cecilia. "Transnational Parenting and Immigration Law: Central Americans in the United States." *Journal of Ethnic and Migration Studies* vol. 38, no. 2, 2012, pp. 301-22.

Parreñas, Rhacel. *Children of Global Migration: Transnational Families and Gendered Woes*. Stanford University Press, 2005.

Phoenix, Ann. "Transforming 'Non-normative' Motherhood: Retrospective Accounts of Transnational Motherhood in Serial Migration." *Radical Psychology*, vol. 9, no. 2, 2010, www.radicalpsychology.org/vol9-2/phoenix.html. Accessed 30 June 2016.

Sassen, Saskia. "Global Cities and Survival Circuits." *The Globalization and Development Reader*, edited by J. Timmons Roberts and Amy Bellone Hite, Blackwell, 2015, pp. 195-215.

Takeda, Atsushi. "Emotional Transnationalism and Emotional Flows: Japanese Women in Australia." *Women's Studies International Forum*, vol. 35, no. 1, 2012, pp. 22-28.

Yeates, Nicola. "Global Care Chains." *International Feminist Journal of Politics*, vol. 6, no. 3, 2004, pp. 369-91.

Zarembka, Joy M. "America's Dirty Work: Migrant Maids and Modern-Day Slavery." *Global Woman: Nannies, Maids and Sex Workers in the New Economy*, edited by Barbara Ehrenreich and Arlie Hochschild, Owl, 2002, pp. 142-53.

FILMS

Wang, Wayne, director. *Maid in Manhattan*. Colombia Pictures, 2002.

Brooks, James, director. *Spanglish*. Sony Pictures Entertainment, 2004.
Prado, Anayansi, director. *Maid in America*. 2005.
Velasco, Veronia, director. *Mother Nanny*. Unitel Pictures, 2006.
Jones, Kirk, director. *Nanny McPhee*. Universal Pictures, 2006.
Iñárritu, Alejandro G., director. *Babel*. Paramount Classics, 2006.
Cox, Tim, director. *Mammoth*. IFC Films, 2006.
Pulmonic, Robert, director. *The Nanny Diaries*. MGM Studios, 2007.
Taylor, Tate, director. *The Help*. Dream work Studios, 2011.
Chen, Anthony, director. *Ilo Ilo*. Film Movement, 2014.

2.
Madre/Moneda

The Moral Value of Motherwork in Immigrant Nanny Personal Narratives

ELIZABETH CUMMINS MUÑOZ

IN RECENT DECADES, global migration trends have shifted toward a feminization of migration, as more and more of the domestic work, nursing, elderly care, and childcare in the global north is performed by women who have left their own homes, children, sick, and elderly behind.[1] In my own local community, these broad global changes—brought on by the complicated intersections of globalized economies, state policies, gendered power dynamics, and class- and race-based social structures—can be keenly felt by anyone who takes the time to see the domestic work and care work so often invisible to the public eye. In the following discussion, I consider one form of this labour, transnational nanny work, as it manifests itself in the personal narratives of two migrant women in Houston, Texas. For each of these women, such invisible work becomes quite concrete when it translates into remittances that serve as a lifeline for loved ones back home. And for each, the particular nature of the emotional labour involved in dependent care work blurs the lines between love and work, and between mother and employee, as they struggle to reconcile the lived experience of choices that are both right and wrong. For these women, mothering is like a coin with two faces—one that provides and one that loves. This *madre moneda*, or mother coin, signifies both economic value and emotional value, but can only land with one side up.

MOTHERING AND MOTHERWORK

Although sometimes used interchangeably, motherwork is separate from and inextricably related to the practice of mothering. In these pages, "motherwork" describes the daily labour necessary to care for dependent children, whereas "mothering" refers to a set of actions that respond both to affective bonds as well as to social constructions of motherhood, an institution deeply embedded in gendered social structures (Nakano Glenn; Segura). For women who leave their homes, and often their biological children, to care for the children of others, the peculiar nature of transnational nanny work activates cultural constructions of motherhood that are often incompatible. Conflicts arise as emotional bonds are formed only to be broken and multiple tensions compete to divide a mother's resources between mothering her own children and devoting motherwork to those of another. Another conflict deeply significant to the migrant nanny's sense of self involves the competing moral values attributed to the work of mothering within this transnational economy. On the one hand, motherhood is associated with an emotional value based on the relational interaction that is inherent to caring through affective bond and physical presence. On the other, an exchange-based economic value is ascribed to work that provides for one's children materially with the income earned through motherwork.

These two distinct values are associated with gender roles in the patriarchal cultures characteristic of many women migrants' home countries, in which the dual responsibilities of parenting—to care for emotionally and to provide for materially—are managed by assigning the tasks to mothers and fathers, respectively.[2] Through repeated cultural narratives enforcing these gendered roles, a woman's parenting identity becomes tied to the moral value system embedded in her local culture's motherhood ideal—a sense of right and wrong based on relational interaction and nurturing through "the embodied, fleshly contacts that signal intimacy" (Kittay 57). As Rhacel Salazar Parreñas has noted, transnational mothers are called upon to take up the roles of both father and mother in an expanded definition of motherhood that incorporates material provisioning, or breadwinning, into the role of "mother" (93). For these women, the inability to respond simultaneously to both sets of values can result in deeply felt personal conflicts. In the case of migrant nannies who are mothers, the distance separating them from their transnational children both enables breadwinning and also precludes the intimate physical presence that breeds affective bonds. At the same time, the nanny's daily work confuses the boundaries between motherwork for economic exchange and the emotional relationship associated with the practice of mothering. This paradox manifests itself at the level of identity, wherein what is "good" in one context is "bad" in another. For Pati and Sara, two migrant nannies who live this conflict in their past and present, the irreconcilable nature of these conflicting constructions of "good" mothering is apparent in the competing selves that appear in their personal narratives.[3]

In the following pages, I present these two women's stories and reflect on the larger cultural, economic, and sociopolitical forces shaping them. Pati and Sara are both Central American immigrants living in Houston, Texas, and working as nannies in the homes of American families. Both women are mothers of American-born children, and both are daughters who share the experience of having lost the presence of their mothers to migration when they were young. My analysis of these recorded conversations is neither sociological nor anthropological, but approaches both the interviews, as well as the documents resulting from them, as cultural texts produced in a specific context and shaped by the sociopolitical locations of each participant and by the spaces in which the interviews were conducted. As such, I reflect on their stories not as objective statements of fact but as negotiations of self-identity undertaken in full awareness of my own social and cultural position.

I met Sara and Pati through my social capital as a neighbourhood mother with a fluent command of Spanish. Pati is the friend of a woman I employed to clean my own home, and I met Sara at a local park. As an educated, Anglo, upper-middle class woman who has often employed others to clean my home and care for my children, I share a great deal with the women who employ Pati and Sara; my position as a writer and student of Hispanic literature and culture was made clear in my presentation of the project. As such, it is possible that these women came to the interviews with a sense of my role as a sympathetic proxy both for their employers and also for a larger American audience. I accept and assume this implicit role with a deep sense of responsibility. I am aware that—although the subaltern may never truly speak—Sara and Pati communicated something urgent to me in our conversations, and I am obligated to transmit what I have understood of that communication, filtered though it may be. What I heard in Pati's and Sara's stories was the intimate negotiation of meanings within each woman's narrative understanding of her experience. In essence, their stories are portraits of the identity-articulating processes at the local site of the globalized forces that define and limit their opportunities. They reflect a deep struggle to affirm the dignity of their choices and to define the good in their mothering within competing moral imperatives. I heard the pain of this struggle in their voices, and I read it on their bodies.

SARA'S STORY: "I'M FATHER AND MOTHER TO THEM, *SOY PADRE Y MADRE PARA ELLOS.*"[4]

Sara is a young woman in her twenties from a poor rural area of El Salvador. She describes her hometown in terms of extreme poverty and recalls a childhood in which she and her siblings only bathed when the rain water had filled the collection tanks. Sara's mother emigrated when Sara was nine years old; her father, a former *guerrillero* in the El Salvadoran civil war, had already left for the United States. She and her three little sisters spent their brief childhoods in their hometown with their grandparents. By thirteen, each girl had married; by fifteen, the oldest two had followed their parents north, each with their own babes in arms.

While our children played in the park, I listened to Sara's story unfold, shaped by my own careful questions. In her narrative, she describes two primary conflicts. On the one hand, she struggles with her identity as both mother and daughter as she seeks to acknowledge the good and understand the bad in the conflicting demands of transnational mothering. The second conflict, born of the first, extends this question to the project of migration itself, and asks in retrospect if the material gains resulting from her family members' decisions to migrate were worth what she describes as "the disintegration" of her family.

From the beginning of our conversation, Sara acknowledges the fundamental economic need at the root of her mother's choice to migrate. She describes her family's recourse to gleaning recently harvested fields and hunting iguanas in search of food, explaining that her mother was "the source of our sustenance." Still, Sara frames the negative consequences of her mother's absence with equal clarity: "When you don't grow up with someone, you love her, but it's not the same as when you're with her." She recalls her inability to comprehend the distance her mother had travelled, and confesses that she and her sisters thought that their mother wasn't telling the truth about being able to come home to visit: "We thought she just didn't want to come back." Although Sara insists with a strong voice that she always understood and forgave her mother, her tone becomes low and deep when referring to her sister's judgment: "She hasn't gotten over it. She throws it in our mother's face that her life was the way it was because our mother abandoned her. It's a feeling. Look, that's what happens when people from countries like El Salvador travel here and leave their children back there. They suffer a lot. Because the kids, there are a lot who never forgive them." Sara does not count herself among those who will not forgive, and her narrative reveals a strong connection between this generosity of perspective and her own experience as a working mother in the U.S.

When I ask her about her U.S. employment experience, Sara describes a series of domestic service positions ranging from fulltime, sixteen-hour-a-day servant work, to once-a-week cleaning jobs. One experience she recounts illustrates the many ways in which gender, race, and class circumscribe both her motherwork and her mothering. As a fulltime nanny and housekeeper for a family with young children, Sara earned $350 working forty hours a week. "I was a slave for them," she insists. "I cleaned the house, picked up the little girl from school, walked the dog, picked up the drycleaning, shopped for groceries, everything." Sara recounts how, shortly before her employer gave birth to the family's second baby, she announced her own second pregnancy. Within two months, she was replaced and dismissed. She recalls the couple's explanation in their words: "You're an excellent worker ... but we want someone who doesn't have any problems." As she reflects on this incident, her reaction retains the confusion she experienced at the time: "I wanted to die because what did I do wrong?"

Sara expresses a deep sense of guilt for the care she feels she was withholding from her own son, as she gave her time, patience, and attention to the charges in her care. She explains that her child's caregiver, an uncle's wife, did not tend to him well. In her view, this inferior care caused the child to become ill: "He's been very sickly, in part because of my *descuido*, the care I didn't give him, because of my job." She describes a boy who has grown increasingly vocal about his frustration with his mother's time away; he has reproached her for her absence and her mothering style. "I've given so much of myself to work that I'm losing my children's love," Sara concludes.

Although her son lives with her, the mothering experience Sara describes parallels the emotional conflict common to transnational mothering. "I feel bad," she explains, "because I leave my kids to come and take care of [theirs]. I treat them better than mine because I have to be kind and available for everything they need." Sara describes a local version of the global care chain—a dynamic identified by many scholars of global migration and care work, in which globalized inequalities enact a progressive decrease in the quality of care from wealthy nations to poorer ones (Hochschild, *The Managed Heart*; Chavkin; Maher; and Salazar Parreñas). In a local response to global forces that reduce economic opportunity at home and increase opportunity abroad, women from poorer countries with export-oriented economies and decreasing state support for families migrate to wealthier countries to participate in a growing service economy and take on the care work left behind by increasingly professionalized women. This dynamic leaves a significant care deficit in sending countries, which is addressed by lower-quality care, as elderly grandparents or working relatives, often with children of their own, step in to look after the children left behind (Kittay; Salazar Parreñas; Herrera). On a macro level, the sending states generate value by exporting care without expending domestic resources to compensate; on a micro level, transnational families experience subpar care that perpetuates the structural violence inherent in global inequalities.

Sara lived this dynamic as a transnational child, and her mothering experience as a migrant care worker is similar. She enables her employers to fulfill American middle-class mothering ideals by exchanging the motherwork she would devote to her own children for compensation, a portion of which is dedicated to securing less valued and more poorly paid care for the children she leaves at home. Although her motives continue to be shaped by a global economy requiring her to send remittances to her grandmother and aunts back home, the emotional pain she felt as a transnational child is activated in this local space. The pain extends its reach to her sense of self as a mother and causes her to identify with her own mother's difficult choices: "I feel bad, and I identify with my mom, because I tell myself, she did the same thing; she left us to give us something better. The only difference was all that distance."

Despite this damage to the emotional value of her mothering, Sara strongly and confidently affirms the economic value of her wage-earning work as a parent. She explains that her children are U.S. citizens and she intends to create a future for them. For Sara, this is made concrete through the home she secured for her children: "I got a house, thinking of creating a better future for them. I tell myself, 'Well, they're from here, why would I take them to my country?' ... But getting a house means I have to work a lot because I am father and mother to them." Sara applies this characterization to her mother as well, and finds parallels not only in their shared profession but in their husbands' shortcomings. She describes her physically abusive father with the same language she uses to refer to her own husband: "He's not the best husband around." As a result of their men's refusal to take responsibility for their families, Sara and her mother must each be both father and mother to their children. This engenders conflicting identities—both breadwinner and caregiver—that can be understood in terms of the embodied experience of gendered social systems.

These gendered expectations run deep. Despite the potential for redefining motherhood in the context of migration and transnational mothering, scholars recognize the tendency for both sides of transnational communities to reinforce traditional gender roles, often redoubling expectations of intense emotional labour on the part of the absent mother.[5] These dynamics reflect a normalization of gender differences in parenting that is felt on a deep emotional level by all involved. Even though Sara may take pride in her ability to create a financial future for her children in the U.S., the painful internal negotiations of the moral value of her own mothering practices give rise to a narrative tension in her personal story.

Sara's account of her family's migration experience reveals a persistent ambivalence about the choices her mother made. On the one hand, she acknowledges her mother's hand in advancing the family's material position: "I don't blame her because I know that she did it for the same reason I leave my kids with someone else—to eat well." On the other hand, she gives credence to her sister's unforgiving blame. When I prompt Sara to give her evaluation of the family's migration strategy, she says that the choice to pursue separate paths destroyed the family unity: "When we came here, the family came apart." But she preserves her own sense of self as a good mother by maintaining that her mother's choice to provide material care over emotional nurturing was not the reason for the family's heartaches.[6] Instead, she turns to the culture of the United States to explain the failure of her family's migration: "In El Salvador, women are raised to be maids and housewives, to obey their husbands and everything. They come to a different culture. The women are liberal.... They're free to make their own decisions without having to ask their husband's permission first." In her parents' case, this cultural change resulted in her mother leaving her father, precipitating her family's disintegration. After reflecting, Sara concludes, "This country can give you a lot, but it takes away a lot, too. It takes more than it gives because it gives an economic life, but it takes away family."

When I ask directly if she would make the choice to migrate again, Sara does not hesitate: "If I could turn back time, I'd stay in my country ... definitely, without thinking twice." Her voice is strong and articulate, much the same as the tone she uses to refer to the home she has acquired for her American-born children. Perhaps with these contradicting declarations she has found a way to be both mother and father—a good mother who would stay behind for the sake of the family and a good father who would leave to make a better life for her children. Whereas Sara struggles with the conflicts inherent to mothering her own children in this transnational economy, Pati's story reflects the other side of the coin: the struggle to manage motherwork for hire.

PATI'S STORY: "DON'T LOVE THEM LIKE YOU DO, *NO LOS QUIERAS CÓMO LOS QUIERES.*"

When I spoke with Pati, a young mother in her thirties from a small town in El Salvador, she was eight months pregnant with her second child. Pati's mother had left the family for the U.S. when Pati, the youngest of four, was six years old. Because their father had abandoned them, Pati and her siblings spent their childhood with various aunts and grandparents until each migrated as adults to reunite with the family in Texas. When I prompted Pati to talk about her experiences as a nanny in the United States, her responses led to many threads that combined to form a single story: the events leading up to and following the unexpected and abrupt ending to her employment with an American family whose children she professes to love as she does her own.

Shortly after she arrived, Pati found work with an American family through her mother. The child was two months old, and for the next seven years Pati lived in the family's garage apartment and cared for the young boy and the baby girl, who would be born two years later. She describes the couple's behaviour toward her as infused with respect on every level. They were professional, polite, and a model for Pati's own future relationship and parenting. During her time with this family, Pati grew to love the children. She devotes much of our conversation to affirming and analyzing this love, and says more than once that she loves the children as much as she does her own: "I adore them. I always saw them like they were my own.... All day long! From seven-thirty to six in the evening. I was the one who took care of them when they were sick, feeding them twice a day.... But I saw them grow up, watched them develop. And it was beautiful, beautiful." In these reflections, Pati sets up a hindsight perspective in which she always understood and accepted the emotional vulnerability inherent to her situation. She relays the advice she received from fellow immigrant nannies with more experience: "Don't love them like you do. Start withdrawing this affection because from one day to the next when they don't need you, they're not going to care what you feel." But Pati concludes that she had no choice because to do her job meant to love the children; there was no separating the work from the bond. "For me to do my job well," she explains, "I have to love what I do."

When she became pregnant, Pati tells me that her employers were unfailingly supportive. To illustrate, she recounts the man's insistence that she stop working when he learned her doctor had ordered her to rest. "'Go home and rest, do it for me,'" she remembers him saying. She smiles when she repeats his command, wearing a faraway look of nostalgia that she has summoned several times in her story and which serves to build the tension and frame the past in terms of the present: "I never forgot those words."

Shortly after Pati's daughter was born, the husband lost his job, and the wife explained that they could not afford to employ Pati until he found a new position. According to Pati, her employer assured her that her job was safe, and that as soon as the husband found employment, Pati would be invited to return to work with all the same arrangements they had discussed— including the significant benefit that she would be able to bring her infant daughter with her. In the one year interim, Pati babysat for the family here and there and did small jobs for people within her employer's network—all of whom, she reminds me, were aware of her employer's long-term plans for Pati. At the close of that year, Pati became pregnant with her second child and immediately told her employer of the pregnancy in full confidence. Shortly thereafter, the woman informed her that the husband had secured a position but the family had hired another nanny, a foreign university student. She asked Pati if she could work for them until the new nanny could start.

Pati's shock and confusion was compounded by the details of the job transfer, and she began to reevaluate the nature of the relationship she had built with the family over the years: "They gave her the car that they had bought for me, for my use. They gave her the credit card at the same time ... a cell phone, an iPod, at the same time, right there in front of me. ... So, it isn't how I thought it was. Because I thought it was a special affection they had for me." Her tone is forceful when she says this, the intonation rising on the word "me." She leans in and her voice cracks with emotion, revealing a tension in her body between pain and anger.

Despite her confusion at the time, in hindsight Pati is able to articulate the disconnect at the source of her sense of betrayal: "I began to consider a lot of things, that part of all this wasn't something I had earned; it wasn't something I had built up, a special affection.... They are wonderful people, with anyone. But there was never an appreciation, a special sense of value for me." From the beginning of her story, Pati insists that on a purely analytical level, her employers cannot be faulted for their actions: "I mean, it's not anyone's fault. It's not anyone's fault. It's not the nanny's fault, it's not my boss's fault that I ended up pregnant either. It's not my fault." She calls on two arguments to justify her employers' actions on their behalf. First, her pregnancy would affect her motherwork because of the physical nature of the job. Second, Americans are particularly disposed to litigation, and a pregnant woman doing physical work in a family's home would leave them vulnerable to being found at fault if an accident were to happen.

Pati rationalizes her employer's choices in other areas as well. When I ask her to reflect on her own approval of her employer's decision to work away from home, Pati answers with a story. In a discussion about her impending maternity, Pati recalls telling her employer that she personally would not choose to leave her child to go to work. The comment left the woman visibly upset, as she thought Pati had judged her as a bad mother for working outside the home herself. Pati's response to her employer is telling: "Do you know what the difference is between me not leaving my child and you leaving yours? It's because you go to an office, and I would be going to take care of other children ... because the work is different. If I had to work the way you do, I would look for a good person to take care of my children and I would leave them." Given this logic, it is reasonable that a woman would do what she had to do to make sure her children were given full attention while she was away at her office job. In all, Pati has constructed herself a clear map of the relative economic value of motherwork and emotional value of mothering. When the practice of mothering is expanded to include breadwinning, this expansion cannot be justified if the mother's resulting employment calls for motherwork that is dedicated to other children; the boundaries between work and love are too ambiguous. Unfortunately for Pati, this logic breaks down when she applies the same analytical attitude to her own mother's choices.

When her mother left six-year-old Pati to emigrate to the United States, she found a position as a nanny for three American children, the oldest of whom was also six years old. She would stay with this family for the next twenty-five years. When Pati arrived in the U.S., her mother continued to look after the youngest child, now a teenager. Pati recounts a memory from one morning soon after her arrival, when she accompanied her mother to take this boy to school. When he hopped out of the car, her mother kissed him goodbye and told him she loved him. As Pati reflects on this exchange, she has difficulty maintaining her objective composure: "When I came here, and I saw my mom with these kids who were already eighteen years old, and telling them, 'Sweetheart, I love you, take care,' in front of m—" Here, Pati begins to cry. "It was like, 'Why? Why with him and not with me?'" She breaks down at this point in our conversation. Although I recognize that she is wounded and vulnerable and still quite confused by her most recent betrayal, it is also true that her embodied emotions, the tears and the speechlessness and the hunched over sobs, tell their own story, and escape the analysis and objective logic of choices based on economic need.

Two moral judgments play out in Pati's story, both within the binary gender meanings of patriarchy. The good parenting attributed to breadwinning is associated with the "masculine"—mind, reason, economic value, and individual success. The good in the caregiving parent, on the other hand, is attributed to the "feminine"—body, emotion, relational value, and collective collaboration.[7] In her analysis of her mother's impossible choices, Pati characterizes the path her mother was forced to take in the same terms that Sara uses to describe her own situation: each woman had to be "*padre y madre*" at the same time, father and mother both. The conflict at the heart of this mother coin lies in the inevitable contradiction of the moral rights and wrongs ascribed to gendered parenting constructions in the patriarchal contexts within which each is evaluating her mother's choices and her own. When woman-mother is essentialized and mothering and motherwork are associated with "feminine" qualities, they carry the same power structure inherent to patriarchy; motherhood and its work and practices are cast as subordinate to the masculine values of public labour and reason. This same gender-based power differential is responsible for a global economic and social system in which parents and loved ones must choose breadwinning over nurturing.[8] When I consider Pati's and Sara's stories in the context of these complicated value systems, I observe a complex and often structurally violent network of constraints and expectations. Transnational economies intersect with social constructions of gender, race, class and nationality, all of which play out in a global care chain of unequal resources. This complicated dynamic manifests in Pati's and Sara's identity-making narratives as they try to make meaning out of their choices at the crossroads of competing ideals.

THE RELATIONAL SELF: TELL ME, *CUÉNTAME*

In this reflection, I have attempted to understand Pati's and Sara's personal narratives as local responses to global processes. In negotiating the meanings ascribed to motherhood in a transnational context, both women assert local agency in response to the pressures of globalism. Denise Segura and Patricia Zavella describe a "subjective transnationalism" by which migrant women expand their economic and social agency in an effort to redress economic need, while simultaneously redefining accepted ideals of family and motherhood (3). These scholars maintain that this process "maximize[s] women's survival and mobility" (27). In Pati's and Sara's personal narratives, I find an expression of agency that moves beyond material survival, to encompass a value system that is alternative to the masculine logic of economic exchange and social power, one that takes into account the longings of the heart.[9]

These longings are at the heart of the emotional violence I perceive in Sara and Pati's stories, a violence that is is clarified for me by the work of Eva Feder Kittay. In her philosophical examination of the emotional harm experienced as a result of migrant care work,

Kittay affirms that the particular nature of dependency care work generates a moral harm when it is exercised in the context of global migration. Kittay uses Hochschild's concept of the "global heart transplant," which describes the transfer of affection that results when the intimate nature of care work breeds emotional bonds in the absence of a migrant caregiver's own loved ones. In this dynamic, the displaced love that the carer cannot give through close contact is "poured into" the physically present child whom the caregiver is charged to look after (Hochschild, "Love"). In her methodical examination of this dynamic through the lens of human rights, Kittay posits a "right to give and receive care" that is born of the ethical premise that all individuals are inherently relational and that relationships based on emotional bonds are integral to the carer's sense of self. In this context, the emotional violence experienced by transnational mothers and children is inflicted when the right to give and receive intimate care is revoked, thereby threatening their integral self as relational beings.

Kittay asserts that this core sense of a fundamentally relational self is more fully developed in women because of their socially imposed identification with the feminine values of affection and emotional bond (62). When women such as Pati, Sara, and their mothers negotiate social and economic systems requiring them to sell their motherwork for economic value, they are denied their right to care according to the emotional values of mothering. When transnational and migrant mothers seek to reconcile the privileged masculine value system of economic exchange with their own highly developed, feminine sense of self as relational, affective beings, the contradiction breeds conflict that can be heard in their narrative voices and read in their embodied telling. At the same time, the interview space in which these personal narratives were elicited can be understood as inherently interactive, as it privileges and honours the relational self through the act of witnessing.

Narrative researcher Catherine Kohler Riessman, in her exploration of the complicated positioning of the interviewer as interpreter, appeals to Ruth Behar's 1996 call for ethnographic interviewers to be "vulnerable observers" (193). "When we enter the lives of others and write about them," Riessman observes, "we become witnesses" (194). With this in mind, I have struggled to present faithfully the information Pati and Sara shared with me. Although the promise of objectivity inherent to scholarship offers distance from the tricky vulnerabilities of personal engagement, I recognize that Pati and Sara did not protect themselves from such vulnerabilities when they opened their hearts to me, hungry for validation and understanding. In choosing to honour the relational nature of these interviews, I must, then, consider my own personal interpretive filter.

Throughout these conversations, Pati and Sara respond to my questions, prompts that many times reveal my own reactions to their stories as each of us shapes our identities in the moment of telling. At times, I can hear my desire to justify the choices they recount within the moral systems of my own mothering ideals and those of my imagined readers—asking Pati, for example, "Do you believe that it was really necessary for [your mother] to emigrate?" At others, I realize I have led them to predetermined conclusions, such as when I ask Sara if she identifies with her mother's excruciating choices. Then, there are moments in which I give in wholly to the emotion in their narrative, empathizing with the children who love without knowing and the women who love without understanding: "And did you understand this when you were a child?" I ask Pati about her mother's reasons for migrating, "because sometimes the only thing that's there is the absence."

When I reflect on these embodied narrative exchanges, I see myself guiding, responding, shaping, and often straining with body and mind and ears to listen for the key that will grant me distance. Even though I have employed women like Sara and Pati, and even though these pages would not have been written without the daily intimate attentions of the women who cared for my own growing children, I want to hear that I am not a part of this problem. But we are each of us in our own ways both victims and enablers of global economic, political, and social systems that have taken up residence in the personal identities and private bodies of women like Sara and Pati. In the local spaces of our intimate lives, these global systems engender the "pain and possibility"[10] of enduring choices that are both right and wrong, both wrong and right.

ENDNOTES

[1]For a discussion of the feminization of migration, the service industries of the global north, and the emergence of transnational families, see Segura and Zavella; Ehrenreich and Hochschild; Chavkin; Maher; Hondagneau-Sotelo; and Salazar Parreñas.

[2]See Denise Segura for a discussion of the distinct patriarchal constructions of family in working-class Mexican and middle-class U.S. cultures.

[3]These interviews form part of a larger project, a cross-genre presentation of my conversations with eight migrant nannies from Mexico and Central America who live and work in Houston, Texas. The names of all interviewees have been changed.

[4]All the direct quotations taken from the interviews have been transcribed and translated by me. At times, I have chosen to maintain the Spanish for phrases and words whose particular meaning is both important to the text and also difficult to translate.

[5]In her study of Filipino transnational families, Rhacel Salazar Parreñas observes that the children studied maintained gendered care expectations of a mother even when she had migrated away from the physical home and that they reported feelings of resentment and abandonment toward migrant mothers far more than they did toward fathers (125-132).

[6]For discussions of the redefinition of "good mothering" among transnational mothers, see Hondagneau-Sotelo and Avila (406-409); and Hondagneau-Sotelo (26-27).

[7]In her study of social constructions of mothering, Evelyn Nakano Glenn lays out this gender-based binary and the power structure within which it operates (13).

[8]See in particular Salazar Parreñas, chapter one, "The Global Economy of Care" in *Children of Global Migration.*

[9]In her insightful study of marriage attitudes among multigenerational women in a transnational U.S.-Mexican community, Jennifer Hirsch cautions against simplistic formulations of migrant agency that reduce motivation to economic or social forces, and urges scholars to recognize that all research subjects "deserve the basic humanity of being understood to make decisions not just out of strategy and advantage, but out of love and longing as well" (455).

[10]See Maria de la Luz Ibarra on the opportunities and limits characteristic of immigrant work in the new domestic labour.

WORKS CITED

Chavkin, Wendy. "The Globalization of Motherhood." *The Globalization of Motherhood: Deconstructions and Reconstructions of Biology and Care*, edited by Wendy Chavkin and JaneMaree Maher, Routledge, 2010, pp. 3-15.

Ehrenreich, Barbara, and Arlie Russell Hochschild. "Introduction." *Global Woman: Nannies, Maids, and Sex Workers in the New Economy*, edited by Barbara Ehrenreich and Arlie Russell Hochschild, Metropolitan, 2002, pp. 1-14.

Herrera, Giaconda. "Stratified Workers / Stratified Mothers." *The Globalization of Motherhood: Deconstructions and Reconstructions of Biology and Care*, edited by Wendy Chavkin and JaneMaree Maher, Routledge, 2010, pp. 55-75.

Hirsch, Jennifer. "'*En el norte la mujer* manda': Gender, Generation, and Geography in a Mexican Transnational Community." *Women and Migration in the U.S.-Mexico Borderlands: A Reader*, edited by Denise A. Segura and Patricia Zavella, Duke University, 2007, pp. 438-455.

Hochschild, Arlie Russell. *The Managed Heart: Commercialization of Human Feeling*. University of California Press, 2012.

Hochschild, Arlie. "Love and Gold." *Global Woman: Nannies, Maids, and Sex Workers in the New Economy*, edited by Barbara Ehrenreich and Arlie Russell Hochschild, Metropolitan, 2002, pp. 15-30.

Hondagneu-Sotelo, Pierrette. *Doméstica: Immigrant Workers Cleaning and Caring in the Shadows of Affluence*. University of California Press, 2001.

Hondagneu-Sotelo, Pierrette, and Ernestine Avila. "'I'm Here, but I'm There': The Meanings of Latina Transnational Motherhood." *Women and Migration in the U.S.-Mexico Borderlands: A Reader*, edited by Denise A. Segura and Patricia Zavella, Duke University Press, 2007, pp. 388-412.

Ibarra, María de la Luz. "Mexican Immigrant Women and the New Domestic Labor." *Women and Migration in the U.S.-Mexico*

Borderlands: A Reader, edited by Denise A. Segura and Patricia Zavella, Duke University Press, 2007, pp. 286-305.

Kittay, Eva Feder. "The Moral Harm of Migrant Carework: Realizing a Global Right to Care." *Philosophical Topics*, vol. 37, no. 2, 2009, pp. 53-73.

Maher, JaneMaree. "Motherhood: Reproduction and Care." *The Globalization of Motherhood: Deconstructions and Reconstructions of Biology and Care*, edited by Wendy Chavkin and JaneMaree Maher, Routledge, 2010, pp. 15-27.

Nakano Glenn, Evelyn. "Social Constructions of Mothering: A Thematic Overview." *Mothering: Ideology, Experience, and Agency*, edited by Evelyn Nakano Glenn and Grace Change, Routledge, 1994, pp. 1-29.

Salazar Parreñas, Rhacel. *Children of Global Migration: Transnational Families and Gendered Woes*. Stanford University Press, 2005.

Segura, Denise. "Working at Motherhood: Chicana and Mexicana Immigrant Mothers and Employment." *Women and Migration in the U.S.-Mexico Borderlands: A Reader*, edited by Denise A. Segura and Patricia Zavella, Duke University Press, 2007, pp. 368-387.

Segura, Denise A., and Patricia Zavella. "Introduction." *Women and Migration in the U.S.-Mexico Borderlands: A Reader*, edited by Denise A. Segura and Patricia Zavella, Duke University Press, 2007, pp. 1-32.

Riessman, Catherine Kohler. "Doing Justice: Positioning the Interpreter in Narrative Work." *Strategic Narrative: New Perspectives on the Power of Personal and Cultural Stories*, edited by Wendy Patterson, Lexington, 2002, pp. 193-214.

Walks, Michelle and Naomi McPherson. "Introduction: Identifying an Anthropology of Mothering." *An Anthropology of Mothering*, edited by Michelle Walks and Naomi McPherson, Demeter, 2011, pp. 1-47.

Wrigley, Julia. *Other People's Children*. Basic, 1995.

3.
Of Bodies, Borders, and European Belonging

Trial of a Child Denied and the Sterilization of Roma Mothers in the Czech Republic

ROXANA CAZAN

> OSTRAVA, Czech Republic—Just hours after her second child was born, 19-year-old Helena Ferencikova's joy was dashed. In the recovery room, she discovered that the paper she had signed, not knowing what it said, had allowed doctors to sterilize her. The Vitkovicka hospital in the northeastern Czech Republic says further pregnancies might have killed her. But Ferencikova believes the reason was her ethnicity—Gypsy. (Janicek)

THE STORY ABOVE began the first court case against the coercive sterilization of Roma women in Eastern Europe and constitutes the main act in Michele Coomber's heartfelt documentary *Trial of a Child Denied* (2011).[1] Taking a stand on issues such as Roma rights, motherhood, feminism, racism, and democratic citizenship in Central and Eastern Europe, the almost twenty-six-minute film aims to document the systemic denial of Roma women's rights to bodily integrity and reproductive freedom. Like *No Más Bebés*—a 2015 documentary film directed by Renee Tajima-Peña investigating the coercive sterilization of Mexican immigrant women in the 1970s United States—*Trial of a Child Denied* exposes an untold chapter in the global history of reproductive rights—the plight of the Roma. Their ethnic and racial identities have been contested by normative, homogenous, and national grand-narratives; they have been pushed to the margins of the nation-state, and have been denied access to political representation. Coomber's documentary also sheds light onto one variety of global feminisms focusing on the rights and needs of Roma women in Europe. Through three vignettes portraying Roma women subjected to coercive sterilizations, Coomber's documentary constructs the Roma not just as fated victims of a long-standing xenophobia amplified under communism in the Czech Republic, but also as embodiments of a people in formation, whose exclusion from citizenship illustrates the very failure of European unification. On the one hand, the disingenuous tactics employed by hospitals to coerce Roma women into consenting to sterilization reflect a state ideology in which ethnic minorities constitute unwanted social elements and whose containment and elimination are matters of institutional concern. On the other hand, the enforced sterilizations of Roma women denote the failure to comply with a politics of minority integration and protection required from all European Union member states. Through camera angles, filming techniques, and visual tropes, Coomber alludes to previous moments of ethnic violence against the Roma in the Czech Republic as she alternates between disabled Roma women's bodies and derelict cityscapes, both of which constitute discursive spaces for the performance of civic exclusion.

In this chapter, I argue that as a modern epistemology of what Etienne Balibar calls "the border zones,"—areas in which the state exerts methods of selective control on various populations—the documentary depicts the performance of violent state sovereignty and exclusionary citizenship that Roma in Eastern and Central Europe suffer (Balibar, *We, The People of Europe*, 108). Coomber creatively recovers the Roma's access to European citizenship through an appeal to civic consciousness regarding minority integration in the Czech Republic. Advocating for the global rights of women, the documentary highlights a type of activism that discloses the injustices suffered by populations historically excluded from national histories of state formation. These populations have been colonized and orientalized by white-centred, Western European powers, in two ways. First, the documentary narrates a history of oppression regarding a community whose identity remains otherwise elusive globally; the film forces Western audiences to reexamine Eurocentric definitions of belonging and knowledge formation.[2] Second, the recognition of giving Roma women a public and meaningful voice has a global reach; in this sense, the documentary attempts to empower the Roma in Europe.[3] Coomber draws a metaphoric parallel between the maternal Roma body unjustly injured through sterilization and certain peripheral urban areas constituting "border zones," thereby highlighting that the confrontation between economies of gender, ethnicity, and reproduction can be addressed and understood (Balibar, "World Borders, Political Borders," 73). I appeal to Balibar's notion of the "border zone" as I address the element that constitutes the focus of the documentary, namely the Roma female body, and note the actual geographic areas representing Roma living spaces within the city.

ROMA MINORITY ADMINISTRATION IN THE CZECH REPUBLIC

Unique among the Central and Eastern European states, the Czech Republic joined the European Union in 2004 as a model case of postcommunist transformation and a successful example of European integration. One of the conditions for integration consisted in the alignment of domestic legislation with the so-called *acquis communautaire*—a set of European Union laws and regulations establishing the compatibility between an EU candidate and the other signatory states. An important part of the *acquis communautaire* is the observance of human and minority rights (Ram 28-56). Specifically, Title II, Article 6 of the European Agreement, which establishes the access of the Czech Republic to the European Union, states: "Respect for the democratic principles and human rights established by the Helsinki Final Act and the Charter of Paris for a New Europe ... constitute[s an] essential element of the present association" ("General Principles" 6). Northern Ireland, for instance, challenged its compatibility with *acquis communautaire* in 2014 when its blanket ban on abortions was ruled as a breach in both women's and human rights as established by the European Convention on Human Rights (High Court). In the post-1990 Czech Republic, the role of the European Union, the international socialization of the postcommunist state, and its democratic consolidation have reformed the political culture and civil society in matters regarding minority rights. Subsequent European agreements and domestic policy reforms have urged the

Czech Republic to conduct its ethnic politics in accordance with democratic principles sensitive to human rights issues—such as the accommodation of domestic minority rights, the prevention of ethnic violence, and the establishment of institutions designed for the implementation, sustenance, and development of this politics (European Commission, "Report on the Implementation of the EU Framework for National Roma Integration Strategies"). In showing the Czech Republic's commitment to the European merge and implicitly to the minority rights clauses, Miloš Zeman, prime minister between 1998 and 2002, declared that "We shall not conceive our entry to the EU only as a foreign policy matter, but also as a domestic affair, because the impact of European norms on the Czech law is basically a matter of domestic policy" (CTK News Wire). However, a European Commission Report in 2003, only a year prior to the integration, observed that

> As regards the situation of the Roma minority, the multi-faceted discrimination and social exclusion faced by the Roma continues to give cause for concern. Unemployment affecting the Roma continues to be disproportionately high. Widespread discriminatory hiring practices are still being reported. ("Comprehensive Monitoring Report on the Czech Republic's Preparations for Membership" 34)

Although discriminatory practices against the Roma simmered down after the 2004 European integration, they have continued to be recorded.

Prejudice against the Roma, which reached a peak in the Czech Republic following the fall of communism in the 1990s, has been amply noted. According to a recent estimate, the Roma minority in the Czech state numbers around 300,000 members, representing approximately 3 percent of the total Czech population (European Roma Rights Center, "Compensation Now: Campaign on Coerced Sterilisation"). Following the split of Czechoslovakia in 1993, the Czech citizenship law issued the same year prevented many individuals of Roma ethnicity from claiming full citizenship, which attracted international attention to the plight of this minority. According to the new citizenship law, possessing a criminal record warranted the loss of or guaranteed the impossibility of obtaining citizenship (Ram 40; Hübschmannová). International security specialist Rich Fawn argues that the provisions implemented for the application for citizenship primarily aimed to disenfranchise the Roma and to relegate them to the condition of being stateless (1201). As a result of European criticism, however, an amendment to this law "designed to bring the citizenship application procedures closer to the European model" was signed in 1996 (qtd. in Ram 41).

Concomitantly to the issuance of the citizenship law, the far-right Republican Party openly advocated for violence against the Roma: "In February 1993," Miroslav Sládek, the party leader between 1990 and 1998, "called on Czech mayors to expel Roma from their towns and offered the prize of a car to the most successful" (Fown 1202). Only three years later, the city council in the township of Usti nad Labem sanctioned the construction of a wall along an important traffic artery in order to divide Roma inhabitants from their non-Roma neighbours (Ram 42). Designed as "just a fence ... necessary to protect the 'orderly citizens' from their 'unadaptable and indecent' neighbours," the wall boxed in about 160 Roma residents (Connolly). In her opinion piece, Milena Hübschmannová notes that "the wall in Matični was removed *after* the joint protests of Roma organisations, NGOs, human rights' organisations, and especially after massive criticism from abroad" (Hübschmannová, my emphasis). In particular, the European Commission rightfully proclaimed that the wall damaged the Czech Republic's reputation as a democratic and European nation (Ram 42). Such acts of exclusion directed at Roma bodies render them as indicators for the restrictive delineation of ethnic borders within the Czech nation, which becomes both xenophobic and homogenous (Šťastný; Fawn 1193-1219; Osborn).[4]

As a particular expression of ethnic violence during communism, forcible sterilization toward the Roma supported a supremacist, discriminatory politics popular in Czechoslovakia long before 1990 (Powell).

> In a racist policy similar to the eugenics experiments in the American South, [the communist authorities] attempted to break what they considered a vicious circle of unem-

> ployment, welfare dependency, poverty, high demographic growth and crime through the sterilization of Romany women. (Tucker 210)

Several organizations, including Charter 77, disclosed that "the Czechoslovakian government has paid women to have abortions and even to undergo sterilization, practices ... refer[red] to as genocide" (Kostelancik 316). Eighty-seven cases of sterilization were recorded between 1990 and 2005 alone (Romedia Foundation). Giving birth also represents a specific rite of passage for Roma women. In Roma communities, a female attains "womanhood" only after she becomes a mother. Hence, forcible sterilizations constitute acts of what Slawomir Kapralski calls "semantic" violence (Kapralski 248). This type of aggression illustrates the ways in which the Roma are denied access to a specific ethnic and cultural identity that would allow them membership in the Czech nation.

THE ISSUE OF BORDERS

In his book entitled *We, the People of Europe? Reflections on Transnational Citizenship*, French philosopher Etienne Balibar argues for a transformation in the concept of borders and the idea of the nation-state. Although one may consider this transformation as a global phenomenon of modernity, Balibar pins it to the consequences of the East European states' failed attempt "to homogenize [their] 'civil society'" during communism (82). In the later 1990s, "the borders of new sociopolitical entities, in which an attempt [had been] made to preserve all the functions of the sovereignty of the state, [were] no longer entirely situated at the outer limit of territories; they [were] dispersed a little everywhere" (1). The borders of the new political and economic territories are no longer situated at the periphery, but are dispersed throughout the territory as the zones of confrontation between different political, social, ethnic, and economic classes, and between religious and secular views. They constitute the most important areas for the formation of a new people, of the nation-state, and of democratic citizenship ("World Borders, Political Borders" 71-72). The politics of exclusion that traditionally took place at national boundaries today affect performances of national, ethnic, and racial omissions, and enforce a violence contrary to the nature of European citizenship. In this sense, border zones constitute "the sites of residence of nomadic and minority populations who are the source and target of the obsession with law and order that is so closely intertwined with the obsession with identity" (Balibar 177). These are the spaces where discriminatory actions that have been legitimated to support ideologies of national homogeneity (for instance, under communism) become suspect, and their discrediting reveals holes in the narratives of democratic citizenship, particularly in the European Union.

Although he does not address the Roma issue in Central and Eastern Europe, Balibar does discuss in his theory of borders the exclusionary nature of the present-day European state, which helps problematize not only the notions of territory and economics but also European citizenship as unfairly granted to certain populations and not others. The principle of the border zone can also help shed light on displacements and disjunctures created by globalization. As with many populations across the world expelled to the margins of the nation—Indigenous populations, Palestinians living in occupied territories, Syrian migrants, and many others—the Roma in the Czech Republic occupy a geographical and political space in formation, which concerns the constitution of both nation and citizenship and demands analysis.

In her compelling documentary, Coomber symbolically depicts instances of Balibar's exemplary "border zone" in the Czech Republic on two levels. First, she constructs the bodies of sterilized Roma mothers as metaphors for a critique of ethnic violence. By revealing the coercive nature of the women's sterilization procedures, Coomber insists that hospital authorities consciously hid their culpability in an attempt to normalize xenophobia without raising suspicion. Second, the filmmaker geographically delineates the urban spaces inhabited by the Roma as stages for the performance of social, civic, and economic exclusion as she alludes to xenophobic incidents in the recent history of the Czech Republic. By promoting a public discourse about the intersection of gender, ethnicity, citizenship, and reproduction, Coomber sets out to engage civil consciousness and to elicit a commitment for resolution regarding the status of the Roma in Central and Eastern Europe. Coomber's documentary highlights the case of the Roma in the Czech Republic to argue that citizenship is understood in the age of globalization as a precarious status in which some individuals, often women, must fight for the recognition of rights by over-performing civil responsibilities. Only after having documented, disclosed, appealed, and validated their sterilizations as violations of their cultural, gendered, and bodily integrity can Czech Roma maternal bodies emerge as sites of resistance, agency, and democratic citizenship.

TRIAL OF A CHILD DENIED

Coomber's expository documentary assembles several monologues into an argumentative frame to reveal Czech prejudice against the Roma and to demonstrate that sterilizations deny Roma's sovereign citizenship. Without the presence of a commentator, the interviews arrange themselves into a narrative and offer the impression of objectivity. Coomber intercuts Helena Ferencikova's, Helena Balogova's, and Elena Gorolova's monologues with scenes filmed in court and at meetings of a Roma women's commission established to address the Council of Europe at Strasbourg. The three women's testimonials are enhanced by interviews with hospital delegates, legal representatives, and the women's spouses, who offer their interpretations of the events. Because the documentary is filmed in Czech and captioned in English, one must remain aware of translation challenges. The current analysis is based on the English captioning.

The opening shot establishes the rhetorical situation of the documentary in which the female body represents a liminal, indeterminate site for the performance of discrimination against the Roma community through enforced sterilization (Albert; Šimůnková; Denysenko; European Institute for Gender Equality; "Forced Sterilization of Romani Women—A Persisting Human Rights Violation"; "UN Presses Czech Republic on Coercive Sterilisation of Romani Women"). The viewer is invited into an obstetrics operational theatre where a deserted surgical bed is surrounded by sinister equipment. The first interviewee, a male medic, explains the surgical process of tying a woman's fallopian tubes during a sterilization procedure and offers a quick demonstration on a piece of intravenous drip tube, which mimics the actual organ. Although tube ligation became a practised sterilization method in London in the early 1800s, the psychological repercussions were not clearly studied or understood. Only recently have researchers began to underscore the high occurrence of remorse in patients sterilized immediately after fetal delivery (Zurawin and Sklar). Despite the global controversy, tubal ligation as a method of contraception generates, the doctor's unaffected explanation of the sterilization process indicates that concern for the patient's emotional disposition has no place in this setting. As a representative of state, the doctor illustrates how women's bodies become objects on which he, the male agent, can perform his expert and state-sanctioned medical operation (Haas). The surgeon represents the vehicle of a complex metaphor, as he embodies the rigid authority of the hospital, the patriarchal power of public institutions, and the voice of procedural law. This tripartite tenor of Coomber's opening metaphor induces an awareness of the state's omnipresence, coded both male and white. Aided in his routine by a female nurse to whom he appears to explain the procedural steps of fallopian tube ligation, the surgeon looks up at the camera only for a brief moment at the end of his performance to indicate that he is in fact addressing the viewer.

Despite the doctor's insistence on the accuracy of the procedure, obtaining a patient's informed consent is called into question with the next scene. The camera introduces Helena Ferencikova lying on a surgical table in a decrepit intensive care unit while the soundtrack carries a dramatic tune above the noise of a heart monitor. Visually prompted to infer Ferencikova has suffered a tube ligation, the viewer learns that the woman consented to sterilization while debilitated by pain and that the need for such a procedure had not been discussed with her prior to her labour.

> I was lying there pregnant when I went into labour, had delivery pains and my water broke.... Those pains are horrible. I don't think that any woman could ever read in that kind of pain. Any woman would simply sign it and

> not care. Such pain would easily make you jump out of the window. You simply want everything to be over. I think I was sterilized because I was a Roma woman and they didn't want Roma to have too many children.

Ferencikova questions the hospital's technique of obtaining consent and interprets the doctor's ulterior goals as she acknowledges her inability to make an informed decision, which helped the hospital to fulfill its discriminatory agenda.

With her confession, Coomber argues that consent needs to be understood as a result of the ability to discern a procedure from another. Whereas Ferencikova situates debilitating pain as the motivator for her decision, other women in Coomber's documentary claim illiteracy as the barrier for expressing informed consent. For instance, Helena Balogová admits that "I didn't know what they did to me because I can't read or write, so I signed what I shouldn't have signed." All women, however, interpret their sterilizations as acts of ethnic and racial violence against the Roma. The doctor's expert justification of the procedure may be read as a means to demonstrate that these women would not have been able to understand the urgency of their situation, and therefore, would not have been able to offer their informed consent given this communication rift. However, their recognition of racial discrimination and of the echoes of earlier xenophobic incidents against the Roma in the Czech Republic suggests that these women would have been capable of rational comprehension. Reasonably then, the court justices Coomber captures on camera admit that "informed consent isn't a question of just a few minutes," which shows that the process might have been superficially covered by hospital administrators and that the patient was forced to give her consent without thinking it through.

Related to sterilization, the lack of cultural sensitivity to the notion of purity—*mahrimé*—within the Roma society represents another form of bias that Coomber examines, albeit subtly. As a practice of rendering the body free of contaminants, sterilization determines the border between cleanliness and pollution, between virtue and dishonour. In Roma culture, the lower body is considered symbolically impure or *mahrimé* because it houses the organs responsible for intercourse, reproduction, parturition, and bowel movements. Therefore, "[t]o be *mahrimé* means not only to be defiled, it also represents a danger to the community by introducing evil and unbalance" (Grigore 15). Traditions around the event of birth rise from the belief that menstrual blood renders women impure (Matras 88). Predicated on the blood taboo is the practice according to which recent mothers must undergo a process of purification. Understood in this sense, sterilization equals decontamination, which allows these women resocialization with other members of their community. In hopes of being purified, Ferencikova (and the other Roma women in Coomber's documentary) could have easily interpreted sterilization as a cleansing that would permit her to cross the impurity boundary set by parturition.[5]

Another type of cultural insensitivity toward Roma traditions is the unacknowledged social importance of a woman's ability to give birth (Ortner 69).[6] Ferencikova underscores the importance of reproduction in affirming women's gender roles within the Roma community to which she belongs: "Roma people are simply used to having more children. A Roma woman is precious because she gives children to a Roma man, right?" Notwithstanding the patriarchal power dynamics that establish said role, reproduction assigns a Roma woman her social standing and acknowledges her gender. In a Romanian Cortorari[7] Roma community, "a female baby acknowledged as such at birth can only become a Cortorari woman once she procreates in wedlock" (Tesăr 115; Toma and Fosztó 283). As the first and foremost gender performance, parturition constitutes a necessary act legitimizing the category of woman. Fertility denotes a core theme in the mythology of Moravian Roma, collected and transcribed by Rudolf Daniel circa 1955 (Pavelčik and Pavelčik 22-24). In a 2004 article on Roma reproduction in Serbia, Jelena Čvorović similarly argues that a Roma "woman's highest value is her reproductive capacity ... if [she] bears many children, she is respected and treated well" (225). In this vein, Elena Gorolova, the third Roma interviewee in Coomber's documentary, puts it rather dramatically: "An apple tree which stops bearing fruit is no longer worth anything in the garden ... that's how we women feel, we have lost our mission."

Ferencikova, however, explains that regardless of tradition, her husband is pleased with her and that the catalyst of their marriage is love: "I know my husband loves me and is going to stay with me. We have two children, and that is enough. The main thing is that we love each other." Despite her confessing to the power of love, the setting in which Coomber chooses to depict her—a bed in a children's room decorated with toys—embeds Ferencikova into the narrative of desirable reproduction and underlies her search for social justice.

Using Ferencikova's story as a framing device, Coomber outlines a collective ethnic politics by illustrating a shared understanding of the modes of social, political, and civic engagement available to the Roma in the Czech Republic. Ferencikova interprets the events as follows: "If [the hospital] cared for me, they would have asked me ... but they didn't give me any chance to think it over as if I was some kind of little guinea-pig." Her husband sketches a similar portrayal of the racism and xenophobia the Roma have historically endured in the Czech Republic: "The Czech Republic judges Roma people badly because they say we're not educated and we do bad things. There is discrimination in the Czech Republic. We feel it a lot." The man uses the pronoun "we" to draw a line—indeed, a border—between the Roma community in the Czech Republic and the rest of the nation. However, "we" also proposes a self-reference that allows the audience to identify not only with the Roma but also with other communities of women equally harmed. This develops an empathetic relationship between viewers and the viewed, between "our" bodies and those selected for sterilization. Through the plaintiffs' testimony and protest, the documentary explains how Roma women do not have access to civic rights the same way as non-Roma Czech citizens do. For instance, Elena Gorolova says, "I came to Strasbourg because the Council of Europe invited me to attend the exhibition of our group, the group of women who've been sterilized. I was at home for such a long time and I just wanted to shout it out. That's why I'm shouting it to the world." She engages in a certain type of democratic citizenship in which civil disobedience can be performed through public protest. Hoping that the Council of Europe would lend them a listening ear, the women ask for the type of justice expected in a multicultural and borderless Europe. In similar ways, through visual anthropology, the documentary "shouts" to the world that these Roma women have once again been injured on account of both their ethnicity and their gender.

For Coomber, the sterilized bodies of Roma women in the Czech Republic become sites on which democratic modernity and communist traditionalism meet. Interpreting the hospital's malpractice as a remnant of a formerly prevailing ideology of national homogeneity, a male medical professional describes a communist tradition in which the doctor has ultimate agency and decision power over the life of a patient. In other words, it is not the doctor's fault but rather their ideological upbringing under communism, which has shaped the medical culture writ large: "They simply had that way of thinking that they've been taught at schools during communism." Testifying to the politics of exclusion practised under communism, which bordered on eugenics, another male interviewee confesses: "the old regime didn't even try to conceal that large Roma families for them were the cause of many social problems ... it was believed that the Roma population was of less quality not only in terms of health but intellect, too." Although both men agree that such coerced sterilization deserves to be punished in Western European countries, in the Czech Republic, conveniently identified by the speakers as a state that despite its EU membership does not quite qualify as European, "the doctors are guilty in the same way we all are." With this statement, guilt is displaced from the perpetrators of violence to the state that sanctions violence against minorities and to another instance of the collective yet indeterminate "we."

Although Coomber situates the female body as a generative territory despite its sterilization, another border zone—the area in which a new people and a new consciousness emerge—is delineated on a literal level through the employment of geospatial referents such as rivers, buildings, courtyards, streets, and fences. This aesthetic together with its political project are visually mapped on a contemporary urban geography. The camera moves outside of the operating room—the spatial location at the start of the documentary—and focuses on a window, then exits the building through the window to reveal areas recognizable as Roma settlements. The filming motion unites two representations of Balibar's "border zone"—the women's recovering bodies and their pauperized neighbourhoods—in order to emphasize Roma marginalization and statelessness.

While interviewees utter their part, the camera rolls over a panoramic view of the cities of Ostrava and Most, surveying Roma vicinities. The long-shot angle captures a wide landscape strewn with modern apartment buildings that contrast with the decrepit houses in which the Roma live—a figurative ethnic enclosure, which the camera captures in close shots. In the words of Zoltan Barany, "In the absence of a Romani 'homeland' or 'mother state,' no external actor"—not even the Czech state—"is sufficiently ... concerned ... to offer protection and enforce ... rights" (328). Thus, Roma marginalization gains symbolic figuration in Coomber's documentary. The spatial barrier is a compelling visual trope reminiscent of the wall erected in Usti nad Labem and establishes the meagre resources the Roma have access to as another indication of their status as undesirable. In fact, the three vignettes the documentary presents are visually connected by similar interludes. The camera connects Ferencikova's ordeal to Helena Balogova's and Elena Gorolova's through the topography of the border. For instance, in Ostrava-Přívoz, the viewer enters a marginal space as the camera rolls along an unfinished brick wall and glides over the frames of former windows now walled up as if to designate an indisputable barrier. The dull red bricks contrast with the luminous green of the space outside, enclosed by a wall—a yard converted into a playground—and through colour, the bricks symbolically remind viewers of a regime that took forceful measures to criminalize Roma culture and to eradicate Roma identity (Fawn 1213). The viewer sees a decaying building through the eyes of a child who notices the utter disrepair while a vivacious group of more Roma children play in the rubble.

In all three vignettes, Coomber depicts Roma children at play. This cinematographic tactic engages the belief that the uncontrolled reproduction of certain groups of individuals, often racialized, backslides the nation into a state of postcommunist destitution. During such moments, the filming slows down, allowing the audience to focus on the images and to decode their symbolic use. The portrayal of Roma children who appear unaware of the state-sanctioned xenophobia singles them out as the indirect victims of forcible sterilizations. These images also conjure global memories of moments in the twentieth century when the institutionalization of similar ideologies facilitated diabolical measures of population extermination during the Holocaust, the Bosnian civil war, the second Sino-Japanese War, the 1984 Sikh riots in India, or the Burundi mass killings, to mention just a few. In all these cases, the targeted populations were racial or ethnic minorities whose biological lives and reproduction—the birthing and upbringing of children—constituted a threat to the wellbeing of the majority.[8]

The link between bodies and borders is undeniable. Representations of the body, reproduction, or biometrical practices, and physical or mental health issues are all tangled up in notions of class distinction and ethnic belonging. Traditional beliefs that set a female body closer to the natural word and thus inferior to men, as Sherry Ortner's work indicates, represent the first border separating men and women established along gender lines. That certain ethnic groups have a favourable national representation over others highlights the existence of another type of border drawn along ethnic lines and manifested through bodies. As globalization sets in motion an increased flow of bodies, ideas, and practices, it also often leads to conflicts between bodies, ideas, and practices. Women's bodies play an important role in determining the borders of the nation, the purity of the community, and the authenticity and reproducibility of groups. Across certain borders, women's lives are devalued or sexualized. In an attempt to raise attention to the fact that some lives do not matter as much as others, the 2008 Campaign for Compensation for Coercively Sterilised Romani Women was launched at a Women's Worlds Congress in Madrid, Spain (European Roma Rights Center, "First Court Victory in Central Europe on Coercive Sterilisation of Romani Women; Ostrava Court Finds Violations of Dignity as a Result of Abuse by Czech Doctors"). The advocates appealed to global human rights activists because the governments of the countries where forced Roma sterilizations had occurred failed to take action despite constant lobbying. However, their singular efforts are not enough. Films, such as Coomber's or Tajima-Peña's, aim to divulge that such racialist phenomena continue to plague the world. They indicate that reproductive crimes such as forced sterilizations do not occur only within certain communities; rather, they have the potential to affect all women. Finally, they underscore that global feminist agendas must address the experiences and perspectives of women of colour, working-class women, and, certainly, Roma women.

ENDNOTES

[1]My gratitude goes to Abby Palko, Dorsía Smith Silva, Laila Malik, Sarah Stapleto, Victoria Adams, Brandi Pettijoh, and Elizabeth Frierson for helping me edit and enhance this chapter. All the errors are my own.

[2]When represented in cultural artifacts, the Roma are by and large caricaturized across the globe. Some examples include the following: American TLC produced shows such as *My Big Fat Gypsy Wedding*, *American Gypsy*, or *Gypsy Sisters*; the Turkish series *Gönülçelen*; the Venezuelan telenovela *Kassandra*; and Bollywood interpretations of Gypsy culture and dance in *Mangal Pandey: The Rising* or *Pardesi*. The more realistic and complex representations of the Roma such as those produced by director Emil Kusturica and musician Goran Bregović remain widely unknown.

[3]The documentary has been aired at the International Film Festival in Amsterdam and on CNN International.

[4]Public intolerance against the Roma continued in the new millennium. Though not very frequent after 2000, these events illustrate the Roma's unremitting exclusion from European citizenship.

[5]There is no indication that the hospital may have reacted to Roma practices that build on the concept of women's inferiority as oppressive and patriarchal.

[6]One must notice that both the assignation of females to the responsibility of reproducing the community and the elements of defilement associated with their reproductive biology constitute signs of a cultural evaluation of women as inferior to men. However, a critique of this is neither the object of my paper, not the task of Czech OB/GYN professionals.

[7]Cortorari is an exonym that refers to an ethnic community of

Roma from Transylvania, Romania, who speak the Romanes dialect called Cortorari. The term is derived from the Romanian word *cort*, meaning "tent" and which refers to traditional living spaces of the community.

[8]Aware of the political import of their documentary despite of being warned that this was not "the most glamorous subject" for a debut film, producer Dana Wilson and director Michele Coomber reveal their intention to CNN reporters: "questions remained over the extent of modern-day eugenics and the spokesperson of the health ministry admitted that had this occurred in a country like the UK, medical staff would have been terminated. The issue is not simple however" (*Trial of a Child Denied)*.

WORKS CITED

Albert, Gwendolyn. "Forced Sterilization and Romani Women's Resistance in Central Europe." *Different Takes*, vol. 71, 2011, dspace.hampshire.edu/bitstream/10009/925/1/popdev_differen-takes_071.pdf. Accessed 5 Mar. 2015.

Balibar, Etienne. "World Borders, Political Borders." *PMLA*, Translated by Erin M. Williams, vol. 117, no. 1, 2002, pp. 71-78.

Balibar, Etienne. *We, The People of Europe. Reflections on Transnational Citizenship*. Translated by James Swenson. Princeton University Press, 2003.

Barany, Zoltan. "Living on the Edge: The East European Roma in Postcommunist Politics and Societies." *Slavic Review*, vol. 53, no. 2, 1994, pp. 321-44.

Connolly, Kate. "Gypsies Trapped behind 'European Wall of Shame.'" *The Guardian*, 24 October 1999, www.theguardian.com/world/1999/oct/24/humanrights.kateconnolly. Accessed 5 Mar. 2015.

Čvorović, Jelena. "Sexual and Reproductive Strategies among Serbian Gypsies." *Population and Environment*, vol. 25, no. 3, 2004, pp. 217-42.

Denysenko, Marina. "Sterilized Roma Accuse Czechs," *BBC*, 17 Mar. 2007, news.bbc.co.uk/2/hi/europe/6409699.stm. Accessed March 5, 2015.

European Commission. "Comprehensive Monitoring Report on

the Czech Republic's Preparations for Membership." *European Commission*, 2003, http://ec.europa.eu/neighbourhood-enlargement/sites/near/files/archives/pdf/key_documents/2003/cmr_cz_final_en.pdf. Accessed 5 Mar. 2015.

European Commission. "Report on the Implementation of the EU Framework for National Roma Integration Strategies." *European Commission*, 2014, http://ec.europa.eu/justice/discrimination/files/roma_implement_strategies2014_en.pdf. Accessed 5 Mar. 2015.

European Institute for Gender Equality. "Elena Gorolova, Czech Republic," *Women Inspiring Europe Resource Pool*, 26 Nov. 2012, eige.europa.eu/more-areas/women-and-men-inspiring-europe-resource-pool/elena-gorolova-0. Accessed 5 Mar. 2015.

European Roma Rights Center. "Compensation Now: Campaign on Coerced Sterilisation," *European Roma Rights Center*, 2008, http://www.errc.org/article/compensation-now-campaign-on-coerced-sterilisation/2965. Accessed 22 June 2015.

European Roma Rights Center. "First Court Victory in Central Europe on Coercive Sterilisation of Romani Women; Ostrava Court Finds Violations of Dignity as a Result of Abuse by Czech Doctors." *Minority Electronic Resources*, 2005, www.minelres.lv/mailing_archive/2005-November/004310.html. Accessed May 7, 2015.

Fawn, Rick. "Czech Attitudes towards the Roma: 'Expecting More of Havel's Country?'" *Europe-Asia Studies*, vol. 53, no. 8, 2001, pp. 1193-1219.

"Forced Sterilizations of Romani Women: A Persisting Human Rights Violation." *Romedia Foundation*, 7 Feb. 2013, romediafoundation.wordpress.com/2013/02/07/forced-sterilization-of-romani-women-a-persisting-human-rights-violation/. Accessed 19 Sept. 2015.

Grigore, Delia. "Family and Health in the Traditional Rromani Culture." *Introduction to Roma Culture: Exploring Cultural Diversity for Family Doctors,* Eds. Sara McKelvey, Julie Ray, and Penelope Riseborough, Romanian Family Health Initiative, 2007, pp. 1-44.

Haas, Elizabeth. "Women's Health. Good Health for Her: Issues in the Czech Republic." *Expatz.cz*, 4 Oct. 2007, www.expats.

cz/prague/article/health-medical/womens-health/. Accessed 31 Jan. 2016.

High Court of Justice in Northern Ireland. "The Northern Ireland Human Rights Commission's Application in the Matter of an Application for Judicial Review by the Northern Ireland Human Rights Commission In the Matter of the Law on the Termination of Pregnancy in Northern Ireland" *Northern Ireland Courts and Tribunals Service*, 2014, No. www.courtsni.gov.uk/en-GB/Judicial%20Decisions/PublishedByYear/Documents/2015/%5B2015%5D%20NIQB%2096/j_j_HOR9740Final.htm. Accessed 28 Jan. 2015.

Hübschmannová, Milena. "The History of the Roma in the Czech Republic after the Fall of Communism." *Rombase* 2002, http://rombase.uni-graz.at/cgi-bin/art.cgi?src=data/hist/current/after-communism.en.xml. Accessed 5 Mar. 2015.

Janicek, Karel. "Gypsy Women Confront Czechs on Ugly Legacy." *The Washington Post*, 17 June, 2006, www.washingtonpost.com/wp-dyn/content/article/2006/06/17/ AR2006061700396_pf.html. Accessed 7 May 2015.

Kapralski, Sławomir. "Democratization in the Post-Communist Europe: A View from the Margins." *Polish Sociological Review*, vol. 163, 2008, pp. 245-62.

Kostelancik, David J. "The Gypsies of Czechoslovakia: Political and Ideological Considerations in the Development of Policy." *Studies in Comparative Communism*, vol. 22, no. 4, 1989, pp. 307-21.

Matras, Yaron. *The Romani Gypsies*. Harvard University Press, 2015.

Ram, Melanie H. "Democratization through European Integration: The Case of Minority Rights in the Czech Republic and Romania." *Studies in Comparative International Development*, vol. 38, no. 2, 2003, pp. 28-56.

Ortner, Sherry B. "Is Female to Male as Nature Is to Culture?" *Woman, Culture, and Society*, edited by M.Z. Rosaldo and L. Lamphere, Stanford University Press, 1974, pp. 68-87.

Osborn, John E. "Liberal Humanism Abandoned: The Paradox of the Post-Communist Czech Republic." *Occasional Papers of East European Studies*, Woodrow Wilson International Center for Scholars, Washington, DC, July 2011.

Powell, Chris. "Time for another Immoral Panic? The Case of the Czechoslovak Gypsies." *International Journal of the Sociology of Law*, vol. 22, 1994, pp. 105-121.

Šimůnková, Monika. "Czech Republic: Compensation for illegally sterilized women in negotiation," *Romea.cz*, 20 May 2013, www.romea.cz/en/news/czech/czech-republic-compensation-for-illegally-sterilized-women-in-negotiation. Accessed 5 Mar. 2015.

Šťastný, Jiří. "Češi propadají anticikánismu, každý druhý tu Romy nechce, zjistil průzkum." *iDNES.cz*, 2010, zpravy.idnes.cz/cesi-propadaji-anticikanismu-kazdy-druhy-tu-romy-nechce-zjistil-pruzkum-1qx-/domaci.aspx?c=A101209_161615_domaci_js. Accessed 5 Mar. 2015.

Tesăr, Cătălina. "Becoming Rom (Male), Becoming Romni (Female) among Romanian Cortorari Roma: On Body and Gender." *Romani Studies*, vol. 22, no. 2, 2012, pp. 113-140.

Toma, Stefánia, and Lásló Fosztó, *Spectrum: Cercet ri Sociale despre Romi*. Kriterion, 2011.

"Trial of a Child Denied." *CNN World's Untold Stories*, 7 July 2008, edition.cnn.com/CNNI/Programs/untoldstories/blog/2008/07/trial-of-child-denied.html. Accessed 22 June 2015.

Trial of a Child Denied. Directed by Michelle Coomber, Mortal Coil Media, 2011.

Tucker, Aviezer. "The New Jews." *Telos*, 1993, pp. 209-16.

"UN Presses Czech Republic on Coercive Sterilisation of Romani Women," *European Roma Rights Centre*, 4 Sept. 2006, www.errc.org/article/un-presses-czech-republic-on-coercive-sterilisation-of-romani-women/2626. Accessed 5 Mar. 2015.

Zurawin, Robert K., and Avi J. Sklar. "Tubal Sterilization." *MedScape*, 16 Oct. 2012, emedicine.medscape.com/article/266799-overview. Accessed 5 Mar. 2015.

4.
Transnational Mothering Online

Community Blogs by Diasporic Indian Mothers

SUCHARITA SARKAR

I had not known before how great is the burden of pain for the mother who raises a child. One can only know it through one's own difficulties and experiences.
—Rashsundari Debi (qtd. in Sarkar 191-92)

We are a new generation of mothers in India, of the information age. Of satellite TV and internet; Of smaller families and fewer children; Of mommy blogging and sharing stories. On the threshold of modernity and traditionalism. What is it like to parent at a time like this in India? Let's talk!
—Preethi ("Let's Talk Motherhood" par. 1)

INTRODUCTION: THE CONSTRUCTION OF INDIAN MOTHERHOOD

RASHSUNDARI DEBI'S EXPERIENCE of motherhood in 1876 as a solitarily suffered "burden of pain" and Preethi's exploration of mothering in 2011 as "sharing stories" differ diametrically in their access to a shared maternal discourse expressed by mothers themselves. These two juxtaposed extracts expose the long-time silencing of mothers, the deeply felt need for sharing experiences, and the gradual emergence of maternal voices. Historically, motherhood in India has been glorified—in Hindu scriptures and customs—whereas mothers have been systemically disempowered and made vulnerable by the "meaning attached to the idea of motherhood" (Krishnaraj 22).The hegemonic meanings of good motherhood—constructed and controlled by Brahminical caste patriarchy and approved only within the limits of heterosexuality, endogamy, and son preference—have erased the agency and experience of mothers, and, instead, have perpetuated expectations that mothers should always serve and sacrifice for their family. These imposed constructs of motherhood are often internalized by mothers themselves: "South Asian women are often socialized to perform motherhood in a way that neglects their selfhood" (Sangha and Gonsalves 3). Thus, Indian motherhood has been represented and regulated by others, rather than through agentic self-expression by the mothers themselves.

But this female and maternal silencing has also been tenaciously, though sporadically, resisted by women writing about themselves. Development of female education from the nineteenth century onward contributed to the rise in autobiographical and protest writings by women. Simultaneously, however, the nationalist construction of motherhood extended the social role of mothers as reproducers of the ideal Indian nation. In post-1947 sovereign India, the traditional construct of domesticated motherhood was undermined by the rising number of educated and working mothers. Several factors have complicated the postcolonial discourse of motherhood: constitutionally guaranteed equal rights; the post-1991 neoliberal market dynamics devaluing reproductive labour of stay-at-home mothers as compared to the productive labour of working mothers; the ascendancy of Hindu nationalist ideology reasserting the intensive role of mothers in nurturing aggressive Hindu sons; the urban and global migration flows dismantling traditional co-parenting family structures; and the growth of the Internet, which offers participatory spaces for self-fashioning and connecting.

The complex backdrop of motherhood in preglobalized India has shaped the representations and expressions of sub-continental and diasporic Indian mothers after globalization. Contextualized against the historical silencing of mothers and the dominant cultural expectations of motherhood, this chapter aims to study how two community blogs by diasporic Indian mothers—*Masalamommas* and *Indian Moms Connect* (IMC)—use modern information and communication technologies (ICT) to negotiate with motherhood constructs and perform mothering in their self-controlled, transnational, online spaces. I will analyze and theorize specific blog entries in relation to the blogs' overt declarations of intent. This analysis deploys the distinction and imbrication between institutionalized motherhood and experiential mothering in the contexts of "diaspora" and "transnationalism." Although these terms "are often used interchangeably," diasporas are constituted by "co-ethnic and cultural identification" with the homeland, while transnationalism derives more from "*elective* modes of identification" and the "the multi-striated connections they give rise to" (Quayson and Daswani 2-4; my emphasis). I shall use the term "diasporic" to refer to the location and identity of the mothers and the term "transnational" to refer to the networks of connection. However, there are necessary overlaps because identity and networks are not discrete concepts; in fact, they are functionally interrelated in mom blogs.

The mom blogs interrogated in this chapter belong to privileged and mainstream intersections—urban, educated, heterosexual, predominantly Hindu, upper caste and middle class, with access to computer-mediated communication. They exclude many other mothering experiences disadvantageously implicated in North-South global inequities. In the subsequent sections, I investigate how middle-class diasporic Indian mothers use the transnational blog space as a discursive site to replicate, resist, and refashion institutionalized motherhood and articulate the challenges of mothering in globalized situations. In doing so, they disrupt the dominant construct of the silent, subjugated Indian mother and enable multiple maternal voices to emerge, connect, and create new meanings of mothering and motherhood.

GLOBALIZATION AND ONLINE COMMUNITIES OF DIASPORIC INDIAN MOTHERS

Globalization as a process is marked by time-space compression and is characterized by the relative ease with which people, cultures, capital, and commodities travel transnationally. Ato Quayson and Girish Daswani emphasize that diaspora and transnationalism are "two key concepts" which can organize our understanding of "identity and globalization in today's world" (2). Whereas diaspora is marked by nostalgia for the real or imagined homeland, Johannes de Kruijf defines transnationalism as a state of being simultaneously and dynamically embedded in the society of origin and the society of settlement, and this embeddedness is forged and sustained by linkages and continuing exchanges (6-7). The mom bloggers studied here are hypermobile and connected maternal migrants who can engage with other mothers in diasporic or indigenous locations. They can negotiate with their homelands and adopted lands in multiple ways through the dynamic, interactive, and transnational space of their blogs.

Diaspora spaces are conceptually "inhabited not only by those who have migrated and their descendants but, equally, by those who are constructed and represented as indigenous" (Brah 178). The mom-blogs studied here have a wide community of bloggers, including those who reside in South Asia, those who have migrated abroad, those who are second or third generation immigrants, and even those who have South Asian partners, thus being transnational in the literal sense of reaching beyond or transcending national boundaries. These diverse locations and genealogies lead to multiple ways of understanding and performing motherhood, and these blogs offer a rich terrain of maternal differences as well as identities. My focus in this chapter will be on select blog posts by diasporic Indian or Indian-origin Hindu mothers, although these transnational blog-spaces are voluntarily inhabited by a much wider demographic.

Masalamommas—launched in June, 2011 by Anjum Choudhry Nayyar in Canada—addresses the "*modern* South Asian working or stay-at-home mom" juggling "family, extended family, sometimes a career and ... *cultural expectations*," yet who has sufficient resources of time and money to engage with "fashion, education, balancing [the] household budget, cool tech and gear *must-haves* to the latest health and parenting news" ("About Us" pars.1-3, my emphasis). Similarly, *Indian Moms Connect*—founded by Preethi in 2011 with six key team members and over 150 contributors from cities in the United States, Australia, Europe, and India—also specifies its target readership of "global *urban* Indian mothers" who feel the need, and enjoy the leisure, "to *get together and discuss* the issues of the *daily job of parenting*" (Team IMC, "About the Team" par. 1, my emphasis).

It may be critiqued that these blogging communities are predicated upon the "social exclusion [of] non-blogging, non-wired and non-computer literate women" (Stadtman Tucker 207). Yet these very privileges of middle-class affluence constellate with diasporic experiences of displacement and marginalization to create deep maternal anxieties that form the impetus to connect and share stories in these blogs. These anxieties are rooted in the stresses of the "daily job of parenting" in the new home, as well as in the "cultural expectations" of the old home (Team IMC, "About the Team" par. 1). Diasporic mothers are expected to preserve and transfer the cultural legacy of the *desh* (home country) to their children and to protect them from the corrupting cultural influence of the *videsh* (adopted or foreign country) (Mishra 5). This pressure to resist the fast-paced flows of globalization that threaten the homogeneity of Hindu cultural identity escalates maternal guilt. Geetha, a blogger on *Indian Moms Connect*, articulates the persistent fear felt by diasporic mothers of being judged as bad mothers if they fail to suitably Indian-ize their children: these mothers "strive to teach their kids their family tradition and culture" through "umpteen efforts" to "celebrate major Indian festivals, visit places of worship, read stories from Indian scriptures, emphasize the importance of mother-tongue, expose the kids to Indian Music and Art forms, etc" (Geetha par. 6). Yet Geetha accepts that acculturating forces might lead her son to have "different aspirations than our dreams and expectations" (par. 7). Geetha also engages with the complex network of cultural expectations existing among first-generation migrant mothers, their homeland-dwelling parents, and their own second-generation diasporic children, and she seeks a balance between the demands of the homeland and the needs of surviving in the new land. Linking her happiness to the balance between her extended family in the homeland and her friends in the adopted land, Geetha uses the fluidity of the transnational blog space to reconcile with her in-betweenness.

Nayyar deploys this search for balance as the impetus to create *Masalamommas*. She uses the "cultural conversations" in the discursive blog space to resolve the questions she was "struggling with": "How do you balance your need to be realistic with cultural celebrations as a mom of this generation with your need to respect elders' expectations?" ("When Motherhood" par. 10). Diasporic Indian mothers have to navigate the double isolations of motherhood and migration, and as technology-enabled "third-wave mothers," they may choose to "cultivate an online persona to restore their self-concept as cultural citizens and to relieve ... their sense of displacement" (Stadtman Tucker 201). Group blogs join acts of self-validation to build transnational online communities that "create an approachable space for mothers to share their experiences" and "hopefully learn from each other" (Team IMC, "About IMC" par. 1; Nayyar, "When Motherhood" par. 9). By voluntarily participating in such blog spaces, mothers reconfigure their diasporic motherhood roles through self-chosen, supportive, and transnational networks. Thus, the mothers' individual agency as well as their collective conversations helps them grapple with the challenges of diasporic mothering through an ongoing, evolving process.

COMMUNITY BLOGS AS MATERNAL RESOURCE

De Kruijf suggests that computer-mediated communication is a part of "the coping strategy of migrants" to deal with "dislocation and relocation" (9). For diasporic Indian mothers, this coping strategy is mainly three-fold: as mothers, they require advice on nurturing their children in new locations; as migrant Indians, they require resources enabling them to reproduce Indian cultural ideals; and as individuals who have a self beyond the maternal, they require support of a like-minded, nonjudgmental community and a creative space of their own. The flexible blog format, which is based on slow, asynchronous conversations, is ideally suited for time-constrained migrant mothers. As de Kruijf writes, the blog space "enables non-physical co-presence ... and allows instantaneous as well as suspended interaction" (9). Both *Masalamommas* and *Indian Moms Connect* are founded and maintained by mothers who aim to create an empathetic, accessible, diversified, and participatory maternal space through online resources as well as customized advice, and offline support through community and consulting activities. ICTs such as community blogs "support the transformation of family networks into transnational ... networks" (de Kruijf 9). Although these blogs function as surrogates of homeland families, their support or advice is not intrusive, coercive, or rigidly imposed. The mothers control the dynamics of their interaction with the blogs, and they can selectively and flexibly use the blogs' versatile resources to manage their individual mothering experiences.

Both blogs have hyperlinked sections offering advice on motherwork, and maternal and child health. Advice given by medical experts is a cost-saving strategy often useful in new locations. *Masalamommas* has a dedicated advice section called "Saheli Circle," which aims to "foster dialogue" between the readers and expert columnists (who are often mothers themselves) on such issues as pregnancy care, single mothering, and work-home balancing ("Saheli Circle" par. 1). "Saheli" means "female friend" in several Indian languages: as the experts belong to the maternal community, their advice is less intimidating and more approachable. Some blog posts bridge the gap between the diaspora and homeland by offering advice consistent with homeland mothering traditions. For instance, *Indian Moms Connect* shares postpartum recipes that aid lactation (which were traditionally fed to new mothers by their own mothers); yet these recipes are simple enough for busy mothers in nuclear families to make for themselves (Divya par. 1). Through such easily replicable cultural markers, these blogs facilitate the realization of the mothers' "homing desire," which is the diasporic desire for "cultural identification" with the homeland (Brah 189).

The blogs discussed here provide resources and links to mothers who wish to teach dominant constructions of Indian culture to their children through ethnic markers such as food, language, dress, and festivals. *Masalamommas* strategically cross-promotes other "mompreneurs" like "Gnaana" who sell culture-specific commodities like customized "developmental toys and educational material to teach children ... about South Asian cultures" (Nayyar, "Gnaana" par. 5). *Indian Moms Connect* has a section called "IMC Treasure Box," which markets sets of India-themed stories, craft projects, and recipes; their online venture, "IMC Marketplace," promotes digital mompreneurs (Team IMC, "What's IMC Been Up To?").

Despite the overt commodification of culture, these blogs also offer many free resources, such as recipes, homemade project ideas, and downloadable apps. For instance, one writer recommends films, books, and apps that can teach "mythological stories of Hinduism" (Sekhar par. 1). Diasporic subjects have been critiqued as being "antimodern" in their "capacity for ethnic absolutism"; and many of the posts discussed here do "re-create their own fantasy structures of homeland even as they live elsewhere" (Mishra 17). Yet despite the obvious Hindu ideological affiliations expressed in these posts, the bloggers also resist the hegemonic absolutism of such affiliations by consciously adopting an inclusive, multicultural approach. Anandini Sekhar, for instance, admits that although her recommendations are limited "to the Hindu faith," she also wants to learn about "similar media tools for other faiths." In this way, she validates "cross-cultural learning ... and sharing" (par. 13). Vinay Lal has critiqued the regressive and "ossified conception of faith" that "cyber-diasporic" Indian American Hindus often exhibit, especially those advocating right-wing Hindu nationalism (147). I argue, however, it is the very polyphony of the cyber-diaspora—as represented by the multitudinous maternal voices on transnational community blogs—that allows for more personalized, flexible, and protean interpretations of faith to coexist with and even counter the organized, conservative domination of diasporic Hindu nationalism.

Hindu patriarchal constructs of sacrificial motherhood are also subverted through blog resources catering to maternal self-image, self-confidence, and general selfhood. *Masalamommas* has a section called "Shape your Life," which focuses on "getting your body in shape" and equates it with "getting your life in shape" (Dhindsa par. 1). Such rhetoric may be read as expressing a "postfeminist sensibility" that resexualizes and feminizes maternal bodies through the "dominance of a makeover paradigm" (Gill and Scharff 4). Yet such postfeminist critiques are complicated if we contextualize transnational Indian makeover paradigms against the traditional, homeland disapproval of mothers choosing to spend time and effort on themselves. The cult of motherhood idealization prevalent in Hindu patriarchal ideology desexualizes mothers (Aneja and Vaidya 36-37). This denial of embodied maternal desire has been internalized by women, especially in conservative homeland families—leading to a generational disapproval of contemporary mothers who express their desire for self-care or "me-time." Blogger Kajal Desai articulates this context when she writes of the "discrepancy between our views and those 'back home' on the importance of health and wellness" for mothers (par. 3). When *Masalamommas* claims its members are "strong, passionate, ambitious and sexy," it goes beyond the postfeminist cult of maternal beauty to communicate a strategic defiance of the Indian cultural trope of maternal self-abnegation ("About Us" par. 9).

CONTESTING GOOD INDIAN MOTHERHOOD

Such resistant readings are also a valuable tool in theorizing how these blogs negotiate with the sociocultural construct of good Indian motherhood. The processes of globalization and neoliberalism—with increasing numbers of educated and working mothers—have both challenged and recodified these hegemonic constructs. Although popular Indian media iconizes the "aggressive, confident, urban" new woman (and mother) as "representing globalized India," this same public cultural discourse also reemphasizes the "core" Indian values of the New Woman by anchoring her to "the patriarchal household—as mother, wife, and sister"—and subjecting her to "new forms of patriarchal oppression" (Oza 22, 30). Rupal Oza further links the "traditional modernity dyad" with the "dual construction of Indian versus Western" and suggests that the "new Indian woman had to be modern but not so modern as to transgress into 'Westernized' modernity" (31). This ambivalent and paradoxical construction of the modern-yet-traditional mother is especially significant in the context of diasporic Indian mothers who are located at the frontlines of old-new, Indian-Western cultural negotiations.

Masalamommas and *Indian Moms Connect* engage with this debate in multiple and often contradictory ways. Globalized Indian mothers have to constantly, and anxiously, balance the diasporic tightrope between protecting homeland culture (to conform to their Indian expectations) and assimilating with the culture of the adopted land (to live up to their global aspirations). This makes them vulnerable to new norms of performing globalized Indian good motherhood. Some blog posts reinscribe the culturally laden Hindu "divine role of motherhood" in mothering practices, essentializing the "journey of motherhood" as the *Navarasas* (nine emotions) (Deo pars.1-3). Such blog posts associate all positive mothering emotions with the baby's milestones rather than with the mother's selfhood; erase any pain felt by the mother at her loss of freedom; and categorize maternal fear as only the fear of failing to become "good mothers" (Deo par. 4). In effect, these posts reformulate conservative constructs of motherhood as coercive prescriptions of maternal perfection. Nayyar posts about hosting "the perfect dinner party" because, as "South Asian moms ... hosting a dinner party is ... about welcoming people into your homes, sharing your family, your values ...with others," and then she appends recipes and tips suggested by a white, male, commercially sponsored chef (Nayyar, "Tips" par. 2-6). Such posts recreate old patriarchal expectations of ideal maternal domesticity—and exploit middle-class anxieties about respectability—in globalized, neocapitalist, neopatriarchal contexts.

Despite such formulaic reconstructions of good motherhood, these blogs allow space for counter-discourses articulated by mothers themselves. *Masalamommas* includes radical maternal voices questioning the need for obedience in children: "Is this a cultural expectation (or pressure) we subconsciously instill in our children?" (Khetarpal par. 7). Jasjit Sangha and Tahira Gonsalves have demonstrated how mothers are playing "an active role in setting the terms and conditions in which culture is reproduced in the South Asian diaspora" by "making decisions about which South Asian values to impart on their children" (5). In a post on celebrating children's birthdays as "cultural milestones," Nayyar includes diverging views by mothers—some who spend lavishly to "keep it traditional and tie in as many cultural elements" as they could, and some who prioritize cost cutting over "image"—and encourages the reader to decide for themselves (Nayyar, "Striking the Right Balance"). Thus, by distributing decision making among bloggers and readers, these transnational blog spaces collectively empower the community of mothers and enable them to decide and design their own performances of Indian mothering.

Sometimes, personal and familial decisions extend to wider political debates. *Masalamommas* adopts a consistent and conscious strategy to be culturally inclusive by resisting the religious intolerance of right-wing Hindu nationalism as well as the racist politics of the Global North. It encourages posts by Muslim bloggers and promotes outreach activities, like Meet a Muslim Family, "to be proactive to dispel myths about their religion and culture" (Nayyar, "Meet a Muslim Family" par. 1). *Indian Moms Connect* also speaks out against gendered politics. It critiques the inadequacy of governmental initiatives, such as the "#SelfieWithDaughter" project, which reveal that Indian "patriarchal society definitely gives more importance to a boy than to a girl" but is ineffectual in "actually help[ing] the girl child … in any way" (Team IMC, "#SelfieWithDaughter"). By overtly participating in the political, these group blogs transgress dominant norms of submissive Indian motherhood to venture (though intermittently) into more self-aware and feminist terrains.

Even within the domain of mothering practices, *Indian Moms Connect* has contributors who encourage fellow mothers to normalize self-doubt and exercise agency by disregarding "unsolicited advice": "As we gain comfort with our new body and role, constraints and privileges; we also begin to feel confident about taking the call for our kids," trusting their own judgment rather than depending on external advice (Arora par. 4). This increasingly confident articulation of the maternal self—which coexists with contradictory and regressive ideologies and positions—makes the transnational Indian community blog space a dynamic and discursive site for maternal identity creation. Even such culturally sanctified, but classed and socially tabooed topics such as breastfeeding are reclaimed and publicly debated by the mom bloggers: a working mother of two children declares that breastfeeding is a personal choice and "really no one [else]'s business." She feels "relieved" with "no sense of guilt" when she stops breastfeeding earlier than medically recommended, and she supports the decision of any other mother who "doesn't want to feed" (Team IMC, "Is There a Right Age?" pars. 3-8). Such posts are usually followed by supportive comments by readers. Maternal solidarity is expressed in these blogs as a community-building strategy, and it has therapeutic effects on the bloggers and readers. By sharing a diverse array of mothering stories and maternal resources, ranging from the traditionalist to the progressive, these online communities "provide mutual support" for varied and atypical mothering subjectivities (Team IMC, "About IMC" par. 1).

REDEFINING TRANSNATIONAL INDIAN MOTHERING COMMERCIALLY AND AUTHENTICALLY

A recurrent criticism against mom blogs is that despite serving a "therapeutic purpose by normalizing maternal imperfection and shattering the myth of maternal bliss," they neither address the "structural context of motherhood" nor attempt to "transform society" (Stadtman Tucker 208). Globalized Indians have been further critiqued as they often persistently satisfy conservative inclinations even when using ICT as a bridge space for creating and transmitting cultural identities (Skop and Adams). Although it is undoubtedly true that transnational Indian mom blogs often reassert neoliberal, postfeminist, and propatriarchal reconstructions of motherhood, it is also true that they include and encourage alternative mothering experiences. *Masalamommas*, for instance, has many in-depth posts on stepmothering, mixed marriages, single mothering, and "raising daughters amidst gender bias… [and] infertility" (Nayyar, "When Motherhood" par. 14). Instead of radical and structural social resistance, they offer diverse articulations that may resonate and even inspire change at individual levels.

Another recurrent criticism is the commodification of blogs, which supposedly dilutes the authenticity of maternal self-articulation and protest (Connors 94). Hence, when mom blogger Shweta Jacob claims to have been motivated by a book "to continue to pursue success in [her] career," her self-transformation becomes suspect because the post is also a promotional review for the book in question (Jacob par. 6). Catherine Connors dismantles the criticism against commercialized mom blogs because such criticism extends the gendered assumption that motherwork should not have monetary value; it is also very possible that commercialization may not corrupt the authentic writing practices of bloggers (95). Thus, we may interpret the increasingly commercialized, market-oriented, and sponsored online and offline presences of these mom blogs in dual ways. When *Masalamommas* hosts a South Asian inspired baby shower, it is a marketing opportunity for the sponsoring brand and natal experts, as well as a fetishization and trivialization of cultural markers such as ethnic dresses and artifacts. But it also continues the homeland mothering tradition of *godh bharai* (fill the lap) and a real-time opportunity for diasporic Indian moms-to-be to share stories, fears, and advice with other in similar situations (Nayyar, "Masalamommas Hosts"). *Indian Moms Connect* claims that "We hope to partner with you in your motherhood and life journey whether as a parenting platform or a place to start your business" (Team IMC, "What's IMC Been Up To?" par. 5). This profit-oriented venture may also be read as providing financial opportunities to other mothers, thereby extending the network of support structures offered by the blog from the personal and cultural to the economic. Any critique of the consumerism of homeland culture and transnational spaces needs to acknowledge the real benefits to individual mothers provided by these forms of cultural production and consumption.

Although the transnational Indian community blogs question the cultural construct of motherhood and provide space for diverse, individual mothering voices, their resistance is not revolutionary, collective, sustained, or systemic. When *Masalamommas* self-identifies as "empowered women and mothers," or when *Indian Moms Connects* addresses an emancipated "new generation of mothers," it is both a declaration of intent and market friendly spiel; empowerment is conditional, limited, conflicted, and often superficial. Yet, contextualized against the Indian legacy of maternal subordination and erasure of the lived experiences of mothers, even such minor redefinitions and meaning-making conversations have significant value and potential. De Kruijf states that "a crucial feature of transnationalism as online behavior is its transformative potential," which is realized in the experience, practice, and externalization of transnationalism (9). In the blogs studied in this chapter, this transformative potential is expressed through an ongoing, enabling project of self-making—as hyphenated yet Indian mothers, as globalized yet individualized migrants—that is sometimes regressive, sometimes tentative, and sometimes assertive.

A similar, and similarly fragmented, process is also collectively emerging in mom blogs in the Indian subcontinent. In fact, the transnational blog space connects diasporic and homeland mothering communities more intimately, intricately, and immediately than was possible in the old isolated diasporas. When Preethi, in the quote at the beginning of this chapter, addresses the "new generation of mothers in India," she is referring to this scattered and privileged, but increasingly bridged, community of diasporic and homeland mothers, who can transform traditional motherhood roles to more assertive and connected mothering by "sharing stories." It is through these gradual shifts from prescriptive motherhood to pluralized, self-defined mothering and through the extension of support, choices, and spaces that these transnational blogs are redefining Indian mothering in globalized and empowering ways.

WORKS CITED

"About Us." *Masalamommas,* 2014, masalamommas.com/about-us. Accessed 14 Jun. 2014.

Deo, Alpana. "Navrasas (Nine Emotions) of Motherhood." *Indian Moms Connect*, 2 Jun. 2015, www.indianmomsconnect.com/2015/06/02/navrasas-nine-emotions-motherhood. Accessed 18 Aug. 2015.

Aneja, Anu, and Shubhangi Vaidya. *Embodying Motherhood: Perspectives from Contemporary India*. Sage and Yoda Press, 2016.

Arora, Praneeta. "Judging Mom: Self-Doubts of a Mother." *Indian Moms Connect,* 15 Sept. 2015, www.indianmomsconnect.com/2015/09/15/judging-ourselves-as-moms-self-doubts-of-a-mother. Accessed 17 Sept. 2015.

Brah, Avtar. *Cartographies of Diaspora: Contesting Identities*. 1996. Routledge, 2005.

Connors, Catherine. "Meter Politikon: On the 'Politics' of Mommyblogging." *Mothering and Blogging: The Radical Act of the Mommyblog*, edited by May Friedman and Shana L. Calixte, Demeter Press, 2009, pp. 91-111.

de Kruijf, Johannes G. "Introduction: Migrant Transnationalism and the Internet." *Indian Transnationalism Online: New Perspectives on Diaspora*, edited by Ajaya K. Sahoo and Johannes

G. de Kruijf, Ashgate Publishing, 2014, pp.1-17.

Desai, Kajal. "Staying Fit While Pregnant." *Masalamommas*, 8 Apr. 2015, masalamommas.com/2015/04/08/staying-fit-while-pregnant. Accessed 18 Aug. 2015.

Dhindsa, Binu. "Shape Your Life: Fitness Tips with Binu Dhindsa." *Masalamommas*, 21 Feb. 2013, masalamommas.com/2013/02/21/shape-your-life-fitness-tips-with-binu-dhindsa. Accessed 12 Jan. 2015.

Divya. "Ghee-Garlic Rice." *Indian Moms Connect*, 24 Jan. 2013, www.indianmomsconnect.com/2013/01/24/ghee-garlic-rice. Accessed 18 Aug. 2015.

Geetha. "Wish I Had It All!—Thoughts of an NRI Mom." *Indian Moms Connect,* 23 July 2015, www.indianmomsconnect.com/2015/07/23/ wish-i-had-it-all-from-an-nri-mom. Accessed 18 Aug. 2015.

Gill, Rosalind, and Christina Scharff. Introduction. *New Femininities: Postfeminism, Neoliberalism and Subjectivity*, edited by Rosalind Gill and Christina Scharff, Palgrave Macmillan, 2011, pp. 1-17.

Jacob, Shweta. "How 'The Momshift' Helped Me Follow My Dream." *Masalamommas*, 29 Apr. 2014, masalamommas.com/2014/04/29/how-the-momshift-helped-me-follow-my-dream. Accessed 18 Aug. 2015.

Khetarpal, Roma. "Does Obedience Make a 'Good' Kid?." *Masalamommas*, 10 Sept. 2015, masalamommas.com/ 2015/09/10/does-obedience-make-a-good-kid. Accessed 15 Sept. 2015.

Krishnaraj, Maithreyi. "Motherhood, Mothers, Mothering: A Multi-dimensional Perspective." *Motherhood in India: Glorification without Empowerment?*, edited by Krishnaraj, Routledge, 2010, pp. 9-43.

Lal, Vinay. "The Politics of History on the Internet: Cyber-Diasporic Hinduism and the North American Hindu Diaspora." *Diaspora,* vol. 8, no. 2, 2009, pp. 137-72.

Mishra, Vijay. *The Literature of the Indian Diaspora: Theorizing the Diasporic Imaginary*. Routledge, 2007.

Nayyar, Anjum Choudhry. "Gnaana: A Fresh, Modern Way for Kids to Connect with Indian Culture." *Masalamommas*, 14 Sept. 2011, masalamommas.com/2011/09/14/gnaana-fresh-modern-way-for-kids-connect-indian-culture. Accessed 10 Jan. 2015.

Nayyar, Anjum Choudhry. "Masalamommas Hosts a South Asian Baby Shower." *Masalamommas*, 24 Nov. 2014, masalamommas.com/2014/11/24/south-asian-baby-shower-hosted-masalamommas-huggies. Accessed 10 Jan. 2015.

Nayyar, Anjum Choudhry. "Meet a Muslim Family Aims to Remove Misconceptions." *Masalamommas,* 21 Apr. 2015, masalamommas.com/ 2015/04/21/meet-a-muslim-family-aims-to-remove-misconceptions. Accessed 12 Aug. 2015.

Nayyar, Anjum Choudhry. "Tips to Throw the Perfect Dinner Party." *Masalamommas*, 30 May 2015, masalamommas.com/2015/05/30/tips-to-throw-the-perfect-dinner-party-by-chef-michael-smith. Accessed 12 Aug. 2015.

Nayyar, Anjum Choudhry. "When Motherhood Meets Community." *Masalamommas*, 7 Aug. 2013, masalamommas.com/2013/08/07/when-motherhood-meets-community. Accessed 10 Jan. 2015.

Oza, Rupal. *The Making of Neoliberal India: Nationalism, Gender and the Paradoxes of Globalization.* Routledge, 2006.

Preethi [Preethi Chandrasekhar]. "Let's Talk Motherhood." *Indian Moms Connect*, 1 Aug. 2011, www.indianmomsconnect.com/2011/08/01/lets-talk. Accessed 3 Jan. 2014.

Quayson, Ato, and Girish Daswani. "Introduction—Diaspora and Transnationalism: Scapes, Scales and Scope." *A Companion to Diaspora and Transnationalism*, edited by Girish Daswani and Ato Quayson, Wiley Blackwell, 2013, pp. 2-26.

"Saheli Circle." *Masalamommas*, 2015, masalamommas.com/saheli-circle-2. Accessed 10 Jan. 2015.

Sangha, Jasjit. K., and Tahira Gonsalves. "Introduction: Contextualizing South Asian Motherhood." *South Asian Mothering: Negotiating Culture, Family and Selfhood*, edited by Jasjit Sangha and Tahira Gonsalves, Demeter Press, 2013, pp. 1-14.

Sarkar, Tanika. *Words to Win: The Making of Amar Jiban: A Modern Autobiography*. 1999. Zubaan, 2013.

Sekhar, Anandini. "Hindu Mythological Stories for Today's Kids." *Masalamommas*, 12 Dec. 2013, masalamommas.com/2013/12/12/ hindu-mythological-stories-todays-kids. Accessed 12 Jan. 2015.

Skop, Emily, and Paul. C. Adams. "Creating and Inhabiting Virtual Places: Indian Immigrants in Cyberspace." *National Identities*, vol. 11, no. 2, 2009, pp. 127-47.

Stadtman Tucker, Judith. "Mothering in the Digital Age: Navigating the Personal and Political in the Virtual Sphere." *Mothering in the Third Wave*, edited by Amber E. Kinser, Demeter Press, 2008, pp. 199-212.

Team IMC. "About IMC." *Indian Moms Connect,* 2015, www.indianmomsconnect.com/about-us/about-imc. Accessed 10 Jan. 2015.

Team IMC. "About the Team." *Indian Moms Connect*, 2015, www.indianmomsconnect.com/about-us/about-the-team. Accessed 10 Jan. 2015.

Team IMC. "Is There a Right Age to Stop Breastfeeding?" *Indian Moms Connect*, 3 Aug. 2015, www.indianmomsconnect.com/2015/08/03/is-there-a-right-age-to-stop-breastfeeding. Accessed 18 Aug. 2015.

Team IMC. "#SelfieWithDaughter." *Indian Moms Connect*, 5 July 2015, www.indianmomsconnect.com/2015/07/05/selfiewithdaughter. Accessed 18 Aug. 2015.

Team IMC. "What's IMC Been Up To?" *Indian Moms Connect*, 14 May 2015, www.indianmomsconnect.com/2015/05/14/whats-imc-been-up-to. Accessed 18 Aug. 2015.

5.
The Doing of Mothering from the Margins

GAVAZA MALULEKE

FEMINIST SCHOLARSHIP OF MOTHERHOOD and mothering—which has long highlighted the themes of social practices of nurturing and caring for dependent children—has begun to attend to gendered patterns of migration, along with attention to such factors as race, class, and culture. Recent studies have started to focus on migrants and the new family configurations resulting from to the dispersion of family members across national borders. Some of these family configurations include the various ways in which migrant women employ strategies to deal with mothering from a distance in an arrangement known as "transnational motherhood"—such as the Latina immigrant women who work and reside in the United States while their children remain in their country of origin (Hondagneu-Sotelo and Avila 548). Furthermore, studies focusing on mothering practices of expatriate families, whose plan is to return to their home country once their contracts are finished, have shown that families develop strategies that enable their children to succeed in the host country as well as successfully reintegrate back into their home country (Nukaga 68). Additionally, Njoki Wane examines the strategies employed by single migrant mothers in their host country and how they create communities of support ("Reflections" 106).

Similarly, this chapter examines how migrant women raising children in the host country deal with the notion of motherhood. I investigate this question from a transnational feminist perspective by examining the forum discussions of members of the African Women in Europe (AWE) online network who discuss varying experiences of being African mothers in different countries in Europe. Drawing on Judith Butler's notion of gender as a performative act, I examine the category of gender with a focus on mothering from the interstices of being women, having African ancestry, and living in Europe.

Solidarity, as it is used in this study, is taken from Chandra Talpade Mohanty's definition, in which she places "mutuality, accountability and the recognition of common interests as the basis of the relationships among diverse communities" (7). Instead of enforcing a commonality of oppression, this definition of solidarity locates communities of people who have chosen to work and fight together (Ibid). Mohanty's notion of solidarity is useful for what is happening in the African Women in Europe (AWE) platform as it envisions solidarity as "always an achievement, the result of active struggle to construct the universal on the basis of particulars/differences" (Ibid). This is critical as the recognition of difference in the AWE platform is highlighted in many instances, which demonstrates how solidarity is forged while respecting and acknowledging differences. Furthermore, although the members are faced with mothering in host societies where issues of race, culture, and class are relevant, these issues are not necessarily experienced in the same way. Moreover, these issues are further complicated by the members' need to maintain strong ties with their country of origin (Levitt and Glick Schiller 1002). Using Sara Ruddick's insight that mothering involves both power and powerlessness, I explore the many dimensions and ambivalences within the process of mothering among the AWE members (343).

METHODS

In this chapter, I draw on empirical data gathered as part of a PhD project that focused on how the online platform, AWE, positions itself from a transnational feminist perspective. AWE is made of about 550 members, constituting of women from all over Africa who live in different parts of Europe. It is a private platform in English. The founders decide who can join, and members have to pay a lifetime membership fee of twenty euros as a form of commitment to joining and participating in the platform. Members not only exchange ideas online but also have offline meetings. These meetings are organized in different cities and are mainly small gatherings geared to fostering friendships across Europe. Members are encouraged to create and join different subgroups within the platform to generate discussions as well as groups of shared interests. Participation consists of discussions with other members in the forums, posting discussion topics, and writing blogs, and the discussions posted on the online platform range from current affairs to support inquiries. I have concentrated on discussions that centre on motherhood, family, and children, which I have taken from ten forum discussions. I have used critical discourse analysis to examine the ways in which social power and inequality are "enacted, reproduced and resisted by text and talk in social and political contexts" (van Dijk 18). I explore discourse as something produced, circulated, distributed, and consumed in society. The overall intent is to ensure that different discourses, not only from within the host society but from the country of origin, are accounted for and examined.

MOTHERING FROM THE MARGINS

> "At home in Nigeria, all a mother had to do for a baby was wash and feed him and, if he was fidgety, strap him onto her back and carry on with her work while that baby slept. But in England she had to wash piles and piles of nappies, wheel the child round for sunshine during the day, attend to his feeds as regularly as if one were serving a master, talk to the child, even if he was only a day old! Oh, yes, in England, looking after babies was in itself a full-time job."
>
> —Buchi Emecheta, *Second Class Citizen*

As the protagonist in Buchi Emecheta's *Second Class Citizen* compares the mothering experience in Nigeria to the one in England, the reader can easily observe how different these practices are to her. The author portrays Nigerian mothering practice as "simple" and "less complicated," whereas mothering in England may as well be a "full-time job." The interesting aspect, however, is not the comparison as such, but the protagonist's ability to have an awareness of both mothering practices through the process of her migration from Nigeria to England. The awareness and knowledge she portrays also reflects the liminal phase characterized as "ambiguous, neither here nor there, betwixt and between all fixed points of classification" (Turner, "Dramas" 232). However, this betwixt and between as portrayed here cannot be associated with transmigration whereby migrants are simultaneously connected to more than one society. The middle voice, as portrayed by Emecheta, seems to be experienced in the mothering practice of England while at the same time, holding on to the other mothering practice she left behind in Nigeria suggesting a transitional moment where which she is neither what she was (a mother in Nigeria) nor what she will become (a mother in England).

The protagonist's betwixt and between position, in which she recollects the past because she has encountered a different experience in the present, is also a space in which the subject recognizes both mothering experiences and is faced with the choice to either articulate how she reconciles these experiences or do nothing, as mothers on AWE express. In an excerpt taken from the discussion, "Raising Our Kids in Two Cultures," this position becomes clear when one member says the following: "Personally I think it's a challenge. It is a good opportunity for our children to experience both sides. But for our partners we have to explain to them and somehow agree to be in between. It's not easy. There is a big difference between the African culture and the European culture. One has to live for several years in each country to understand a little bit." For this member, raising children in two cultures is a challenge because a big difference exists between African and European culture. However, she acknowledges that it is good for children to experience both sides. In addition, this member does not explain which European or African culture she is talking about as both cultures appear to be homogeneous. Yet this is not entirely surprising, since the platform is framed as African women in Europe. She also does not privilege either culture as being better, but focuses more on how both cultures can be experienced by the children and thus, highlighting the idea of being "in-between." This "in-between" position suggests an insider position in both cultures because as explained by the member, "one has to live for several years in each country." However, the exposure to both cultures by living in each country also suggests a distance or disconnect to both of these cultures at one time or another. It can then be argued that her marginality stems from experiencing both cultures and thereby being privy to the positive and negative sides that exists in both cultures. Interestingly, she uses this liminal position at the margin to create and forge solidarity with the other members when she asserts that it becomes their (her and the members') responsibility "to explain" and "to somehow agree" with their respective partners on the importance of exposing their children to both cultures. The members can find solidarity in the knowledge that they are at the margins; this liminality puts them in a position of power through which, though with difficulty, they can take the initiative to persuade their partners to see the importance of both cultures for their children.

In this posting, it is clear that the exposure to more than one culture through migration forms part of this marginality. However, for some members, this experience can also occur in one's home country, yet because of the platform's migration focus, only issues linked to that experience tend to be privileged. In another discussion titled, "How Important Is Your Mother Tongue," a member posits the following:

> I had problems with my son, who even back home did not want to learn my mother tongue, preferring Kiswahili instead. However, we left home for U.S. and Europe when he was only eight, and it was not long before he began to have trouble conversing in Kiswahili. Help came in the form of sending him home during summer holidays when he turned twelve.... He asked to be sent home as he found Austria a little challenging for him and wanted to reconnect with his extended family back home. It worked miracles; at seventeen, he is now comfortable with the language and plans to spend as much time back home as he can.

In her situation, her son had the option to learn her mother tongue (which she does not identify) as well as Kiswahili, which is the official language of some countries in East Africa, and he preferred Kiswahili instead of her mother tongue. This is a common experience in many African countries. For instance, in South Africa alone, there are eleven official languages and because I learned English as a first language at school, my parents encouraged me to be fluent in my mother tongue, Xitsonga, as a way for me not to lose the language and cultural practice. Similarly, this member shows that this was an issue she encountered in her home country, where Kiswahili and a number of other languages exist alongside each other. This story also exposes a liminality because she found herself wanting her son to learn her mother tongue, whereas her son preferred to speak Kiswahili. In Southern Africa, urban areas tend to be melting pots of languages; thus, one's hometown or province is where the mother tongue is spoken by many people. For instance, if she was residing in the urban areas, then her liminality of being "in-between" would have been reflected in the 'home' (read: rural area) and not 'here' (read: urban area) where, although her language might be spoken, Kiswahili would be the predominant language. Although she cites this liminality as an issue, Kiswahili no longer posed as much of a problem once she moved internationally. Now, her son was faced with the loss of Kiswahili in Austria as well as other challenges. She does recount his liminality, yet she can still help her son. Although her ability to send him home during the summer is an important part of the story and hints at a stable financial situation and middle-class status, she only says that it worked in her situation and does not suggest it as something all the members should do. Through her son's experience of liminality, she displays a liminality of her own as a parent; this is how she can find a connection with the other members. However, the way in which she solves her problem is not something all members can do.

Furthermore, this member gives us a glimpse of the potentiality inherent in this space. As Victor Turner explains, "liminality may perhaps be regarded as the Nay to all positive structural assertions, but as in some sense, the source of them all, and, more than that, as a realm of pure possibility whence novel configuration of ideas and relations may arise" ("Symbols" 97). There is a tendency to assume that the liminal position is a negative space where one feels invisible, homeless, and lost. Although this is an important part of the experiences, Turner argues for recognition of other aspects of it. When this member was in her home country, she wanted her son to learn her mother tongue. However, once she moved to Austria, and he started to struggle with Kiswahili, it was more important for him to reconnect with extended family by sending him back home. Kiswahili started representing home and became a language she was comfortable with him learning. This whole experience reconfigured how she thought about languages and mother tongues. The liminal position—the exposure to everything and nothing—is a space full of possibility, which becomes evident in this platform through the members' quest for solidarity.

MOTHERING AS A PERFORMATIVE ACT

Mothering is a central theme in the AWE online discussion. The centrality of mothering and the use of "women" in the framing of the platform as "African Women in Europe" may insinuate that womanhood is linked to mothering and, therefore, may imply a gender identity. However, for this study, I argue it is important to move away from a fixed gender identity and start from Butler's assertion that "if gender is instituted through acts which are internally discontinuous, then the appearance of substance is precisely that, a constructed identity, a performative accomplishment which the mundane social audience, including the actors themselves, come to believe and to perform in the mode of belief" (520). If gender is constituted through acts, then the notion of "woman" and therefore mothering can also be seen as a performed construct.

Following Ruddick, I focus on what mothers do rather than on what they are, and argue that the word "women" in AWE means that women do mothering. Focusing on the performative dimension of "doing" mothering is integral to this chapter because this is how this platform came into existence. The founder of AWE related in an interview that one of the reasons she started this website was to get advice and support from other African women on how to deal with her son's being bullied in kindergarten for having curly hair. Dealing with the various challenges of motherhood motivated her to start the website. Her actions resonate with Ruddick's argument that maternal practice responds to the "historical reality of a biological child in a particular social world" (346). It is evident through her words that even though maternal practice is linked to the notion of women through the word maternal, the basis for the practice is not based on biological wiring but on performative acts responding to the children's various experiences. This posting captures a significant dimension of this issue:

> Especially creating time to play with your kids, I cannot remember playing with my parents only with my brothers, sisters and neighbours. Most of us African women we have this problem. So we buy toys and think this will do the job. [O]f [course] not!!! We need to show them how to play with the toys and get down on the floor and do those brrrrrmmmmm brummmm (driving a car) or reading books, bed time stories and singing and dancing.

The commenter views her childhood experience of playing more with her siblings and neighbours and less with her parents as an African mothering practice. This mothering practice may still persist in her home country; however, it seems through migration she has been exposed to an alternative way of mothering and wants to adopt this variation. This posting makes the case for why "women who mother" should not be seen as a stable identity, but rather as "the act that one does, the act that one performs, is, in a sense, an act that has been going on before one arrived on the scene" (Butler 526). This member shows this kind of performative act of mothering precedes her and continues today, but the performance can also be subverted in the face of changing conditions. For example, she suggests changing their maternal practice through more involvement and play with their children.

THE DOING OF MOTHERING UNVEILED

By focusing more closely on the members and their performative acts of doing mothering and the conditions that inform these performative acts, I observe what conditions are recognized as relevant by the members. This section is subdivided into three parts. The first focuses on how children's voices inform mothering. The second highlights the importance of help and support structures in mothering, and the final one demonstrates how mothering can be seen as a way to preserve cultural heritage.

Children's Voices Inform the Doing of Mothering

Mothering is in many ways informed by the needs of the children. As such, it comes as no surprise that children's voices permeate the discussions on the AWE platform. In the discussion, "Why Am I So dark," a member posts about an issue she finds apprehensive, but it has not yet happened. She sought to get advice from the other members: "I am waiting for my kids to one day ask me this question. 'Why am I so [much] dark[er] than others?' Or 'why are you so dark coloured and dad so light?' What is the most diplomatic way to explain this? I just want to be ready with a good answer. What did you tell your kids?... I would love to hear [how you] respond[ed] to this." This member is in an interracial relationship where a difference in skin colour between the parents is apparent. Moreover, she and her family reside in a place where dark-skinned people are not as common. She worries that her children will question their difference from others. Although the question has not been asked by the children yet, this member anticipates it will be asked and is planning how to answer it, which highlights the importance of the social context in shaping the experiences of the child. In mothering, parents or those charged with mothering are confronted with and anticipate a myriad of questions from their children to which they feel it is their responsibility to give the best possible answers. Furthermore, the post reveals that "many mothers early develop a sense of maternal competence, a sense that they are able to protect and foster the growth of their children" (Ruddick, 344). The need for this maternal competence becomes clear when viewing the mothering practice as a process of repetition. As Irene Gedalof (paraphrasing Luce Irigaray) explains,

> the woman as mother is positioned as place, the 'still silent ground' upon which the masculine subject is constituted, and as long as she serves that symbolic function she cannot take a place of her own or even take place, that is, exist and define an identity of her own as long as the positioning

> of woman/mother as a place is said to be—a site of stasis and repetition-as-same against which the dynamism of time is produced. (90)

However, this discussion post also challenges the idea that although mothering is repetitive, the context that informs the practice and how the competence is developed will always differ.

This member frames her question by specifically focusing on racial difference in an interracial relationship. Although some members who are mothers may share similarities in that they are mothers to mixed race children, her situation is specific to her because of the context of her lived experience and the way in which she has chosen to approach the issue. Furthermore, she also develops her maternal competence by seeking advice and learning from other members in the AWE platform. In so doing, she accomplishes two things. First, she establishes a relationship with those members who respond to her request for support, which is where solidarity is forged. Interestingly, in establishing the relationship, she also lives out Gedalof's argument that "there is always the possibility of a repetition that undoes, a repetition that communicates agency and produces something new" (92). By bringing this issue and framing it in this manner, this AWE member highlights a repetition of mothering as informed by the children's needs and demands. Yet at the same time, in repeating this on an online platform and sharing it with members who are both mothers and nonmothers, her post demonstrates that not only is this mothering practice unknown to her but her newly acquired performative acts may result in a mothering practice different from how she was raised. This action illustrates that repetition in the mothering practice does not necessarily stay the same even when it seems familiar. Mothering is a fluid and always-in-process construction.

The Doing of Mothering Requires Support and Help

Needing help and support are also central themes on the AWE platform. For these members, mothering is not an easy task, especially when juggling it with careers and studies. Figuring out how to gain support and help becomes all the more important. Members also communicate that all the responsibility of the mothering practice should not fall on those doing the mothering. Aside from the member who differentiates between the experiences of getting help at "home" and in the "Western world," all the discussions in the posts I have examined focus on how help can be sought or gained within the new context. This need for support is very much centred on being in Europe, although aspects related to being African are occasionally also explored. In the discussion, "Dysfunctional Society," a member shares her parenting experience:

> Parents need help and support to handle the stresses and strains of life. This can be someone who takes the kids off for a while allowing parents time to recharge and reenergize. Back home, it is easy to rely on relatives and hired help for this However, it is a different story out in the western world, where things are very different. Other types of help could be counselling services where people can go to seek nonjudgmental help and advice. Lack of help can drive parents to the brink and unfortunately those who suffer are the children.

For this member, parents need support to have time on their own to recharge, so that they can better take care of their children. However, this posting points to a factor that was not brought up in the other related discussions. According to her, the situation is different for her and some other members because they have all been exposed to mothering with the help from relatives and hired help in their country of origin or what she calls home. The mothering practice that she links to home echoes the concept of "othermothering," which suggests children do not only belong to their biological parents but to the community at large. In practice, women help other mothers, but these practices can go beyond racial and gender boundaries (Wane, "Reflections" 112), particularly since they now have to contend with mothering in the Western world where things are different.

Doing Mothering as Part of Cultural Preservation and Heritage Discipline:

The topic of discipline came up in the discussion forum, "Raising Our Kids in Two Cultures," where it was closely linked to the notion of culture. However, because culture as a concept is context specific and hard to define, it is important to mention that I use the term based on how the members use it. In this excerpt, one member points out the difficulty for parents raising their children in two cultures, particularly when married to a non-African partner:

> Those of you married to non-[A]frican partners even have a triple burden. I know that from experience I had the same problem with my ex-boyfriend [who is] a [G]erman, ... he didn't like it one bit that I yelled at the boys or even talked loud to them. It was our biggest problem but again I saw that what he was saying was absolutely true we agreed on telling the boys just once to do something if they didn't ... consequences followed which ranged from grounding them to not letting them watch TV or even cutting off their pocket money. How I managed to successfully pull my boys through up to this time is that I simply combined the positive things from "my" [A]frican upbringing and the positive things here in Germany plus the day-to-day changes the kids were going through. On the whole, I think there's no laid-down patent manual about how to bring our kids up between two cultures all we have to do is trial and error because however we want to inflict the [A]frican culture into them their current culture will always dominate and what might work for one kid will never work for another I see that with mine.

For this member, being in a relationship with someone who had a different upbringing exposed her to a different way of parenting her children. This is a situation found in many contexts. However, because of the way this platform is framed as part of forging solidarity, this member highlights her situation as being linked to intercultural relationships. Shouting and yelling as a parenting style is one that is practised in many families whether in Europe or Africa. Yet because she is in a relationship with a German man, she takes his different upbringing and his parenting style as linked to being German. This suggests that the platform's positioning and the way it is framed influence how the members articulate certain issues. Even though the notion of culture is used very loosely by this member, especially when she talks about African or even German culture, there is awareness that all cultures consist of both negative and positive aspects. Through her encounter with her ex-boyfriend, a liminal position emerges in which she can see that certain aspects she relates to her African upbringing are not positive, just as she sees certain types of parenting within the German context as negative. This marginal position occurs in moments of challenges, and although she finds having different parenting styles from her boyfriend problematic, a negotiation process begins in which she can see both sides and even start to question the validity or rigidity of her African upbringing. The quotation marks she places "my" in front of the African upbringing suggests a questioning of the homogeneity of African upbringing.

After sharing her own experience, this member proceeds to generalize her opinion and include the other members. For this particular member and, it seems, for others as well, there is a need to pass her African culture to her children through mothering. As Wane asserts "African women are the guardians of traditional knowledge ... and through narration, women pass on knowledge of African cultures and ways of knowing" ("Mapping" 186). Iris Marion Young builds on this idea and asserts that "traditional female domestic activity of women, which many women continue today, partly consists in preserving the objects and meaning of home" (332). For Young, "the work of preservation ... involves teaching the children the meaning of things among which one dwells, teaching the children the stories, practices, and celebrations that keep particular meanings alive" (333). The member's assumption that all the other members involved in mothering are or should be passing their culture to their children starts to make sense in this context. In the context of this platform this need for preservation of culture through the mothering process is heightened by a loss of control in interactions with the local culture, where a sense of powerlessness is at play. Even though parents might have the power to "inflict" the African culture on their children, the local culture can also have a significant influence on the child's upbringing.

Language:

Many of the platform members see language as an important tool in mothering, as it allows them to preserve their cultural heritage among other things. In the forum discussion, "How Important Is Your Mother Tongue," one member responds to the discussion in the following way:

> For children, it is easy to learn a new language. I am an adult and am struggling with my German. The more languages they learn the better for them in the future. I talk to my children in English and my husband speaks to them in German. I can't imagine going to Kenya and my children can not talk to my relatives. I will spend the holiday translating.

According to this member, the more languages children learn, the better it will be for them in their future. This decision is informed by the fact that she wants her children to communicate with her relatives in her mother country. Although this assertion is supported by other members, not all members share this perspective. As shown here:

> I start conversing with my thirteen yr old in [S]wahili and before I know it, we both have switched to English.... I just need to try harder than I am at the moment. Honestly ... when we went to Kenya for the first time and saw how my daughter was getting frustrated to speak to her grandma, I actually felt embarrassed. I promised myself to be speaking to her more in [S]wahili but Alas ... it's not happening. The Europeans came, conquered and lived in Africa for many years, and they never forgot their language.

Although both members are from Kenya, their views on which languages to teach as the mother tongue differ. The member in the first posting teaches her children English, which is an official language in Kenya and can be assumed to be a language she views as a mother tongue. At the same time, the member in the second posting prefers to speak Kiswahili, which is the other official language in Kenya, instead of English. The reference to European colonialism by this member alludes to the notion that Kiswahili may be considered more of an African language and hence more acceptable than English. Although Kiswahili is considered an indigenous language, similarly to how English was brought to Kenya by British colonialism, Kiswahili was a trade language from the coast that spread across the country (Ogechi 143). This means neither language is necessarily the mother tongue to these women; however, the use of English and Kiswahili as a medium of communication in urban areas explains why both languages may be seen as such by them. Ama Ata Aidoo expresses the anguish of the African mothers who left family behind when asserting that,

> in spite of these ordeals that African mothers have endured, her children do not truly appreciate her and add to her suffering by returning with grandchildren with whom she cannot communicate, those who speak only 'English, French, Portuguese, etc. and she doesn't!' (123)

Following this argument, there is still a difference between Kiswahili and English in that for the member who only teaches her children English, she is going to add to her mother's suffering by bringing back grandchildren with whom she cannot communicate. Although this situation argues against the dependency of Africans on colonial languages, it cannot be assumed that all African mothers are only conversant in the local language instead of being multilingual. These two postings take differing standpoints on the language debate and show how a stable, fixed idea of an African identity is very problematic when thinking about solidarity. Nonetheless, these members teach their children their mother tongue to foster better communication with relatives in the home country, even though their situations differ. These members want to have their children connect to their home country, yet every situation articulated here is distinct and cannot be assumed to be experienced in the same way.

Besides fostering communication with relatives abroad, some members also want to ensure that the children are fluent in the languages of the host country: "Mother tongue is very important but I think the children should be very good in the language of their other countries too because if I hear the [T]urkish kids out here speak [G]erman it's nothing but very appalling, that's why most of them have no chance of really doing well in school." This member's perspective is informed by the discourse surrounding Turkish children living in Germany who cannot speak German well and therefore struggle at school. Her mothering practice is motivated by her need to ensure that her children can do well in school. The local context seems to take centre stage in what the mothers find is an important language for their children to learn. The importance of children learning the language of their host country is also echoed by another member; however, she sees this as the reason why many parents struggle to speak to their children in the mother tongue. This is what she says:

> I think a lot of us do struggle when teaching/talking to our kids [in] the mother tongue. First and foremost, when we are abroad our main concern is for the children to pick up the local language ... for your case is it Dutch that they teach in school? Otherwise, it will be paying for International school to learn English which is widely spoken in Kenya. We should try all we can to talk to them in one African language popular in your home country. Learning the mother tongue gives them a sense of identity and also they respect themselves more as [having] African origins.

Even though she sees the parents' preoccupation with the local language as a hindrance to teaching the children the mother tongue, the member still sees it as a viable option. She encourages everyone to teach their children an African language popular in the home country, shifting away from the notion of a mother tongue to a popular language in the country of origin. This suggests that the concept of the mother tongue in many African countries is not as simplistic as it might seem. As pointed out in those earlier postings, the members identified English and Kiswahili as mother tongues, but both of these languages are more likely just widely spoken and not viewed as mother tongue by all who speak them. In this discussion, it is evident that mothering includes the responsibility to ensure that children can adapt and do well in school. Moreover, they also need to ensure that their children's sense of identity is sustained. Here, the liminal position of being African and being in Europe is important in that the children need to be exposed to an African language in order to respect their place of origin. Yet it seems that this is only important because they are in Europe and not living in Africa. Young suggests that the "possibilities of the repetition that undoes, or that recollects forward in order to birth something that is both new and familiar, could be a way of getting at the dynamic messiness of the work of inhabitance that is still rarely articulated in the scholarship on migration" (95). This argument exemplifies what is happening in this platform where members would like for their children to learn their mother tongues, which is part of the repetition; however, this repetition seems to be that of "undoing" because what used to be a mother tongue in the past is rather complex. Furthermore, because they want their children to sustain their African heritage, it is more important that they speak a popular African language in their particular country of origin than to not speak any of the languages at all. This can be a way of emphasizing what Young calls "dynamic messiness of the work of inhabitance" (95).

With the mothering process, parents can ensure that they preserve a culture through their children. According to Charles Fonchingong, citing Omolara Ogundipe Leslie, the African culture that they would like to preserve and pass on through their children is itself one of the structures that keeps African women as victims and subordinates (138). However, this argument misses an important factor: mothers are influential in what is taught to their children and thus have more power than is assumed. Mothers help preserve culture by remembering about yesterday (past) and connecting it to what is happening today (present). As Young argues: "the activity of preservation should be distinguished from the nostalgia accompanying fantasies of a lost home from which the subject is separated and to which he seeks to return. Preservation entails remembrance ... Nostalgia is always longing for an elsewhere. Remembrance is the affirmation of what brought us here" (334).

Working with the concept of remembrance as an "affirmation of what brought us here" instead of a "longing for an elsewhere" is critical for this platform. In the discussion of language, members engage with Africa and their specific country of origin in ways that one would assume that their preoccupation with preservation of culture is linked to nostalgia. However, the members illustrate that what they would like to preserve is an affirmation of their identity. This is why they are able to repeat while undoing this repetition when confronted by new situations that require change. Not all members in the platform share the view of cultural preservation, though. One member describes her experience on the importance of mother tongues:

> I am [G]erman, have been in [E]ngland in one and half year. When I came back, I have not been able to speak good [G]erman anymore. It cost me about two month[s] to come back. With my husband I have been speaking [E]nglish all the time, it has been my language, but today, after being back in [G]ermany since eight years,[I] start to struggle in [E]nglish. My daughter who is [G]erman is well, is struggling with every language. She has been speaking fluent [E]nglish with four years, but today she is not passing the class because of [E]nglish. It very difficult with the languages. My own idea to the whole thing is, either you have an intelligence for languages or not. Me for example I am good in math, my kids as well, also why I should be worried about. By the last visit in [A]frica somebody translated for the kids, it has not been nice, but I am quite sure when they would stay there for a while they could communicate as well. It is only a matter of time. They love their [A]frican family, I find this more important.

According to this member, languages are difficult and can complicate children's lives. She asserts that either someone has the ability to learn languages or not. Her children do not speak the language of her husband's country, as she notes during the last visit to Africa, someone had to translate for the children, and this was not a good experience. However, she believes it is more important that they love their African family. Her perspective on the mother tongue topic discussion differs from the other members. Even though it is not mentioned in her post, it is clear that her children do speak German, which is her mother tongue, and, therefore, the other language that they would be learning is for communication with their relatives in Africa. With this analysis, it becomes clear why her position would differ slightly from the other members; her mothering does not have to be preoccupied with preserving culture and heritage because this is already taking place. At the same time, she agrees with some of the other members that language is important to foster communication between her children and the relatives in Africa. Even though she is part of the platform, as a German woman, being in Europe does not have the same consequences as it has for the other members. Additionally, a distance and connection are established at the same time; she can relate to the members' need to teach their children the language to communicate with their relatives in Africa. However, the link can only go so far because her children already speak her mother tongue, and in a way, she is already part of the "we" of the nation. She can easily preserve her heritage. The African members do not share this experience, and, thus, there is a disjuncture between them.

CONCLUSION

As the AWE discussion has shown, mothering is an unstable practice and is constantly negotiated because of the various conditions and influences involved. The members of the platform who have children not only are mothers but are mothering, as demonstrated by highlighting the marginality of their situation and by not assuming a stable idea of motherhood exists. The marginality here is not necessarily negative or positive, but can be seen as both because several members indicate knowledge of their host country and country of origin which simultaneously puts them in a position of power and powerlessness. Their marginal position emerges through interaction with the two locations as well, as when dealing with their children's voices, which seem to permeate some of the forum discussions. The importance of the children's voices in the discussion forums also supports Ruddick's argument that mothering practices have always been informed by the needs and demands of the children and as such, this is repeated even within the migration context.

The experience of being in Europe is an important part of these members' lives. Their encounters with difference and their attempts to deal with these differences reveal a need to stay connected and maintain ties with their country of origin. In examining the importance of support and help to the practice of mothering, the concept of "othermothering" was also carried over to the host country, although not to the extent practised in African countries. Regardless of whether it is hearing children's voices, needing help and support, or maintaining cultural preservation, mothering in this platform reveals that motherhood is not biological but a historical and social construct. The liminal positions of the members reveal that their connections to their country of origin and host country do not only manifest themselves in making comparisons between the two but in a more negotiated experience. These experiences may at times highlight the reinforcement of an outsider-insider binary. In addition, the members discuss mothering as a way to create and establish relationships with one another and share their subjective experiences. Although they are all African mothers from different countries, the participants do mother differently; thus, an analysis of solidarity needs to be more critical of the ways in which such groups frame themselves.

WORKS CITED

Aidoo, Ama Ata. *Our Sister Killjoy*. Longman Publishing Group, 1997.

Butler, Judith. "Performative Acts and Gender Constitution: An Essay in Phenomenology and Feminist Theory." *Theatre Journal*, vol. 40, no. 4, 1988, pp. 519-31.

Levitt, Peggy, and Nina Glick Schiller. "Conceptualizing Simultaneity: A Transnational Social Field Perspective on Society." *International Migration Review*, vol. 38, no. 3, 2004, pp. 1002-1039.

Emecheta, Buchi. *Second Class Citizen*. Heinemann, 1994.

Fonchingong, Charles C. "Unbending Gender Narratives in African Literature". *Journal of International Women's Studies*, vol. 8, no.1, 2006, pp. 135-147. Gedalof, Irene. "Unhomely Homes:

Women, Family and Belonging in UK Discourses of Migration and Asylum." *Journal of Ethnic and Migration Studies,* vol. 33, no. 1, 2007, pp. 77-94.

Hondagneu-Sotelo, Pierrette, and Ernestine Avila. "'I'm Here, but I'm There': The Meanings of Latina Transnational Motherhood." *Gender & Society*, vol. 11, no. 5, 1997, pp. 548-71.

Nukaga, Misako. "Planning for a Successful Return Home: Transnational Habitus and Education Strategies among Japanese Expatriate Mothers in Los Angeles." *International Sociology*, vol. 28, no. 1, 2013, pp. 66-83.

Ogechi, Nathan Oyori. "The role of foreign and indigenous languages in primary schools: the case of Kenya." *Stellenbosch Papers in Linguistics Plus: Multilingualism and language policies in Africa/ Mehrsprachigkeit und Sprachenpolitik in Afrika*, vol. 38, 2009, pp. 143-158.

Ruddick, Sara. *Maternal Thinking: Toward a Politics of Peace.* Beacon, 1995.

Turner, Victor. *The Forest of Symbols: Aspects of Ndemu Ritual*, Cornell University Press, 1967.

Turner, Victor. *Dramas, Fields, and Metaphors: Symbolic Action in Human Society*. Ithaca, NY: Cornell University Press. 1974

van Dijk, Teun A. "Aims of Critical discourse Analysis." *Japanese Discourse,* vol. 1, no. 1, 1995, pp. 17-28.

Wane, Njoki Nathani. "Mapping the Field of Indigenous Knowledges in Anti-Colonial Discourse: a transformative journey in education." *Race Ethnicity and Education*, vol. 11, no. 2, 2008, pp. 183-197.

Wane, Njoki Nathani. "Reflections on the Mutuality of Mothering: Women, Children, and Othermothering." *Journal of the Motherhood Initiative for Research and Community Involvement*, vol. 2, no. 2, 2000, pp. 105-116.

Young, Iris Marion. "House and Home: Feminist Variations on a Theme." *Gender Struggles: Practical Approaches to Contemporary Feminism,* edited by Constance L. Mui and Julien S. Murphy, Rowman & Littlefield, 2002, pp. 314-46.

6.
"Tiger*ish* Mom" in the Dragon's Den

A Journey of Negotiating Culture and Finding One's Voice

AIMEE TIU WU

THIS NARRATIVE PRESENTS my lived experience as a multicultural woman born and raised in the East and educated in the West, and my role as a mother that bears some traits of the stereotypical "Tiger Mother." As an immigrant mother, my story reflects my life in the dragon's den, particularly since I was raised in a traditional Chinese multigenerational household and had to navigate and negotiate many cultural expectations. In addition, as a Chinese daughter-in-law, I still feel compelled to adhere to traditional Chinese values and practices; but at the same time, as a wife and mother, I question the rigidity behind these unspoken social and cultural rules, and their relevance, meaning, and practicality in this day and age. As I have grappled with the dilemma of reconciling my multiple identities, I have discovered the invisibility and challenges experienced by immigrant and multicultural mothers. My goal in sharing my personal narrative is to extend the conversation about these embracing, intersecting, and, at times, contradicting paradigms and identities, and to explore the inner spaces of mothering and motherhood.

DECONSTRUCTING THE NOTION OF "TIGER MOM"

"Tiger Mother" is a cultural reference coined by author Amy Chua in her memoir *The Battle Hymn of a Tiger Mother* (2011). It loosely refers to "the Chinese" way of mothering by illustrating a highly controlling, rigid, and authoritarian parenting approach in which children are denied nonproductive play time and driven to high levels of pressure to achieve success at all cost. Since the book's publication, reactions to this stereotypical, excessively controlling parenting style have divided readers into two camps—those who were infuriated by such harsh parenting and those in awe of Chua's refreshingly authentic disciplinary approach.

Following the ongoing debates surrounding Tiger parenting, the *Asian American Journal of Psychology* published a special issue entitled *Tiger Parenting: Asian-Heritage Families, and Child/Adolescent Well-Being* (2013). Using empirical studies employing both qualitative and quantitative methods, the authors presented research on Chinese American, Korean American, Hmong American, and Mainland Chinese families. In one of the studies, results showed that only 20 percent of parents were classified as Tiger parents (Kim et al. 7). Contrary to popular belief, statistics also point to the fact that most Asian-heritage parents are warm, supportive, and loving toward their children (Lamborn et al. 50; Way et al. 60). In the same journal, a study on Chinese immigrant mothers' perceptions of the contrasts between typical Chinese and U.S. parenting showed that in order to promote their children's holistic development in the United States, they learned to acculturate and become flexible in their parenting beliefs and practices (Cheah et al.). In the same vein, research on Chinese mothers of middle-school students in Nanjing, China, indicated that the mothers' main goals were to raise children who were socially and emotionally well-adjusted so they could become productive citizens of the future (Way et al.). These findings offer a stark contrast to the stereotype that Asian-heritage parents as a group behave like Tiger parents.

Another surprise finding is that Tiger parenting is not linked to the best child outcomes—not academically or socioemotionally. Su Yeong Kim and colleagues, for instance, found in their eight-year longitudinal study that adolescents of Tiger parents were more likely than those with supportive or easygoing parents to feel more alienated from their parents, report greater depressive symptoms, and have lower GPAs (60). Therefore, although Tiger parenting has received much attention, recent research suggests that the myth surrounding Tiger parenting—that children of Tiger parents are the highest achieving, resilient, and most well-adjusted beings—is just that: a myth. Since Ruth Chao's assertion that the Western conceptualization of parenting does not adequately portray the Chinese way of raising children (1111), researchers continue to ask why Asian American children continue to outperform other minority groups academically, despite evidence of authoritarian parenting. In terms of the levels of education, Asian Americans are in the lead with 49 percent having a bachelor's degree or higher, compared to 30 percent white Americans, 19 percent African Americans, and 13 percent Latinos (Ramakrishnan and Ahmad 2). However, a recent study by Hsin and Xie notes that the "Asian-American educational advantage is mainly attributed to Asian students exerting greater academic effort and not to advantages in tested cognitive abilities or socio-demographics" (8416). Moreover, research on Asian American children's educational outcomes has unveiled a surprising finding; instead, the "achievement/adjustment paradox" among Asian American students indicates that despite their academic success, they have lower levels of socioemotional health (Kim et al. 5).

THE DRAGON'S DEN

The dragon's den is used metaphorically in this narrative to refer to the contextual differences of Eastern and Western cultural ideals and expectations as they relate to values, social roles, and expectations. In the Eastern culture, the dragon is a favoured cultural image and an auspicious symbol. It represents benevolence, greatness, power, nobility, and grandeur. Historically, people have shown both respect and fear of dragons. For instance, in Western mythology and literature, the dragon is often depicted as "a symbol of evil," a ferocious creature out to harm humans. However, the Chinese proudly refer to themselves as "heirs of the dragon." Although this explanation may seem simplistic and dichotomous, from a parenting standpoint, the dragon's den also illustrates a highly complex Eastern and Western ideal. This complexity is further enhanced in the changing relationship between a child and a parent in childhood, adolescence, and adulthood.

Although there are intergroup differences in terms of demographics, geographic settlement, religious identities, levels of income, and education, Asian-American culture in general places strong emphasis on family and filial respect. Yet although they share an Asian origin, Asian Americans have very distinct identities, histories, and migration stories. As a result, Asian American children's experiences are deeply varied as well. For example, Chinese and Filipino Americans are the two largest Asian American subgroups in the United States. The Chinese culture is deeply rooted in Confucian philosophy in which authority, filial piety, family hierarchy, emotional restraint, and the value of education are given foremost importance—thus resulting in the practice of preserving social harmony and propriety (Huang and Gove 41). Filipino Americans, on the other hand, experienced a long history of Spanish colonization, followed by U.S. occupation (Bautista 18). As a result, they are heavily influenced by Catholicism, and parenting practices tend to be based more on equality than hierarchy (e.g., patriarchal or age stratification) (Russell et al. 9). The strong family culture emphasizes affection and closeness, and these relationships are often based on Filipino's interpersonal dynamics and cultural concept of "*utang ng loob*" ("debt of gratitude") for others (Rungduin et al. 14).

MOTHERING AND PARENTING IN EASTERN AND WESTERN CULTURES

To fully understand differences in Eastern and Western parenting practices, an appreciation of the cultural values and beliefs that influence parents is warranted. Mothering is a social construct fraught with conflicting cultural interpretations and discourses. Western literature points to an idealized social construct (motherhood) endorsed by a patriarchal society, fueled by cultural assumptions and stereotypes and the categorization of women as either good or bad mothers (Rich 195). In her book *Of Woman Born: Motherhood as Experience and Institution*, Rich (67) wrote "we need to understand the power and powerlessness embodied in motherhood in patriarchal culture." Three decades and two waves of feminism later, Ann Crittenden in 2001, reflected that "for whatever reasons—biology, social conditioning, institutional inertia, choice, or no other choice—children's lives are still overwhelmingly shaped by women, and children are still the focus of most women's lives" (14). True enough, literature on motherhood points to a common theme of "intensive mothering," which mandates mothering as a "child-centered, expert guided, emotionally absorbing, labor-intensive and financially expensive" endeavour, and this remains a normative standard to which mothers are evaluated (Hays 8). Furthermore, "[a] woman's most enduring role in the Western world is that of mother ... [which] is socially constructed around a gendered perception of sex-role stereotypes ...[with] expectations, duties and responsibilities in relation to children" (Allan 57). Over time, Western parenting ideology—perpetuated by popular culture, consumer marketing, and social media—has given rise to the notion of "new momism" (Douglas and Michaels 4) or more specifically:

> The insistence that no woman is truly complete or fulfilled unless she has kids, that women remain the best primary caretakers of children, and that to be a remotely decent mother, a woman has to devote her entire physical, psychological, emotional, and intellectual being, 24/7, to her children. The new momism is a highly romanticized and yet demanding view of motherhood in which the standards for success are impossible to meet. The 'new momism' is a set of ideals, norms, and practices, most frequently and powerfully represented in the media, that seem on the surface to celebrate motherhood, but which in reality promulgate standards of perfection that are beyond your reach. (4-5)

This internal oppressor continues to pit women against one another and affects both stay-at-home and working mothers, creating the so-called "mommy wars" (Steiner 327). The media has amplified the mommy wars through notions of super moms fueling working mothers' guilt in their desire to raise happy and healthy children (Collett 329). Stay-at-home mothers are not spared either, for they face identity challenges of their own as childcare and household chores monopolize their time and energy (Brykman 84).

Similarly, Eastern mothering ideology is strongly influenced by the patriarchal kinship systems of Confucianism, which espouses highly divided gender roles and relegates women to the home sphere (Lim 10). Women are typically socialized into subordinate roles of being a good wife and honouring one's family (Hall 26). Aside from childcare, women tend to be responsible for meals, and this is congruent with Chan's metaphorical use of cooking soup to depict conformation to the social expectations of a good Chinese wife and mother (95). These patriarchal ideals are endorsed by Confucianism and have persistently reinforced the Western ideology of intensive mothering, in which the woman/mother is seen as the most ideal guardian who can provide for the best emotional, physical, and intellectual development of her children (Hays 8).

Over the years, various parenting styles such as "Tiger Moms," "Helicopter Parents," and "Free Range" parents have emerged and received conflicting opinions from the general public. Historically speaking, Western parenting constructs have been largely influenced by the works of Diana Baumrind, Eleanor Maccoby, and John Martin on authoritative, authoritarian, permissive, and indifferent parenting styles (Bornstein and Zlotnik 281). Numerous studies since have examined parenting styles and children's achievement using measures derived from Baumrind's work, which largely focused on well-educated, middle class, North American parents (Steinberg et al; Maccoby and Martin). Authoritative parenting combines parental warmth and discipline, and focuses on the child's development, which has positive effects on children's psychosocial adjustment and academic achievement, since this parenting style acknowledges the child's autonomy (Koerner and Fitzpatrick 136). Additionally, authoritative parenting is also associated with better development and mental health across cultures. In particular, studies have indicated positive outcomes for European American children raised in authoritative homes because this type of parenting involves "parent-child verbal give-and-take which helps facilitate open communication between children and their parents" (Bornstein and Zlotnik 282). Although authoritative parents exert firm control over the child, high levels of parental demand and responsiveness are found to lead to healthy, well-adjusted children (Foo 345; Bornstein and Zlotnik 290).

Authoritarian parenting, the second type of parenting, is described as "hierarchical relationships between adults and children," which are used "to maintain control, sometimes with forceful means" (Huang and Grove 3). This style "may restrict children's autonomy, and is related to low achieving children ... [It is] low in supporting children's needs and interest" (3). In addition, authoritarian parenting depicts children as "submissive to their parent's demands, while parents were expected to be strict, directive, and emotionally detached" (Kordi and Baharudin 217). Research has overwhelmingly suggested that the style is not associated with overall parent-child communication and does not necessarily relate to superior academic performance (Qin 28). Since Chua's Tiger parenting philosophy came into mainstream, the subtle nuance between authoritarian and Tiger parenting should be noted. Although the two can overlap, parenting in ethnic minority families is distinct from the dominant mainstream U.S. culture (Frabutt 245). Su Yeong Kim has clarified that Tiger parenting is characterized by the co-existence of positive and negative parenting strategies (28). Ruth Chao, a leading scholar in multicultural counselling, has also long argued that the authoritarian parenting style does not capture the essence of Chinese parenting, since the notions of control and restrictiveness are radically different between Asian and Eastern-American families (1111). For Chinese parents, strictness is rooted in the Confucian tenet of "*xiào*" or "filial piety," with the intent of fostering harmony in family relationships rather than domination of the child. Hence, Chao has reasoned that parenting concepts and styles developed in the West may not be useful in understanding the traditional parenting ways of Asians (1112).

The third type of parenting, permissive parenting, is seen as "high level of nurturance and clarity of communication, paired with low levels of control or maturity demands" (Bornstein and Zlotnik 283). Permissive parents are conceptually similar to Lenore Skenazy's "free range parents," whereby parents extend considerable trust, space, and freedom to their children to make decisions, grow, and explore without restrictions. Although often criticized for its laissez-faire style and misunderstood as negligent, permissive parents subscribe to "natural, inquiry-based approach to child rearing" (Pedersen 55). Lastly, indifferent parenting is characterized by a parent-centred lifestyle, whereby the parent "is not dedicated to parenting roles and is disinterested in helping foster optimal development of the child" (Bornstein and Zlotnik 283).

Having discussed the conceptual framework that has shaped my narrative, I now shed light on my multicultural experiences. Although the themes I address operate synergistically, I present and discuss them in a chronological order beginning with my home-story, followed by my immigration journey and reflections on my culture and identity, and finally my experience of motherhood.

MY HOME-STORY

My grandparents, driven by economic imperatives, left China in the early 1940s for the Philippines. My grandfather, then sixteen, ventured into an unknown land and had nothing but the clothes on his back. He worked for a distant relative in a province in the middle part of the country and later moved to Manila. Odd jobs and an extended network of overseas Chinese friends who were more than eager to help out a "comrade" made it possible for him to settle into his new home as he sought a better life for himself. Coming from peasant origins, my grandfather envisioned a better life, and leaving China was his only option. After a few years of labour in the Philippines, this sojourner went home to find a bride. Fresh from working abroad, my grandfather's parents arranged a marriage upon his return. The first time he saw my grandmother was when he unveiled her on their wedding day. After a brief wedding ceremony, my grandfather went back to the Philippines to continue working while my grandmother was left in China, pregnant, without her husband by her side. Six kids later, my grandparents had finally saved enough for the whole family to migrate to the Philippines.

Culture/Identity, Heritage and Expectations

Unlike my grandparents, whose immigrant story was driven by economic needs, my immigrant story began in 1995 when crimes against the Chinese Filipino in the Philippines grew into a series of high-profile kidnappings and murders. This societal unrest led many Chinese Filipino families, like mine, to flee abroad. My father decided to move to Canada, as it coincided with the mass wave of migration from Hong Kong. We settled in Richmond, BC, a suburban town adjacent to Vancouver, where most Chinese migrants settled upon their first entry into Canada. As a young teen, the move to the West was exciting, but I struggled to fit in school. Looking back, this was the "mean girls" stage, but the twelve-year-old me felt lost and isolated. Chesney-Lind and Irwin described mean girls as form of bullying and is a "damaging construction of women... [who are traditionally] viewed as nice on the outside but venomous and manipulative inside" (21). Although the experience was mind opening, I was happy to be back in the Philippines, several years later, when peace and order were somewhat restored. Going back to my old school, I had difficulty fitting in once again, since my childhood friends saw me as "that" Western-educated girl when I entered high school.

Being multicultural, I have found that being a Chinese Filipino has always shaped my views, identity, and perception of life experiences. For instance, growing up, I retained the ability to speak Hokkien, a dialect of southern China. My home culture was also very Chinese, and we were brought up to "be" Chinese and "act" Chinese. For example, I was indoctrinated to a few unspoken rules since birth, but the most significant one was filial piety, the lynchpin of Confucianism. *Xiào* is a virtue of enduring respect for one's parents, elders, and ancestors. From the time I was a child, I witnessed how important it was to be good and dutiful to one's parents, especially since I saw how my parents took care of my grandparents. Early on, it was ingrained in me that to demonstrate *xiào* was my duty; I must keep a good name by not bringing shame to the family.

Although women in traditional Asian cultures are considered subordinate (Healey 338), I was fortunate to grow up in a multigenerational household where girls and boys were treated equally. And for the most part, I was a good and obedient daughter, until I hit puberty and realized that the unspoken rules I grew up with suddenly felt oppressive and constricting. All of this coincided with my family's move to Canada, where I saw stark cultural differences between my peers and me. I started to ask why things had to be done in a certain way, why I could not question authority, and why traditions were practised even if they were outdated and inconvenient. This is reminiscent to Qin's longitudinal study on the influence of Chinese immigrants' parenting strategies where she found stark differences in parent-child communication, parental expectations, and parent-child relations among distressed and nondistressed adolescents. My parents strictly adhered to the traditional Confucian tenets in parenting by exercising parental control and emphasizing the importance of education. This parenting approach, according to Qin, results in distressed adolescents, who demonstrate high levels of academic achievement but low levels of psychological wellbeing (22). In hindsight, I experienced more than the normal teenage rebellion; in line with Qin's findings, I was struggling to understand my identity in light of my cultures but my immigrant parents' approach to parenting at that time focused on my academic development rather than the psychological aspect of transitioning into a new environment.

FINDING MY VOICE AS AN IMMIGRANT MOTHER AND ACADEMIC

As I continue my journey and life here in the West, I have found that my Western academic experience has given me a voice to question cultural assumptions, practices, traditions, and beliefs. I find myself open to new ideas and thinking outside of my normative path of a culturally biased mindset. Incidentally, the last few years have been marked by increasingly questioning the traditional notions of *xiào* and reflecting upon the changing times, when these cultural expectations need to be reexamined. For instance, the role of extended kinship living together in a multigenerational household is a culturally distinctive aspect of a traditional Chinese family (Min 117). Similar to other social groups like African American, Native American, and Hispanic American families, "extended family social support is a salient characteristic of minority parenting" (Frabutt 248). Although I acknowledge the importance of extended kin support, I find myself struggling to reconcile traditional Confucian values and my evolving perspective on parenting and family in the West. Recently, my son, who is in preschool, proudly announced one day that he was going to buy our neighbour's house when he got married so he could come and eat at my house every day. I laughingly replied that I did not think his future wife would appreciate that action. Moments like this are affirmation that somewhere, somehow I have passed on values I hold dearly to my children. I am happy that my son sees the value of being close to his family, but I also cannot help but wonder about the impact of change brought about by globalization and shifting cultural ideologies. Similar to how I feel about having some generational differences in perception of family with my in-laws and my parents, I ponder how different will my children's thinking about family be when they become parents.

My grandparents grieved for the loss of their Chinese identity when they left China to establish roots in the Philippines, and my parents may have cringed at our growing Westernized mindset. This loss is due to the contradiction in the cultural beliefs and expectations of their home culture (China) and adopted home culture (the Philippines). After all, "migration involves the loss of the familiar, including language (especially colloquial and dialect), attitudes, values, social structures and support networks" (Bhugra and Becker 19). However, unlike my grandparents and parents, I do not feel strongly about a part of my culture being lost as we moved and assimilated from the East to the West. As Daniel Detzner noted, the younger generations are "embracing individualism and materialism eagerly, while elders consistently emphasize the retention of culture and the importance of family" (100). In my parent's generation, they grew up with very strict adherence to culture and traditions, and they tried to use the same approach to raise my brothers and I. But ultimately, as Min has observed, the changing Chinese American family is "a product of complex interaction between structural factors (i.e., restrictive immigration policies and racism) and cultural factors (i.e., Confucian ethics)" and a result of the changing society (117).

As an immigrant parent, I am keenly aware that my children are Americans; after all, living in the United States is their reality. They have no basis of comparison. In a way, I can understand the need for our elders to hang on to the past, but because of changing times and lifestyle, they are unable to strictly enforce traditional roles and family-oriented values. But times are changing. When my parents visit us in the U.S., I do not see them mourning the loss of a Chinese-Filipino identity in my children. Instead, I see pride and joy in their eyes. And I am keenly aware of my role in "transmitting the cultural traditions and language of [my] country of origin to [my] children and to assist [them] to adjust to expectations of both cultures" (Tumandao et al. 84). This process is called "bicultural socialization," wherein children "acquire the norms, attitudes and behavior patterns of two ethnic groups" (Rotherham-Borus and Phinney 24). This in turn "prepares immigrant children to learn diverse and complementary values, acquire different coping strategies from various cultural and social experiences and attain competence in the multicultural American society" and has been linked to positive outcomes in immigrant children regarding "high self-esteem, positive racial and ethnic identities, achievement motivation, and overall adaptive psychosocial adjustment" (Cheah et al 3). James Frabutt, an action-oriented, community-based researcher focusing on parenting and child development, has noted that "parenting in minority families involves a complex interplay of several factors that impinge upon the nature and quality of parenting" (245). Because of my own migration and acculturation experience, I have come to realize the significance of adapting my parenting behaviour to my new environment in order to prepare my children to assimilate well in their environment. As Alyssa Fu and Hazel Markus have suggested, even if Asian and Western parenting styles are fundamentally different, both culture-centric approaches can motivate children to become successful (739).

As a millennial parent, I also see that my parenting style does not resemble the styles of my parents or in-laws. Although my parents were highly responsive to my academic needs growing up, they did not emphasize my other interests outside academics. My mom was a classic Tiger Mom who did not simply give orders without getting involved. She was in the trenches with me and quizzed me until the wee hours of the morning or shuttled me to and from choir rehearsals. As a parent and educator, I am keenly aware of this difference now and try to balance between being demanding and responsive toward my children's individual needs and interests. For example, my child who is in kindergarten recently asked for skating lessons, and although I would rather she learn math instead, I listened and registered her for a few skating lessons, which turned out to be something she really enjoyed.

As a tradeoff, she had to practice math and reading every night with me. I told this anecdote to my mom and she replied, "Ours is the last generation to obey our parents and the first to listen to our children." Although there is some truth to her statement, I think that millennial parents may have received some stereotypical attention from the media. Moreover, ethnographic accounts of motherhood and parenting from the perspective of millennial ethnic mothers have received little attention and research in the field of social sciences. Therefore, writing this chapter has been a cathartic experience because it has opened up my eyes to surrounding conversations about culture-centric approaches to parenting and motherhood. Through my narrative, I can make some important reflections about the intersections of my home culture (the Philippines) and adopted culture (North America), both of which have contributed significantly to my growth, thinking, and life trajectory. But more importantly, I feel emboldened to share my voice within each culture, and I hope to pass these thoughts to my children. Recently, my daughter, who is five, innocently remarked that she wants to learn to cook so that she can prepare delicious meals for her family someday. In my unguarded "feminist" moment, I blurted out: No, you don't have to learn how to cook. Find a husband who can cook for you and you will be the queen. In afterthought, I felt equally guilty and giddy for saying it because a part of me who has been entrenched in the ideology of intensive mothering says to give our all as women to our families; however, the researcher-academic part of me who has witnessed and lived through the negative implications of this ideology advocates to diminish this harmful notion.

Over the years, I have gained valuable insights from numerous engaging conversations with educators, well-meaning family members, and other mothers. Most importantly, I have learned that (1) the mommy wars is a self-depreciating movement amplified by the media to support and normalize female inequality; (2) there is no exact formula or cookie cutter answer because each child is different; and (3) each family's dynamics and values are different. Having been immersed in communities strongly supporting high academic achievement and being socialized into cultural values that promote "zeal, collectivism, and filial piety" (Noam-Zuidervaart

3), second-generation Chinese parents like me fall into the trap of "success frame," where we tend to subscribe to equally high standards of success (Lee and Zhou 17). But Fu and Markus have highlighted the following:

> motivation is understood to come from within an individual in Western families, while Asian children find strength in parental expectations ... [therefore] ... these findings underscore the importance of understanding cultural variation in how people construe themselves and their relationships to others. Western and Eastern parenting may differ in that European American parents tend to give their children wings to fly on their own, while Asian-American parents provide a constant wind beneath their children's wings. (747)

But there is no denying that parents across various cultures will make sacrifices for their children. Yet this dimension is not highlighted in most studies. Although my approach to parenting is deeply influenced by my own cultural upbringing and acculturation experience, the experience of motherhood has propelled me to believe that my enduring role is that of "beacons of light on a stable shoreline from which [my children] can safely navigate the world. [I] must make certain they don't crash against the rocks, but trust they have the capacity to learn to ride the waves on their own" (Ginsburg and Ginsburg xix). I believe in "lighthouse parenting" and providing a healthy amount of support and challenge for my children in order for them to independently learn stress management (Ginsburg 117). Providing this "holding environment" requires me to be an authoritative parent, who constantly checks in with my spouse to see how we are doing in supporting our children's development and in teaching our children how to actively deal with and manage different cultural contexts and expectations effectively (Drago-Severson 35). In this holding environment, I concur with Kenneth and Ilana Ginsburg in setting high expectations rooted in morality, resilience, hard work, and the ability to adapt to change (xv). After all, my most important role as a parent is to help my children become the best versions of themselves.

WORKS CITED

Allan, Julaine. "Mother Blaming: A Covert Practice in Therapeutic Intervention." *Australian Social Work*, vol. 54, no. 1, 2004, pp. 57-70.

Baumrind, Diana. "Effects of Authoritative Parental Control on Child Behavior." *Child Development*, vol. 37, no. 4, 1966, pp. 887-907.

Bautista, Veltisezar B. *The Filipino Americans: (1763-present): Their History, Culture, and Traditions*. Bookhaus, 2002.

Bhugra, Dinesh, and Matthew Becker. "Migration, Cultural Bereavement and Cultural Identity." *World Psychiatry*, vol. 4, no.1, 2005, pp. 18-24.

Bornstein, Marc H., and Deborah M. Zlotnik. "Parenting Styles and Their Effects." *Social and Emotional Development in Infancy and Early Childhood*, edited by Janette B. Benson and Marshall M. Haith, Academic, 2009, pp. 280-92.

Brykman, Beth. *The Wall between Women: The Conflict between Stay-at-Home and Employed Mothers*. Prometheus, 2006.

Cheah, Charissa S. L., et al. "Understanding 'Tiger Parenting' through the Perceptions of Chinese Immigrant Mothers: Can Chinese and U.S. Parenting Coexist?" *Asian American Journal of Psychology*, vol. 4. no. 1, 2013, pp. 30-40.

Chesney-Lind, Meda, and Katherine Irwin. "Beyond Bad Girls: Gender, Violence and Hype." Routledge, 2008, pp. 21-22.

Chua, Amy. *Battle Hymn of the Tiger Mother*. Penguin, 2011.

Collett, Jessica. "What Kind of Mother Am I? Impression Management and the Social Construction of Motherhood." *Symbolic Interaction*, vol. 28, no. 3, 2005, pp. 327-47.

Crittenden, Ann. *The Price of Motherhood: Why the Most Important Job in the World Is Still the Least Valued*. Metropolitan, 2001.

Douglas, Susan J., and Meredith W. Michaels. *The Mommy Myth: The Idealization of Motherhood and How It Has Undermined All Women*. Free, 2005.

Detzner, Daniel E. "Life histories conflict in Southeast Asian refugee families." *Qualitative Methods in Family Research*, eds. Gilgun, J. E, Daly, K., and Handel, G., Sage Publications, 1992, 100-102.

Drago-Severson, Eleanor. *Becoming Adult Learners: Principles and*

Practices for Effective Development. Teachers College, 2004.

Foo, Koong Hean. "Filial Parenting is not Working!" *Proceedings of the International Conference on Managing the Asian Century ICMAC 2013*, edited by Mandal Purnendu, Springer, 2013, pp. 343-51.

Frabutt, James M. "Parenting in Ethnic Minority Families." *Parenting in Ethnic Minority Families. Journal of Catholic Education*, vol. 3, no. 2, 2013, pp. 245-54.

Fu, Alyssa S., and Hazel R. Markus. "My Mother and Me: Why Tiger Mothers Motivate Asian Americans But Not European Americans. " *Personality and Social Psychology Bulletin*, vol. 40, no.6, 2014 pp. 739-49.

Ginsburg, Kenneth R., and Ilana Ginsburg. "Introduction." *Raising Kids to Thrive: Balancing Love with Expectations and Protection with Trust*. American Academy of Pediatrics, edited by Kenneth Ginsburg and Ilana Ginsburg, 2015, pp. xix-xvii.

Hall, C. Margaret. *Women and Identity: Value Choices in a Changing World*. Hemisphere, 1990.

Hays, Sharon. *The Cultural Contradictions of Motherhood*. Yale University Press, 1996.

Healey, Joseph F. *Diversity and Society: Race, Ethnicity, and Gender*. Sage, 2010.

Hsin, Amy, and Yu Xie. "Explaining Asian Americans' Academic Advantage over Whites". *Proceedings of the National Academy of Sciences*, vol. 111 no. 23, 2014, pp. 8416-421.

Huang, Grace Hui-Chen, and Mary Gove. "Confucianism, Chinese Families, and Academic Achievement: Exploring How Confucianism and Asian Descendant Parenting Practices Influence Children's Academic Achievement." *Science Education in East Asia*, edited by Myint Swe Khine, Springer, 2015, pp. 41-66.

Kim, Su Yeong, et al. "Does 'Tiger Parenting' Exist? Parenting Profiles of Chinese Americans and Adolescent Developmental Outcomes." *Asian American Journal of Psychology*, vol. 4, no.1, 2013, pp. 7-18.

Koerner, Ascan F., and Mary Anne Fitzpatrick. "Communication in Intact Families." *Routledge Handbook of Family Communication*, edited by Anita L. Vangelisti, Routledge, 2012, pp. 177-194.

Kordi, Abdorreza, and Rozumah Baharudin. "Parenting Attitude and Style and Its Effect on Children's School Achievements." *International Journal of Psychological Studies IJPS*, vol. 2, no. 2, 2010, pp. 217-22.

Lamborn, Susie D., et al.. "Hmong American Adolescents' Perceptions of Mothers' Parenting Practices: Support, Authority, and Intergenerational Agreement." *Asian American Journal of Psychology*, vol. 4, no.1, 2013, pp. 50-60.

Lim, Hyun-Joo. "The Intersection of Motherhood Identity with Culture and Class: A Qualitative Study of East Asian Mothers in England." Thesis, University of Bath, 2012.

Min, Pyong Gap. *Asian Americans: Contemporary Trends and Issues.* 2nd ed., Pine Forge Press, 2006.

Noam-Zuidervaart, Krista. "The Construction of the Success Frame by Second-Generation Chinese Parents; a Cross-National Comparison." Dissertation, University of California, Irvine, 2014.

Pedersen, James. *The Rise of the Millennial Parents: Parenting Yesterday and Today.* Rowman, 2014.

Qin, Desiree Baolian. "Doing Well vs. Feeling Well: Understanding Family Dynamics and the Psychological Adjustment of Chinese Immigrant Adolescents." *Journal of Youth and Adolescence*, vol. 37, 1, 2008, pp. 22-35.

Ramakrishnan, Karthick, and Farrah Ahmad. "Part of the 'State of Asian Americans and Pacific Islanders' Series." *Education.* Center for American Progress, 23 Apr. 2014. pp. 1-114.

Rich, Adrienne. *Of Woman Born: Motherhood as Experience and Institution.* Norton, 1976.

Rungduin, Teresita Tabbada, et al. "The Filipino Character Strength of Utang Na Loob: Exploring Contextual Associations with Gratitude." *International Journal of Research Studies in Psychology IJRSP*, vol. 5, no. 1, 2015, pp. 13-23.

Russell, Stephen Thomas, et al. *Asian American Parenting and Parent-Adolescent Relationships.* Springer, 2010.

Skenazy, Lenore. *Free Range Kids: How to Raise Safe, Self-reliant Children (without Going Nuts with Worry).* Jossey-Bass, 2010.

Steiner, Leslie Morgan. *Mommy Wars: Stay-at-home and Career Moms Face off on Their Choices, Their Lives, Their Families.* Random, 2006.

Tumandao Umayan, Maria Luisa, et al. "Mothering and Acculturation: Experiences during Pregnancy and Childrearing of Filipina Mothers Married to Japanese." *BioScience Trends*, vol. 3, no. 3, 2009, pp. 77-86.

Way, Niobe, et al. "Social and Emotional Parenting: Mothering in a Changing Chinese Society." *Asian American Journal of Psychology*, vol. 4, no.1, 2013, pp. 61-70.

7.
Relying on Mothers

Motherwork and Maternal Thinking in Development Empowerment Discourse

MICHELLE HUGHES MILLER

IN 2012, MICHELLE BACHELET, the first woman president of Chile and then-executive director of UN Women, argued of women's relationship to global economic development: "Investing in girls and women is not only the right thing to do, it is also the smart thing to do" ("Women"). As her argument goes, if the global community wants to address global concerns, from extreme poverty to sustainability to growth in developing countries—what I will call in this chapter the "two-thirds world" in line with Chandra Talpade Mohanty's distinction ("'Under Western Eyes' Revisited" 506)—we must nurture and engage the human capital of women.

Such arguments are part of the empowerment of women rhetoric that has been widely used by development actors, UN agencies and personnel, and even transnational feminists and activists in support of the Millennium Development Goals (MDG). I am concerned about this rhetoric, not because I am opposed to investment in girls and women, but because some of the discourse of women's empowerment thinly disguises an interest in women not as women— as in "women's rights are human rights" (Bunch 58) or even as individuals devoid of gender. Instead, in analyzing this rhetoric, I find a not-too subtle assertion that the value of girls and women also lies in their status as mothers or prospective mothers. What women do, then, as they help the world achieve global development is both singular to their activities as neoliberal economic actors and collective to their activities as maternal workers. It is the intersection of these two forms of labour that I take issue with, although my primary task in this chapter is to untangle the discursive construction of maternal work.

Specifically, I consider here some of the discourse of women's empowerment speaking to the purpose of empowering women, its roots in international conventions and rhetoric, and its implications for women as women and as prospective and presumptive mothers. In doing so, I rely on three concepts from maternal theory to unpack this discourse—namely, motherwork, as developed by Patricia Hill Collins, and maternal thinking and maternal practice, as theorized by Sara Ruddick. Although this chapter is largely conceptual, I incorporate illustrations from testimony and reports generated by such entities as the World Bank, UN Women, and other UN affiliates to articulate and inform my arguments. Finally, after I demonstrate the integration of motherwork and maternal thinking into empowerment discourse, I critique my own analysis using some of the tenets of transnational feminism by highlighting the role of motherhood in some regions of the two-thirds world. These transnational feminist arguments challenge my critique of the empowerment discourse by pointing out the culture-specific validity of embracing and endorsing motherwork as development, while they simultaneously challenge mothers' social, political, and economic engagement in development itself. I begin, however, by discussing what is meant by women's empowerment within global doctrine, the MDG, and global economic development efforts.

THE ROOTS OF WOMEN'S EMPOWERMENT: CEDAW

The touchstone of women's global empowerment, the Convention on the Elimination of All forms of Discrimination Against Women (CEDAW), was written to construct a definition of civil rights for women under human rights laws already in existence. The goal was to construct women as men's equals—in opportunities and rights—in the personal and civic worlds. But the justification for this separate convention was for the following reason:

> discrimination against women violates the principles of equality of rights and respect for human dignity, is an obstacle to the participation of women, on equal terms with

> men, in the political, social, economic and cultural life of their countries, hampers the growth of the prosperity of society and the family and makes more difficult the full development of the potentialities of women in the service of their countries and of humanity. (UN, *Convention*)

CEDAW explicitly argues that women should be equal because they cannot fully benefit humanity unless they are. Such arguments are now commonplace, particularly within development discourse. But CEDAW can also be interpreted as calling for women's rights despite women's reproductive activities. By specifically calling on childrearing to be shared, by mentioning family planning and reproductive choice, and by denying discrimination based on procreation, CEDAW puts forward an image of an empowered woman who should not be limited by her role as a potential or actual mother. As such, CEDAW creates the image of an independent entity—a global citizen—whose rights are derived from her humanity and whose empowerment (not entrapment in maternal practice) is essential for her enactment of those rights. CEDAW, however, only started creating the image of women as independent, rational, rights-bearers. Hanna Schöpp-Schilling, who served as a member of CEDAW from 1989 to 2009, argues that women's rights were not yet individualized in CEDAW; rather, the document considered "women as active individuals, but less with respect to their own empowerment ... but rather in the support of and service for others, e.g. family, country, and humanity" (16). She asserts that CEDAW inculcated an instrumentalist understanding of women's empowerment rooted within their caregiver roles within human rights doctrine, even before neoliberal actors embraced the idea. It is to the neoliberal construction of women's empowerment I now turn.

THE MDG: GLOBAL ECONOMIC DEVELOPMENT AND WOMEN'S EMPOWERMENT

The MDG started in 2000 with a promise and a direction: to eradicate[1] extreme poverty, especially in the two-thirds world (UN, *We Can End Poverty*). One critical feminist review of the MDG illustrates that "the MDG framework reaffirms gender, racial and class inequalities" (O'Manique and Fourie 16), even as it purports to address them. Included in the eight specified goals were two that targeted women—promote gender equality and empower women (defined as parity in educational attainment at all levels) and improve maternal health. However, gender equality and the roles of mothers were also embedded in other goals—including a call for women's full, productive and "decent" employment (Goal 1) as the principle means to eradicate poverty as opposed to strong social welfare programs (Jaggar 426) and reference to mothers' educational levels as predictive of child mortality (Goal 4). In other words, gender permeated the MDG, which was the goal of the liberal feminists who lobbied for this inclusion (Calkin 302). The MDG were premised on change to improve individuals' lives, but the avenue to this improvement was, at its heart, economic development. Thus, the MDG integrated a discourse of concern with a discourse of development from the beginning. As women's prominence was highlighted within the concerns, women's status within development efforts became a given. The MDG positioned economic development as an explicit element of women's empowerment, and vice versa. In September 2015, the MDG were replaced with the Sustainable Development Goals (SDG; UN Women, *Women*). In my conclusion, I briefly consider how the SDG continue the focus on women's empowerment central to the MDG.

Within the MDG and various statements endorsing the MDG, we find a definition of empowerment explained by Narayan: "expansion of freedom of choice and action. It means increasing one's authority and control over the resources and decisions that affect one's life" (14). The relationship between empowerment and a free market economy in this definition invokes neoliberalist understandings of personal autonomy and determination as key to economic success. But the importance of this definition, when applied to women, is its reconceptualization of the importance of women's empowerment for the economy, what some scholars (Kabeer 436; Cornwall and Rivas 397) have referred to as the "instrumentalist view." The World Bank recognizes the social justice value of women's empowerment, which "is intrinsically worth pursuing" (Malhotra 3). As a goal itself, however, women's empowerment in terms of educational attainment, economic engagement, or improved health outcomes is in competition with other policies and other potential recipients (Kabeer 435). But as a means to an end, the enhancement of economic success for individuals, communities, and nations through women's empowerment justifies the global community's concern with women's lives. Women become a resource that should be set free of their structural constraints and become entrepreneurs. Their empowerment is our collective success.

Early in the campaign, the role of empowering women was made explicit: "To promote gender equality and the empowerment of women as effective ways to combat poverty, hunger and disease and to stimulate development that is truly sustainable" (UN, *United Nations Millennium Declaration*). By 2010, the claim had become much more pronounced: "Gender equality and the empowerment of women are at the heart of the MDGs and are preconditions for overcoming poverty, hunger and disease" (UN, *The Millennium Development Goals Report* 4). From 2000-2010 women's empowerment was constructed as essential to MDG success; such discourse effectively privileged the instrumentalism of empowerment. Rather than embracing women's empowerment as a human rights issue or a social justice imperative, the discourse spoke to the effects of such empowerment on others. This was, in part, a political choice. Hania Sholkamy, for instance, has argued that this construction was one way to make women's rights (or empowerment) palatable within conservative Muslim societies because it emphasizes what women can do for the societies, rather than for themselves if they become empowered through expanded resources, opportunities, or freedom of choice (86).

The far-reaching nature of women's empowerment was articulated on multiple occasions but rarely as explicitly as this excerpt from a statement by the UN's Secretary-General, Ban Ki-moon, in 2011:

> This year's International Day of Rural Women falls at a time of heightened awareness of the important contribution women are making to social progress... Study after study has demonstrated that rural women are pivotal to addressing hunger, malnutrition and poverty. They are the farmers and nurturers, the entrepreneurs and educators,

> the healers and helpers who can contribute to food security and economic growth in the world's most remote and vulnerable settings ... More than 100 million people could be lifted out of poverty if rural women had the same access to productive resources as men. (UN, "Secretary-General's Message for 2011")

This discourse is both instrumental and complex, as women are presented in their culturally defined roles as nurturers, educators, healers, and helpers alongside their productive roles as farmers and entrepreneurs. Women, according to this, do it all for the benefit of millions of people. Such discourse reflects what Mohanty has stated in *Feminism without Borders*: "women's bodies and labor are used to consolidate global dreams, desires, and ideologies of success and the good life in unprecedented ways" (147).

The desire for women as labourers within development discourse is an even greater issue if we remember that labour is frequently oppressive under global capitalism (Jaggar 428, 430; Mohanty, *Feminism* 141-143; Roberts 218-19). From maquiladoras to migration, efforts to broaden women's labour force participation have often been problematic. Linda Lindsey concludes, "over half a century of research demonstrates a pervasive global pattern connecting development programs to women's impoverishment, marginalization, and exploitation" (8). Thus, although the call in these development campaigns is for women's economic participation to improve conditions for everyone, the outcomes of women's labour are not entirely dependent on the agency of the women involved; rather, they are controlled by the vagaries of global capitalism.

Women's empowerment, then, inculcated in neoliberalism, is allegedly about choice. Enhancing "women's capacity for self-determination" is, for Naila Kabeer, the essence of empowerment (452). This position aligns Kabeer with Narayan's definition, above, and the development discourse. But Kabeer is cognizant of the context within which choice is made. She argues that empowerment is the ability to make choices in situations and contexts that had previously denied women this right or ability to choose. Resources that women can access and can conceive of accessing, their ability to act on these resources, and the outcome achievements of those actions may be indicators of empowerment, but they may also be less than transformative if they occur within domains already specified by gender, such as within maternal practice (450). Indeed, Malhotra notes that "the household and interfamilial relations are a central locus of women's disempowerment in a way that is not true for other disadvantaged groups" (5).

MOTHERWORK AND MATERNAL THINKING AS ELEMENTS OF EMPOWERMENT

As Mohanty has reminded us, "globalization recolonizes women—it 'writes its script' on women's and girls' bodies" (*Feminism* 235). Thus, the construction of "Third World" women workers are defined in terms of their relationships with home and family (143). They are not only neoliberal actors but mothers too, and in that capacity, they are conscripted into a role within development discourse. Lindsey describes this conscription as follows: "globalization's powerful, long-standing effects can be harnessed to improve a woman's life through employment, education, and entrepreneurship, enhancing her own and her family's well-being" (8).

In 1994, Patricia Hill Collins provided us a definition of motherwork: "'work for the day to come,' is motherwork, whether it is on behalf of one's own biological children, or for the children of one's own racial ethnic community, or to preserve the earth for those children who are yet unborn" (48). African American women's home labour benefits the family—"in collective effort to create and maintain family life in the face of forces that undermine family integrity" (47). Motherwork might occur within what Aida Hurtado has called a "politicized private sphere," in which mothers "manage to create and protect in an otherwise hostile environment" (849). In addition, Collins argues that "individual survival, empowerment, and identity require group survival, empowerment, and identity" (47). Writing about physical survival in particular, Collins notes that mothers of colour perform motherwork to ensure survival: "without women's motherwork, communities would not survive, and by definition, women of color themselves would not survive" (50). A similar risk of survival could be articulated for children within many marginalized or vulnerable communities and has been expressly incorporated into MDG and goal number four, which talks about reducing child mortality. Yet the interconnection between child survival, community survival, and the work of mothers to facilitate both is largely presumed rather than lauded. Collins acknowledges that motherwork is not evenly shared and notes the toil it can take: "this work often extracts a high cost for large numbers of women. There is loss of individual autonomy and there is submersion of individual growth for the benefit of the group" (50). I see the applicability of this concept of motherwork in the discourse surrounding women's role in development in the two-thirds world. In particular, I wish to show the expectation of motherwork within these documents, and how they fail to acknowledge the effects of this labour on women's lives.

In addition to motherwork, mothers engage in what Sara Ruddick calls "maternal thinking" (24). The reality of a biological child and its needs leads to mothers responding to children's demands, what she terms maternal practice. For Ruddick, maternal practice has three elements: to preserve children (survival), to nurture children, and to train children to be acceptable social actors (17). Because of these responsibilities, mothers develop a discipline of thinking that changes how they interact with the world. From Ruddick's perspective, the development of this discipline of thinking could take place for any caregivers engaged in maternal practice, regardless of gender (25, 40). However, such care is predominantly the work of women; thus, mothers are perceived to engage in maternal thinking arising from their commitment to maternal practice. For Ruddick, maternal thinking is a way of making sense of the world through the lens of mothering to meet the needs of children. Mothers' commitment to social justice or community development, for example, could be related to their maternal practice.

The relationship between Ruddick's conceptualization of maternal thinking and Collins's understanding of motherwork is important; in my integration, motherwork derives from maternal thinking. As Collins explains motherwork, the demands of preservation, nurturance, and acceptability exist within the labour of African American mothers to ensure the survival and success of their and others' children within a hostile, dangerous social world. Although the contexts of African American mothers' motherwork are not articulated by Ruddick—who has been criticized for generalizing across mothers rather than acknowledging the differences among them (Aanerud 24)—African American mothers' motherwork represents a form of maternal practice and maternal thinking. Thus, for my purposes, motherwork is endemic to mothering within marginalized or vulnerable communities, and maternal thinking, or the discipline constructed by the needs of children, may affect the choices of mothers in those domains. In making this argument, I do not claim that such mothers are victims of either their circumstances or development discourse, but I do claim that development actors do not acknowledge the effects of the discursive construction of the "empowered mother" on the mothers themselves.

Given the focus on extreme poverty within the MDG, the target for women's empowerment is women within economically vulnerable communities. As mothers, they face the demands of maternal practice along with significant resource limitations. It is their maternal thinking, then, and their "work for the day to come" that is the target of development actors—specifically their maternal labour on behalf of children and their thinking about the needs of all children (their own and others). In this way, to transform the conditions under which children live and improve their chances of survival, development actors have identified intervention strategies that often target mothers. They are supported in doing so by research that suggests mothers are a better source of change than other community members. For instance, the 2012 World Development Report, a summary report on gender inequality and development created by the World Bank, highlights research that found "increasing the share of household income controlled by women, either through their own earnings or cash transfers, changes spending in ways that benefit children," whereas research on men's income increases actually worsens the experiences of girls (5). Ranjit Kuar argues that the maxim guiding development efforts is explicitly gendered, and I would add explicitly maternal: "Educate a man and you educate one person, educate a woman and you educate an entire family" (292). In short, these words are echoed across the UN and within development discourse itself: "When women are empowered, their families, communities and nations are stronger and more resilient and vibrant too" (Bachelet, "National Gender").

The 1995 Beijing Platform for Action, where much of the contemporary global feminist agenda emerged, supported this integration of development and motherwork, ironically through its efforts to redress what it saw as an undervaluing of women's maternal practice:

> Women play a critical role in the family ... Women make a great contribution to the welfare of the family and to the development of society, which is still not recognized or considered in its full importance. The social significance of maternity, motherhood and the role of parents in the family and in the upbringing of children should be acknowledged. (UN, *Beijing Declaration*)

In making this statement, the authors both recognize maternal practice and reify its contributions to the social world. The effect of such discourse is both the presumption of motherwork on behalf of the next generation and its additional labour burden. Although both are concerns, it is the essentialist nature of this presumption that I want to highlight because of Collins's concerns about the cost of motherwork on mothers and Ruddick's claim that maternal practice and its corresponding maternal thinking could be realized by anyone. Yet it is not. The cost of motherwork and the need to think about children's needs within development actions are responsibilities that have not been shared. Moreover, there is an acceptance within development that intervention strategies should reflect this pattern. For example, when given power in local decision making in India, the women chose to increase access to public goods like water and sanitation. This action was considered emblematic by the authors of the World Development Report as they concluded: "Women's endowments, agency, and opportunities shape those of the next generation" (World Bank xx). This discourse moves from encouraging women's empowerment to encouraging women's empowerment because of their maternal thinking—they will simply make more inclusive decisions that will benefit a greater number of individuals. For Andrea Cornwall and Althea-Maria Rivas, this is similar to "painting women as the deserving subjects of development's attentions because of their inherent qualities" (399)—in this case, their motherhood.

Choice is defined as the essential element to illustrate women's empowerment. However, Kabeer's concern about the context of choice is left to the wayside because the World Bank and other development actors rely upon mothers' choices within those patriarchal domains. Thus, the call for women's empowerment is the call for a greater reliance on maternal thinking and assumes that mothers, more so than others, think about the needs of their (and others') children, families, and communities. And because this maternal thinking occurs within vulnerable communities, mothers are assumed to perform motherwork to increase the survival of all. This strand of development discourse reflects a colonization or appropriation of women's motherwork—specifically their labour to create local (and global) economic viability through their choices and actions.

The Girl Effect campaign helps to further unpack this construction of the empowered mother. Their website claims that "the world is systematically passing on poverty from generation to generation, while neglecting the one group with the unique potential to break this cycle: adolescent girls." Funded by transnational corporations (including Nike) and private foundations, The Girl Effect works in several countries, such as Ethiopia and Nigeria, to broaden girls' participation in education and economic development. However, Adrienne Roberts notes that the "business feminism" the corporations endorse weds "gender equality and corporate profitability" by essentializing girls while naturalizing the expertise of corporations (and development) to know how to fix complex, gendered social problems (223, 226). Furthermore, Ofra Koffman, and Rosalind Gill argue that in making their arguments, The Girl Effect organization differentiates between the "empowered, postfeminist subjects" who are Western girls and the "downtrodden victims of patriarchal values" (85) who are girls living in the two-thirds world. In doing so, they use the spectre of the "Third World Woman" (Mohanty, *Feminism* 23) as the unwelcome future for the victimized two-thirds world girls if Western feminists fail to act (MacDonald 2).

Much of The Girl Effect's online marketing is about branding; the goal is to "reframe the value of girls" and to ensure their inclusion in development discourse. To do so, the campaign uses media. The three-minute video, "The Girl Effect," uses animated imagery to argue that if twelve-year-old girls have access to healthcare and stay in school, they will become economically independent, which will lead to their ability to choose marriage and children. This idyllic image is portrayed as the alternative to a cycle of poverty and illness, which results when that twelve-year-old-girl, whose "future is out of her control," does not stay in school, gets married at fourteen, is pregnant by fifteen, sells her body to support her child, contracts HIV, and then perpetuates the cycle with her own children. This "negative situation," as the video calls it, is preventable, and the "clock is ticking" to create the girl effect—"an effect that starts with a twelve- year-old-girl and impacts the world." The value of the girl, in this video, is in her ability to break the poverty cycle; thus, becoming a mother is integral to the solution that changes the world. In repackaging girls as the source of global transformation, the organization relies upon their reproductive capabilities. Girls' empowerment, then, is not about their own lives but about their distributive effect on others, including their future children.

In the next section, I briefly discuss how the value of motherhood embedded within cultural practices may interact with development discourse in ways that complicate my critique. In making this self-critical argument, I endeavour to address such mistakes as overgeneralization, oversimplification, and neocolonialism (M'Mworia) that I may have committed in my analysis.

COMPLICATING THE STORY: MOTHERHOOD AS VALUED PUBLIC IDENTITY

In describing feminist activism in Chile, Amy Lind explains how the activists negotiate development practices and resources in their communities and country by asserting their status as mothers (421). Because of the cultural linking of motherhood, women's social status (rooted in patriarchy and heterosexism), family survival, and national development within neoliberal discourse, motherhood became their forum for social change. Lind's analysis hints at a fundamental problem with my critique: within some contexts and for some mothers, the reification of motherhood in development discourse can be potentially beneficial, if not validating. It may also lead to resources not previously available (Radcliffe and Pequeño 1003).

Furthermore, to problematize motherhood within development may be to impose European (or Western) values on other cultures (Radcliffe et al. 393). In part, the issue is a bifurcation between woman as wife and as mother, a claim that Oyeronke Oyewumi makes in her critique of Western feminism's preoccupation with the former (1097). Whereas in Western feminism, the wife is the point of concern because of her experience of patriarchal marriage that reifies a private-public dichotomy, this argument does not always resonate within certain African societies: "Although wifehood in many African societies has traditionally been regarded as functional and necessary it is at the same time seen as a transitional phase on the road to motherhood. *Mother* is the preferred and cherished self-identity of many African women" (1096, emphasis in original).

Development efforts calling for women's empowerment demonstrate their reliance on Western ideology. By calling for women's voice within the home as an indication of women's authority within this presumed patriarchal domain, such discourse assumes women's disempowerment in terms of their relationships to men,[2] not their relationships to their children. Empowering women within their male relationships is the goal; mothers' obligations to their children is a given.

At the same time, by illustrating the value of motherhood to African women, Oyewumi also asks whether empowerment efforts that rely on mothers enhance rather than harm their valuation within societies where motherhood is powerful (Bawa 121) and where "mother" is the "identity and name that African women claim for themselves" (Oyewumi 1097). By separating woman from mother in my critique of development discourse, I may be decentring "mother" from women's held identities in such societies without adequately acknowledging the importance of that identity to their social positions.

Another issue involves mother's labour. Although my critique specifically calls out development discourse for its reliance on motherwork and maternal thinking, mothers still may choose to engage in both and value their engagement in these activities. I do not see mothers as having "non-choices" (Bawa 123). Development discourse includes the argument that women *do* engage in such behaviours; the implication is that mothers, and girls as prospective mothers, *must*. With such discourse, mothers, regardless of their relationship to that status, see their motherwork defined for them, as a strategy for economic development. This construction may have little to do with their needs, interests, or goals for themselves, children, communities, or nations. And Bawa claims this may result in a new "modern normal," in which mothering—though reified in culture—is held accountable to "the approved sociocultural systems where independence, particularly financial, and individualism are the new normal" (128). Motherwork in this context is not only expected but imbued with neoliberal intent. Thus, my concern that motherwork is included in development may ultimately be less important to consider than how motherwork is included.

CONCLUSION

In a 2009 talk on global health, then Secretary-General of the UN Ban Ki-moon observed the following: "People often call an issue on which all can agree a 'motherhood issue.' Ironically, however, motherhood itself has not yet become a motherhood issue" (UN, "Secretary-General"). Although he was explicitly referring to the issue of safe motherhood, his arguments could be broadened to address the concern I have expressed in this chapter: the lack of awareness of the maternal burden unrepentantly integrated into development discourse. Cornwall and Rivas note that one consistent feminist critique of the MDG has been that the goals "make women work for development, rather than making development work for [women's] equality and empowerment" (398). I concur, but this is particularly true in the case of mothers, who have the disproportionate burden to both work for their own equality and that of their family, community, and next generation. Under these discourses, a woman becomes "consolidat[ed into] her role as a mother" (Bawa 123).

I have argued in this chapter that development discourse constructs an "empowered mother" upon whom global economic development partially relies. In addition to their roles as workers, mothers are also discursively expected to engage in motherwork; they are presumed to work and think on behalf of the next generation. And girls, as prospective mothers, find their future maternity constructed as powerful and inevitable, an essentialist interpretation of their economic and social value. To the extent that mothers do this motherwork, they increase the opportunities for their children's (and communities') survival and for the sustainability of development efforts. But this labour may have a high cost for the mothers themselves, as Collins reminds us, a cost that is largely invisible (and possibly irrelevant) in development discourse. Although I have struggled in this chapter with understanding how different cultures' valuations and identities of motherhood could complicate women's experiences of development-imposed motherwork, an effect of the development discourse may simply be more explicit directions for motherwork that have little to do with maternal thinking derived from maternal practice, and much more to do with neoliberal ideology.

Olga Sanmiguel-Valderamma, in her compelling discussion of flower workers in Colombia, has pointed out that empowerment can appear as resistance—to patriarchal motherhood, abusive partners, global social forces, and the absence of community support for the social reproductive labour of mothering (156). Although her research participants' precarious and low-paying labour fuels the global market for flowers and thus fulfills expectations of the women as neoliberal capitalist subjects, their mothering remains privatized with the burden of neoliberal mothering trickling down onto their children, especially their daughters. Nevertheless, according to Sanmiguel-Valderamma, the women with whom she spoke do not feel "trapped" (156) by motherhood; their trap is more global, as their "lives are instead overwhelmingly structured to serve a patriarchal racist capitalist global trading system" (155). As the women engage in motherwork for the survival of their children, their communities, and themselves, it seems disingenuous, then, to claim credit for their empowerment through the development efforts that simultaneously employ, control, and exploit them.

In closing, I previously mentioned that in 2015 the MDG were replaced by the SDG, which continue the rhetoric of women's empowerment as a "pre-condition" for success. This is not surprising, as feminist organizations have provided guidance to the developers of the SDG regarding problems with the MDG. Kristina Lanz, for instance, has asserted the intrinsic value of gender equality in her policy brief, although she did not discuss the role of mothers (3). The SDG do shift the focus to sustainability, and one change in particular highlights the importance of mothers within sustainable development: "We will implement the Agenda for the full benefit of all, for today's generation *and for future generations*" (UN, *Sustainable Development*; emphasis added). It remains to be seen if the burden of benefitting the next generation will be shared across nations, communities, and individuals, or whether it will continue to rely heavily upon the maternal thinking and motherwork performed by mothers.

ENDNOTES

[1] Later, the expression became to "reduce" or to "halve" extreme poverty.
[2] I do not address the heterosexist nature of much of this discourse in this chapter, and apologize for replicating it here.

WORKS CITED

Aanerud, Rebecca. "The Legacy of White Supremacy and the Challenge of White Antiracist Mothering." *Hypatia*, vol. 22, no. 2, 2007, pp. 20-38.

"About Girl Effect." *Girl Effect*, www.girleffect.org/about/. Accessed 24 Apr. 2016

Bachelet, Michelle. "National Gender Mechanisms in European Countries." International Conference on National Gender Mechanisms in European Countries, 25 Sept. 2011, Kiev, Ukraine, www.unwomen.org/en/news/stories/2011/9/national-gender-mechanisms-in-european-countries. Accessed 21 Sept. 2017.

Bachelet, Michelle. "Women as the Way Forward." World Economic Forum, 27 Jan. 2012, Davos, Switzerland, www.unwomen.org/en/news/stories/2012/1/women-as-the-way-forward-remarks-by-ms-bachelet-at-the-world-economic-forum. Accessed 21 Sept. 2017.

Bawa, Sylvia. "Paradoxes of (Dis)empowerment in the Postcolony: Women, Culture and Social Capital in Ghana." *Third World Quarterly*, vol. 37, no. 1, 2016, pp. 119-35.

Beijing Declaration and Platform for Action. Fourth World Conference on Women, 15 Sept. 1995, Beijing, China, www.unesco.org/education/information/nfsunesco/pdf/BEIJIN_E.PDF. Accessed 21. Sept. 2017.

Bunch, Charlotte. "Women's Rights as Human Rights: Towards a Re-Vision of Human Rights." *Women's Rights: A Human Rights Quarterly Reader*, edited by Bert B. Lockwood, Johns Hopkins University Press, 2006, pp. 57-69.

Calkin, Sydney. "Feminism, Interrupted? Gender and Development in the Era of 'Smart Economics.'" *Progress in Development Studies*, vol. 15, no. 4, 2015, pp. 295-307.

Collins, Patricia Hill. "Shifting the Center: Race, Class, and Feminist Theorizing about Motherhood." *Mothering: Ideology, Experience, and Agency*, edited by Evelyn Nakano Glenn, et al., Routledge, 1994, pp. 45-65.

Cornwall, Andrea, and Althea-Maria Rivas. "From 'Gender Equality and 'Women's Empowerment' to Global Justice: Reclaiming a Transformative Agenda for Gender and Development." *Third World Quarterly*, vol. 36, no. 2, 2015, pp. 396-415.

Hurtado, Aida. "Relating to Privilege: Seduction and Rejection in the Subordination of White Women and Women of Color." *Signs, vol. 14, no. 4,* 1989, pp 833-55.

Jaggar, Alison M. "Vulnerable Women and Neo-liberal Globalization: Debt Burdens Undermine Women's Health in the Global South." *Theoretical Medicine*, vol. 23, no. 6, 2002, pp. 425-40.

Kabeer, Naila. "Resources, Agency, Achievements: Reflections on the Measurement of Women's Empowerment." *Development and Change*, vol. 30, no. 3, 1999, pp. 435-64.

Koffman, Ofra, and Rosalind Gill. 'The Revolution Will Be Led by a 12-year-old Girl': Girl Power and Global Biopolitics." *Feminist*

Review, vol. 105, no. 1, 2013, pp. 83-102.

Kuar, Ranjit. *A Panel Analysis of Microfinance's Relevance for Achievement of the Millennium Development Goals: Does Gender Matter?* Thesis, University of Oslo, 2011.

Lanz, Kristina. "Gender Goals, Targets and Indicators for Sustainable Development - Problems and Opportunities: A Briefing Paper for Policy Makers, Lobby Groups and Development Practitioners Interested in Developing Gender-Sensitive Strategies for Sustainable Development." *Eldis*, 2013, www.eldis.org/go/topics/resource-guides/gender/key-issues/gender-and-indicators/the-sustainable-development-goals-the-post-2015-agenda-and-future-opportunities&id=71173&type=Document#.WFAfDn2ssb4. Accessed 23 Apr. 2016.

Lind, Amy. "Women's Community Organizing in Quito: The Paradoxes of Survival and Struggle." *The Women, Gender and Development Reader*, edited by Nalini Visvanathan, et al., Zed Books, 2011, pp. 417-24.

Lindsey, Linda L. "Sharp Right Turn: Globalization and Gender Equity." *The Sociological Quarterly*, vol. 55, no.1, 2014, pp. 1-22.

MacDonald, Katie. "Calls for Educating Girls in the Third World: Futurity, Girls and the 'Third World Woman.'" *Gender, Place & Culture*, vol. 23, no. 1, 2016, pp. 1-17.

Malhotra, Anju. "Conceptualizing and Measuring Women's Empowerment as a Variable in International Development." World Bank's Measuring Empowerment: Cross-Disciplinary Perspectives Workshop, 4 Feb. 2003, Washington, DC, siteresources.worldbank.org/INTGENDER/Resources/MalhotraSchulerBoender.pdf. Accessed 21 Sept. 2017.

M'Mworia, Damaris. "Justice from an African Woman's Standpoint." *Africa Files,* www.africafiles.org/article.asp?ID=3391. Accessed 27 Aug. 2015.

Mohanty, Chandra Talpade. "'Under Western Eyes' Revisited: Feminist Solidarity Through Anticapitalist Struggles." *Signs*, vol. 28, no. 2, 2003, pp. 499-535.

Mohanty, Chandra Talpade. *Feminism without Borders*. Duke University Press, 2003.

Narayan, Deepa. *Empowerment and Poverty Reduction: A Sourcebook*. The World Bank, 2002.

O'Manique, Colleen, and Pieter Fourie. "Gender justice and the Millennium Development Goals: Canada and South Africa Considered." *Politikon*, 2016, pp. 1-20.

Oyewumi, Oyeronke. "Family Bonds/Conceptual Binds: African Notes on Feminist Epistemologies." *Signs*, vol. 25, no. 4, 2000, pp. 1093-98.

Radcliffe, Sarah, with Andrea Pequeño. "Ethnicity, Development and Gender: Tsáhila Indigenous Women in Ecuador." *Development and Change*, vol. 41, no. 6, 2010, pp. 983-1016.

Radcliffe, Sarah, et al. "The Transnationalization of Gender and Reimagining Andean Indigenous Development." *Signs*, vol. 29, no. 2, 2004, pp. 387-416.

Roberts, Adrienne. "The Political Economy of 'Transnational Business Feminism.'" *International Feminist Journal of Politics*, vol. 17, no. 2, 2015, pp. 209-23.

Ruddick, Sara. *Maternal Thinking: Toward a Politics of Peace.* Beacon, 1995.

Sanmiguel-Valderamma, Olga. "Community Mothers and Flower Workers in Colombia: The Transnationalization of Social Reproduction and Production for the Global Market." *Journal of the Motherhood Initiative for Research*, vol. 2, no. 2, 2011, pp. 146-60.

Schöpp-Schilling, Hanna Beate. "The Nature and Scope of the Convention." *The Circle of Empowerment: Twenty-Five Years of the UN Committee on the Elimination of Discrimination Against Women*, edited by Hanna Beate Schöpp-Schilling and Cees Flinterman, The Feminist Press at CUNY, 2007, pp. 10-29.

Sholkamy, Hania. "The Empowerment of Women: Rights and Entitlements in Arab Worlds." *Human Rights, Plural Legalities, and Gendered Realities: Paths Are Made by Walking*, edited by Anne Hellum, et al., Weaver, 2008, pp. 85-99.

United Nations. *The Millennium Development Goals Report.* United Nations, 2010.

United Nations. "Secretary-General's Message for 2011." *International Day of Rural Women*, United Nations, 15 Oct. 2011.

United Nations. "Secretary-General Remarks at his Forum on Global Health: The Tie That Binds." *Secretary-General Ban Ki-moon*, United Nations, 2014.

United Nations. *Sustainable Development: Knowledge Platform*, United Nations, n.d.

United Nations. *United Nations Millennium Declaration*, United Nations, 18 Sept. 2000.

United Nations. *We Can End Poverty: Millennium Development Goals and Beyond 2015*. United Nations, 2010.

United Nations Women. *Convention for the Elimination of All Forms of Discrimination against Women*. United Nations Women, 1 Jan. 2008.

United Nations Women. *Women and the Sustainable Development Goals (SDGs)*. United Nations Women, 2015.

World Bank. *World Development Report 2012: Gender Equality and Development*. The World Bank, 2012.

INTERLUDE

8.
At Sea

JESSICA ADAMS

I'M LYING ON THE cabin sole of our sailboat, breastfeeding and fighting seasickness. The cabin sole of this particular boat, a small, traditional wooden cutter, is a narrow wooden floor running the length of the boat's interior, maybe six, seven feet. We're going against the prevailing wind, tacking back and forth, some miles south of Puerto Vallarta. Seawater is coming in erratic waves over the stern and washing gently around inside the boat. I'm wet. We're all wet. We carry about ten gallons of fresh water on board, so taking a shower after this is over isn't an option. Pouring a few cups of water over ourselves, as my dad would do during his long stays in rural Zimbabwe, is an option. The boat is heeled over, and I'm trying to prop myself up so I don't crush my child. She lies there, nursing calmly. The water, the wind, the motion—it's not strange; it doesn't mean anything in particular. It's life. This is home. I, for the moment, am home.

I don't know exactly why I feel compelled to share this particular anecdote. Perhaps it speaks to a desire for witness or to seek some form of congratulations for my endurance. I'd also just recovered from hepatitis, but, regardless, an intense engagement with the vagaries of the natural world had become commonplace. Maybe it suggests how far I'd travelled from the basic assumptions I had grown up with and from received notions of motherhood I had gathered from my culture. It was a moment, I suppose, at which I felt that I became different. For example, the casual comforts of my previous middle-class life appeared profound luxuries. In other words, I became more like most people in the world. I became, in that sense, unexceptional—stripped for the moment of the privileges attendant to whiteness, middle-classness, Americanness. A sort of baptism, a moment in which boundaries appeared to dissolve. Giving birth struck me that way too—as a breaking down of barriers, a point at which my body was simply human, and I was completely vulnerable to circumstances.

I feared motherhood. Family members were surprised when I turned out to be, in their view, a decent mother. "Jessie's actually a good mom!" they exclaimed to each other, out of my hearing. I was one of those academics who had put the whole thing off—in my case, because of a sense that I'd never get anything done if I had a child and having a child would cut me off from an intellectual and artistic life. One of my graduate professors, herself a new mother, had talked passionately about mother-artists, about how the artistic power of mothers needed to be understood as against the prevailing conception that motherhood somehow compromises women's artistic potential as it distracts them and creates a sieve through which their inspiration leaks. And now I get it. It's not that way at all.

Still, thinking about having a child, I was afraid of the strictures I thought it would place on me. On a gut level, I felt I needed to avoid getting sucked into the dictates of mainstream (as in white and middle-class) American life around babies—around what "motherhood" meant and what it was supposed to mean. After leaving New Orleans for California in the aftermath of Hurricane Katrina, I became professionally rootless, and joined so many others in mourning. Yet I was indebted to the floodwaters for an escape from the seemingly endless search for a tenure-track teaching job. Facing a U.S. president with what appeared to be a backward agenda, preoccupied with the need to live in a more ecologically responsible way, and living with a partner who had recently single-handed his boat across the Pacific, I felt that Mexico was a logical next destination. Children born there could have Mexican citizenship. I'd always wanted to learn Spanish. My husband and I bought a twenty-eight-foot traditional wooden cutter, sold the engine out of it, installed solar panels, got rid of our car, and sailed out under the Golden Gate Bridge, seeking a kind of global future primitive.

Sailing may be the last great way for people without much money, but with some luck, to travel on a grand scale. Not the only way—there are buses, and I have heard that people still jump trains—but it is the one, perhaps, with the most dignity because it has the longest history. The high seas never captivated me as a child. I am forced to admit that after all my years living aboard, I've remained an indifferent, reluctant sailor, plagued by seasickness. And yet. It is the world out there. I tried to put another story together—the seas, as the refuge of artists. Those who live rough, seeking experience. Who crave, above all, time. My family and I probably would have stopped sailing years ago, gone back to something more ostensibly comfortable, if we'd been able to afford it. Instead, we pushed onward, envisioning a new life that did not turn its back on the exigencies of change. Our small family became a unit of survival, the only known thing across an ever-changing geography.

I recently read an article by a woman living in an eight-hundred-square-foot apartment with her three children overlooking Central Park (Neuer). She made a list of things she had learned from this experience, which included how little kids need and how little adults need in order to be happy. I laughed when I read this article, with the author's determined—and, I think, real—cheerfulness in the face of tiny living quarters. I wasn't sure why I was laughing. I read it aloud to my now nine-year-old daughter, with whom, along with my husband, I shared spaces far smaller than the one inhabited by the author for ten years, aboard a series of sailboats, travelling, often staying put, along the Mexican coast, through Polynesia and various parts of the Caribbean, as well as along the eastern seaboard. I have plumbed the rough edges of my personal limitations—as a mother, certainly. And as an American—but I can't really think of myself as exactly American anymore. When people ask where I'm from, sometimes I can barely muster the energy to answer. Who knows? I've lost parts of myself along the way—parts I clung to, parts I don't remember, parts I'm better off without. In leaving U.S. culture behind, like those conducting utopian experiments in generations before mine, I had "dropped out." I did not simply replace my culture of origin with another culture—with Mexican culture, for example. Instead, I hung out in a sort of in-between space. A boat is a sovereignty unto itself in some legal ways; it's a kind of literal floating island, a site in which social norms are bound to become slippery. Hence the necessity of discipline aboard ship. Yet if you focus on the possibilities rather than the dangers of small-scale anarchy, it's peerless as a site of reinvention.

Then again, outside the United States, I'm rarely mistaken for anything other than an American. In embracing a globalized life—as an individual, and as a mother—I have turned into a perpetual stranger, a white middle-class person who has undeniably benefited from white privilege but who has also had what for middle-class whites is the opportunity to experience a deep lack of privilege. Meanwhile, my bilingual, Mexican-born daughter has come to identify herself as Latina. She brushes off our comments to the effect that "Latina" means something she may not be, and indeed perhaps they're irrelevant. She has two blandly white parents, but many of her memories are of growing up in Mexico, the Dominican Republic, and Puerto Rico. She spoke her first words in Spanish.

My identity as a mother has thus evolved in communities far from my family, which itself fragmented long ago. My attempt to parent has taken place as a small act of globalization, if by that term we can mean an attempt at creating, out of a few basic raw materials, a kind of cosmopolitanism on what would be, in the U.S., poverty-level wages. I was leaving my "comfort zone," as they say. Motherhood is interesting as a site of study in part because of a central paradox. It has the ability to create roots; it seems to have almost an imperative to renew the rituals and practices that enable the continuity of "tradition," precisely because it involves the creation of something new and unprecedented.

My comfort zone—middle-class America—seemed so racially monochrome, so ecologically unsustainable, that it had become deeply uncomfortable. I did not want to raise a child in it. In heading out into the unknown, I hoped to throw off many of the traditions I had grown up with in the United States—the de facto segregated neighbourhoods and pervasive racism, the wild impulses of consumerism. I explicitly did not want my child to grow up with the notions (never actually taught by my liberal, well-traveled parents) that I had absorbed in the United States, a kid whose international travel consisted primarily of a few months in France and a couple of trips to Toronto.

Returning by bus to the beachfront town of Barra de Navidad from the birthing center in Guadalajara with our week-old baby (I had narrowly avoided a C-section because the American-born midwife had studied with Mexican midwives who worked out in el campo, where you couldn't just head to the hospital if there were complications), we discovered our bed moldy, everything moldy, inhabited by odd beetles, a large spider. A hurricane had passed while we were away. This seemed not ideal, but OK. Honestly, I was too tired to think about it. My experiences were obviating some of the values of my culture, and I was happily letting go of technology and certain aspects of consumerism—all the stuff—but it was interesting to see what was left, what was most recalcitrant. (It turned out to be things like foodways and space—rituals around mealtimes and food, what kind of space you were "supposed" to inhabit, what "play" meant.)

Part of the point of choosing this life was to enable true co-parenting, to become a unit sharing the day and the work of child raising. In reality, our roles sheared off in different directions. The old stereotypes of mother and father almost instantly reared up and asserted themselves. I was the source of milk, and it turned out that meant almost everything, for a long time. It was my identity, no matter how my thoughts pinged around wildly in my brain. Still, outside the sphere of U.S. culture, I found that "natural childbirth," breastfeeding, co-sleeping—heated points of debate in the States—all seemed not effortless, necessarily, but clearly humane. I hesitate to go too far into these topics because my point is not about what women "should" do, rather about the effect leaving one's accustomed social sphere may have. In her book *Le Conflit: La femme et la mère* (2010), French philosopher Élisabeth Badinter argues that mothering is an ongoing site of women's oppression, thanks now in part to renewed concepts of "ecology." That is, childbirth without drugs, breastfeeding, and cloth diapers have all become tools of the patriarchy. I find it interesting how such a view implicitly accepts a "patriarchal" hierarchy of value. At the same time, from the perspective of one who (without planning it, specifically) used all these modes, it seems like it might not really matter what you do, or don't do. Motherhood is always at base a triangulation of time, guilt, and work, perhaps no one with a child is exempt, and maybe it's simply a matter of how you arrange the variables.

In some ways, global mothering has returned my body to me. I have become more profoundly integrated with the natural world. This is not to say that the process has been easy. Perhaps the "mother-artist" is one who has confronted and lived the complications, the conflict between brain and body, separated by culture and society, in such a way that they become fused and become the site of creativity. After struggling with the usual Western preoccupations around embodiment, I found myself experiencing true, physical hunger. In the Tuamotus, a remote group of atolls west of Tahiti, I tried to write something about being hungry, but I didn't finish it. I was hungry. I was still breastfeeding (I did so for nearly four years—such a convenient food source in the middle of nowhere) and felt a profound craving. I considered how indifferent the natural world was to us, how coldly spectacular—even though, in creating life and giving birth, I'd discovered how ineluctably I made up part of the history of the universe.

So we ate what the local people ate—fish we caught, and coconut, and the eggs of chickens that had eaten coconut, which made the yolks oddly viscous. Breadfruit, I remember, roasted on a fire. The people we met had planted a few tomatoes in the inhospitable coral soil, and were baking bread with flour they had transported from the distant Marquesas to eat at a table they'd constructed under the coconut palms. The few of us there on the atoll waited for the rare provisions from Papeete that came by fishing boat, such commodities as processed New Zealand cheese. A particularly generous Frenchman on a catamaran gifted us once with a quarter of a cabbage. "Are you sure you can part with it?" I recall demanding, breathlessly. I sprouted mung beans until they became long and leggy, their pale leaves spreading inside the jar. I had more at this moment in common with the locals, making do, although they had so much knowledge I lacked—as well as with long-ago white explorers, making their way under sail, encountering things known, if known at all, through guesses, myths, and legends. (I couldn't help visualizing a disorganized montage of rugged pioneers staggering across the plains, Captain Cook's men, ravenous and ill-tempered after their meals of grog and ship's biscuits.)

I had chosen this context of adventure deliberately, but in day-to-day life, the isolation and the reality of the boat meant that old comfort zone was inaccessible. Going out into nature and into unfamiliar cultures, I was interested to see how much I experienced the reality of disorientation and risk. Although I was educated and had parents with some resources, in remote places, we did not have healthcare; there was no doctor if my young child became sick. (We'd brought medicine from Mexico, easily available and cheap.) I did not need health insurance anyway because during all our travels outside the United States, when healthcare was available, it was either cheap or free. I was not able to earn money, at least not much. I was at a linguistic disadvantage, perpetually tongue-tied and at a loss to understand, so that the privileges of my education only took me so far. I was, in other words, stripped of my usual cladding, the insulating gear that keeps some in the United States so blind to the reality of the rest of the world and so punitive in their approach to immigrants, people of colour, the poor. It was not so much a project of participant observation as being scrubbed of the markers that separated me from a perceived other.

It has struck me, moving across different cultural landscapes with a young child, how fluid a child's perceptions are—how specifically one must teach or imply things like racism and gender roles in order for them to exist. My daughter has always had teachers and friends who are people of colour, has had daily interactions with a wide variety of people of different economic and racial/ethnic backgrounds. And I notice that she doesn't react to skin colour as having any particular value. As a Caucasian (the polite term used by my students when I taught at the University of the Virgin Islands), she seems to identify in some ways across what adults may call racial lines. The ideology of "colour blindness" has rightfully gotten a workout with the exposure of racism in U.S. culture, as many people have condemned the idea that whites can simply sweep away history and declare that they don't see colour. The notion of colour blindness is based in an experience (acknowledged or not) of white privilege. And it has been interesting to watch the evolution of my child's consciousness, living since birth among those who in the United States are referred to as minorities. She does not have the same markers of identity that I did, growing up in suburban America.

In saying this, I don't mean to suggest anything beyond simply how blatantly learned race-based (and other) prejudices are. We've all heard the argument that people are simply prone to stereotypes, that somehow the human brain values "like me" as better than "not like me." That there's something natural about the self-other dynamic. Yet this seems to me patently false. This kind of response isn't human or natural. Maybe it's simply a function of the kinds of communities (i.e., nondiverse) in which many people all across the world grow up. Of course, one may argue that those nondiverse communities are a function of human instinct. But again, after having raised a child across cultures, living in close proximity to many types of people, with the supposed "other" not simply as a feature of the landscape but a meaningful player in everyday life, it's amply clear to me that *not* creating racism is a pretty simple process.

I have come to feel that there is something profoundly satisfying in engaging in the constant examination of norms, in always being slightly off balance. The truth is that I am still hungry. I am still seeking. Redefining community has constantly forced me to reexamine myself. I still cannot take certain basic things for granted. I am in some profound way a perpetual observer, yet at the same time, I am bodily integrated into the norms of a series of places to which I know I will never fully belong. And abiding within that simultaneous sense of pathos, fulfillment, and incomplete understanding makes me feel truly and complicatedly alive.

We lived, for a time, in a mythical land filled with black peaks and pineapple fields, papaya, and a beautiful pale purple fruit, the pomme étoile. Custard apple, avocado, mango grew wild on hillsides scattered with sacred places. I paused one afternoon at a spring amid a grove of mape trees, their roots like ribbon candy, and I thought I could feel spirits gazing at me and murmuring in an unintelligible tongue. These were not my ancestors. These gods noticed me, but they were not moved.

WORKS CITED

Badinter, Élisabeth. *Le Conflit: La femme et la mère*. Flammarion, 2010.

Neuer, Batsheva. "Little Space, Large Life: Why We Live in a Teeny Apartment with Three Children." *The Washington Post*, 26 Sept. 2016, www.washingtonpost.com/news/parenting/wp/2016/09/26/little-space-large-life-why-we-live-in-a-teeny-apartment-with-three-children/?utm_term=.a3eb8d3112de. Accessed 21 Sept. 2017.

II.
MOTHERING, GLOBALIZATION, AND NATION

9. Abortion Politics in Edna O'Brien's *Down by the River*

ABIGAIL L. PALKO

BASED ON THE 1992 "X Case," *Down by the River* revisits an abiding concern of Edna O'Brien's: the implications of pregnancy, childbearing, and abortion politics for Irish women, especially state-sanctioned and state-enforced reproduction. Over the course of her prolific career, O'Brien engages with public debates about women's roles as mothers, and her characters represent a variety of challenges to cultural constructions of the Good Mother. In *Girls in Their Married Bliss* (1964; the third novel of *The Country Girls* trilogy), Baba attempts to induce an abortion with hot baths and liquor when she finds herself pregnant by her lover; Kate has herself surgically sterilized after her ex-husband wrests custody of their son away from her in order to avoid the pain of ever losing another child. One of the experimental elements of *House of Splendid Isolation* (1994) is the section in which an aborted fetus speaks. In *Down by the River* (1996), a perfect storm of O'Brien's literary interests—women's sexuality, mothering, and the political shaping of the Irish Republic—converges in her fictionalization of the real-life court case of Miss X. O'Brien depicts a complicated maternal impulse in Mary, her fictionalized Miss X, which mirrors the contradictions in Irish society's response to her. She also exposes the ways in which motherhood, considered the bedrock of the new Irish state in 1922, in reality has proven to be one of the largest stumbling blocks to its modernization and women's full participation as equal citizens. As Jane Elizabeth Dougherty argues of O'Brien's cultural critique,

> In her novel O'Brien shows that these collective ways of knowing, agreed upon in the patriarchal Irish courts and Irish media, as well as created by a patriarchal Western literary tradition and Irish literary canon, preclude a true understanding of the female experience of sexual assault, an experience that remains "unspeakable" in O'Brien's novel, in Irish culture, and in the Western literary tradition. (78)

The result is a work that levies a "political accusation of an Irish-Catholic morality that disregards individual well-being" (van Elk 188); demonstrates through intertextuality "the ways in which classical mythology and canonical literature have both presumed to account for female experience and been entirely inadequate to do so" (Dougherty 79); and, more significantly, explores the development of the eponymous Irish mother's moral subjectivity.

To contextualize this novel globally, it is crucial to note that it was published in the mid-1990s, a moment of great change in both the interplay of reproductive and domestic labour (Chavkin 4-5) as well as geopolitical and economic globalization trends. While the public sphere was undergoing the changes that globalization brought, the private sphere of motherhood, too, was encountering analogous development. Wendy Chavkin defines the "globalization of motherhood" as the "disaggregation of the biologic and care-giving components of motherhood" that has been instigated and driven by the "convergence of dramatic declines in birth rates worldwide (aside from sub-Saharan Africa), the rise of the untrammeled global movement of capital, people and information, and the rapid-fire dissemination of a host of new medical technologies" (3). In this new globalized context, the "fragmentation of biology, care, and relationship ... renders transformed social rearrangements into the biologically tangible" (Chavkin 3). Specific to the Irish economic context, this is the moment when the Celtic Tiger launched, catapulting an Ireland indelibly shaped by generations of poverty into the ranks of the richest countries in the world, a reversal precipitated by Ireland's entry into the European Union. Ireland found itself simultaneously modernizing and entering the global world, and *Down by the River* explores some of the ramifications of the impact of globalization on reproductive labour.

The power of *Down by the River* derives in no small part from its historical basis, the horrific tragedy of the X Case (which followed so closely on the Ann Lovett and Kerry babies tragedies of 1984[1]) and the unrelenting storm and fury that ensued in the Irish media. Irish decisions about women's status as citizens within the context of reproductive rights were now viewed from a more global perspective. In each of these incidents, globalizing impulses clashed with strong nationalist understandings of Irish motherhood to directly affect both the women's reactions to their pregnancies and the community's respective responses. Ruth Fletcher argues that the Irish "stance reflects in part a post-colonial desire to construct a culturally authentic 'pro-life' Irishness in opposition to what has been perceived as a British colonial pro-choice culture" (569); this cultural fight is closely bound up with issues of religious identity.

To briefly summarize the X Case, a fourteen-year-old girl was raped by a man she knew (accounts differ on whether it was a family friend or a classmate's father; the important detail is that it was not her father) and impregnated. Her parents made arrangements to take her to England to obtain a legal abortion, which was illegal in Ireland. The issue moved from the private realm to the public when her parents contacted the local Garda (Irish police force) to see if tissue samples from the abortion could be tested for DNA in order to prosecute the rapist; this, of course, alerted law officers to their intent to procure an abortion for their daughter. The Garda went to the attorney general, who went to court to force her to return to Ireland before having the abortion. When the fallout included great negative publicity, both in Ireland and in Europe, local government officials pressured Miss X's parents into appealing the decision, and in March, she was granted permission to travel freely. She ultimately suffered a miscarriage before she could have an abortion. The X Case generated significant controversy, both regarding the issue of abortion and, more broadly, women's status as citizens of Ireland, since the court prohibited Miss X from leaving the country for nine months, which curtailed her freedom of movement in a way that a man would have never experienced.

Of the case's impact on Irish society, Pauline Conroy writes the following:

> The limited legalization of contraception in 1979 almost instantaneously opened a third divisive period of campaigns over abortion; a subject over which a veil of silence had rested for many decades.... The population were battered and baffled by theological and philosophical positions on the origins of life and the contents of the uterus. As in England in 1938, it was the plight of a child, raped and pregnant, rather than women's rights, which eroded the absolutist position in law: that abortion is always wrong and criminal. (137-38)

Motherhood has been a contested status throughout the history of the Irish Republic because of the conflation of woman with mother, as mother stands as the basis of citizenship in article forty-one, section two of the Irish Constitution; this linkage has an explicit economic basis:

> 1. In particular, the State recognizes that by her life within the home, woman gives to the State a support without which the common good cannot be achieved.
>
> 2. The State shall, therefore, endeavour to ensure that mothers shall not be obliged by economic necessity to engage in labour to the neglect of their duties in the home.

Feminists, activists, and international actors, including the Irish Human Rights Commission, argue that this article abridges women's rights as full citizens and violates articles two and five of the UN Convention on the Elimination of All Forms of Discrimination against Women. The Irish Constitution's eighth amendment guarantees a right to life for the fetus even when the exercise of that right directly conflicts with the mother's wellbeing, creating a further dilemma, as the X Case exemplifies. National debate about these issues unfolded under the scrutiny of the international community. Similarly, this debate plays out in the novel in the various characters' assessments of Mary's maternal fitness.

Situated within the context of the economic inequities exposed by globalization, *Down by the River* highlights the modern hierarchy of class differences that so radically disenfranchises poor women like Mary. This exposition is most compellingly expressed by women in the novel. When politician PJ interrupts his weekend away with his mistress Geraldine to help procure the travel injunction against Mary, Geraldine questions what she sees as an unjust double standard. To his claim that "Look, if it was up to me I'd give her the government jet to get straight back across the salt sea" (158), she asks, "Hundreds of girls go, Jock ... including me ... Why one law for us and one for some poor girl?" (159). Despite Geraldine's urgings, PJ does not intervene to help Mary. Instead, as with many of the other judicial and legal authorities, he portrays himself as the victim: Donal, a senior barrister and friend of PJ's relates of a call from PJ, "He was mental ... chucked a wobbler" (167). PJ justifies the double standard on the basis of Mary's compliance: "Because she came home, stupid" (159). Mary is thoroughly marginalized in the view of the various authorities who wield what Geraldine terms the "mighty ambrosia" of power because she does not competently wield it herself (159). As both PJ and Frank, one of the judges hearing the case, admit, Mary's true sin in this instance was not getting pregnant or seeking an abortion. It was failing to procure one without calling attention to her intention and, worse, for coming home as the court ordered her without obtaining the abortion, putting them on the spot.

Frank's daughter Molly (whose name not insignificantly is a diminutive form of Mary, with implications of a lovingly bestowed nickname) serves as a counterpoint to Mary: she shows what life in a different economic class would have been like for Mary. As the privileged daughter of a Supreme Court judge, Molly is in a position to question her father and submit demands for just treatment, "refusing to get out of the car until he promised to let the girl go to England" (241), whereas Mary cannot wrest basic concessions of her human dignity from her father. Sitting in a position of relative privilege in the new global order, Molly forces

Frank-the-judge to consider the case from the perspective of Frank-the-father by repeatedly asking how he would handle it if she were pregnant, explicitly demanding, 'You would take me to England, wouldn't you?' (242). Frank's answer, sidestepping responsibility, is 'Why the hell did the girl come home?' (242); this response is the clearest (albeit tacit, never explicit) judicial acknowledgment of the double-standard of which Geraldine accuses them.

Down by the River also explores the entangled relationship between the Catholic Church and the Irish state. The novel expresses this imbrication in the descriptions it offers of Irish law as "The law of the land ... The Law of God" (139) and confirms it in Dr Tom's comment that the medical fraternity (and by implication, the rest of Ireland's social structure) is "under the thumbs of the bishops" (142). The construction of "Magdalene versus the nation" (187), which O'Brien progressively and patiently builds up with each successive character's perspective, renders Mary "a pawn in a political battle that she does not understand" (Conrad 104). This political battle entails the painful untangling of the Church and state's entwined influence on Irish life, which has obstructed Ireland's entry into modernity. The fear that such a development invokes is evident in the vitriolic responses to Mary's tragedy, expressed by a series of characters whose sole narrative purpose is to articulate various political and religious points of view. She is summarily condemned by both those close to her, like her best friend Tara's mother, Mrs. Minogue, who finds pleasure in imagining "a night paradise of foul pleasures which the girl enjoyed ... soiled undergarments ... a whore's remains" (150) and strangers, like the woman who calls into the radio to announce, "All you people with liberal tendencies is what's destroying the country ... I'd send her to the laundry she's named after ... I'd make her scrub" (187). The tragic irony that she daily scrubbed herself down by the river in a futile attempt to wash away her father's sexual abuse is ignored by those who know her, some (like Mrs. Minogue) willfully and others (like Betty) fearfully. Furthermore, the truth that her pregnancy resulted from incest is never considered by those who do not know her, even though, as an abstract possibility, it is present in the national consciousness. When Roisin delivers her first speech at a pro-life rally, she dismisses Kitty's concerns as "the incest tosh" (23). This is the only time that the word 'incest' is articulated in the novel, and the scene is prophetically emphatic that pregnancy resulting from incest does not justify abortion. Notably, Kitty "can scarcely bring herself to say the words," the narrator tells us, and her intimations are only indirectly recorded, not marked as dialogue: "It had to be conceded, she had said quietly, that scandals not only existed in dirty rags of newspapers, but happened in families, families all over, so that one read of girls drowning themselves, or giving birth in graveyards and leaving the infant to die" (23).

Not coincidentally, the furor provoked by Mary's pregnancy coincides with national debate about the Maastricht referendum—the moment that Ireland has to decide whether it will join modern, united Europe or not. At any other moment, perhaps, the attorney general could have "sat on it for a pinch of time and put 'Gone fishing' on his door" (246). At this precise moment, however, the Irish are confronted with a Janus-like element of their nature and a need to choose sides, as the debate between two of the judges, Frank and Ambrose, his younger, idealistic counterpart illustrates. Ambrose asserts that "We can't disgrace our country," to which Frank responds, aware that there is no answer that will not cause disgrace, "Our country will not recover from this ... Our Attorney General opened a right can of worms" (252). Ambrose answers Frank's assessment that "'if we don't let her out she might kill herself ... Weigh the deaths ... Two as opposed to one" with an accusation of "horse-trading" (253). As their debate continues, Mary's position as a pawn is emphasized by Ambrose's pivot from her to the nation:

> Ambrose: "You want to canonise her."
> Frank: "Believe me, I don't ... I wish she had gone and done what she had to do and left our lovely constitution with a ribbon round it.'
> Ambrose: "We're a Christian country ... We're a model for the whole world."
> Frank: "We're pagans, Ambrose ... Pagan urges run in our blood ... Pagan love ... Pagan lust ... Pagan hate ... That's why we need God so badly." (253)

The last two sentences encompass the moral component of the debate between Frank and Ambrose. Again, in Frank and Ambrose's attitudes, O'Brien captures the class hierarchy which she accuses of governing Irish life and law. Furthermore, here she starkly lays out the dichotomy of Ireland's desire to be a "model for the whole world" and its "pagan [read pre-modern] urges." These contradictory impulses entrap Mary. As Ingman notes, Mary's body and unborn child "belong to the Irish state; they symbolise what distinguishes Ireland from other nations. If the abortion is permitted, Ireland's alterity would be abolished and her moral integrity threatened. Ireland would become, argue the opponents of abortion in the novel, no better than other nations" (262). In this assessment, resistance to the forces of globalization is framed as a matter of national/religious identity, with those two descriptors being viewed as nearly synonymous.

In order to develop her own moral subjectivity, she must fight those, like Roisin, who would play out the battle on her body: "'It's not your child,' she said suddenly to Mary. "The way your tonsils are yours or your mane of hair." 'It's not yours either,' Mary said, the words a beautiful explosion that seemed to float out of her mouth and blacken the face that was only inches away" (154). The debate rages in the (feminine) private sphere as well as in the (masculine) public one in an echo of article forty-one's reification of the public-private spheres split. Roisin (the radical prolife activist) and Mrs. B (the Fitzs' housekeeper who tends to Mary with a true maternal gentleness) wage a battle to claim God's sanction for their respective stances, in the middle of which Mary miscarries:

> "Kneel," Roisin says.
> "I can't," Mary says.
> "Kneel down and confess before God that you did this."
> "She can't get up ... In God's name will one of you call an ambulance," Mrs. B says, because she sees the look in the eyes, the look she does not like, and in concert with their prayers she holds her; the small frame – askew – whispering in her ear—"You're not going to die ... You're not ... Going ... To die." (260)

Mrs. B's promise concludes the penultimate chapter and is ultimately fulfilled, although the reader is left questioning how effective any victory can be. As Kathryn Conrad argues, "O'Brien suggests that the problems in Ireland run much deeper than one law or another. If there is a solution to those problems, however, it is an impossible one" (104-05). The impossibility of a solution lies, O'Brien suggests, in the imbrication of the personal (Mary's troubles) and the public (the people's conviction that her decision reflects upon their identity), particularly when globalization heightens the stakes of efforts to sustain traditional national identity markers. In this conflict, O'Brien pushes the limits of civil and religious law to demonstrate the extreme, but logical, conclusion of the position exemplified by the eighth amendment, and, thereby, reveals the impact of globalization on a nation still determining how to sustain its national identity in conflicts with a global outlook. O'Brien suggests here that public attention to the negotiation overinvests it with salience.

The text prompts us to see itself as a reflection of the nation's attempted, and ultimately foiled, appropriation of Mary's story. Ailbhe Smyth's collection of essays, *The Abortion Papers: Ireland* (1992)—rushed to press in the intervening months between the Supreme Court's spring 1992 ruling in the X Case and the November referenda on abortion—concludes with a three-essay section on ethics. These analyses are particularly instructive in a reading of *Down by the River* and illuminate the effect of O'Brien's ability to capture the national heteroglossia. Dolores Dooley argues that approaching the abortion debate from the standpoint of a rights analysis necessarily impedes the woman's moral development as it "leads to the displacement and denigration of women as moral decision-makers" (169). She contends that the sociocultural attitude that empowers the enforcement of anti-abortion legislature infantilizes women:

> The current concentration on an unqualified right to life of innocent unborn life implies a *negative evaluation of women* who believe that abortion decisions should, nevertheless, be their own decision not to evade or avoid responsibility but precisely to be able to take 'responsibility' for *their*

> *own* decision, a decision that takes account of *all human factors, emotions, and moral beliefs involved in any abortion decision.* (172, emphasis in original)

Linda Hogan further develops Dooley's request that Irish society permit women to exercise their maternal responsibilities. Hogan identifies both a moral level and a political-medical level to the debate and insists that in the modern state they must be separated: "It is essential ... particularly in Ireland, to recognise that although one's moral convictions are extremely important, and must be considered, personal moral convictions cannot be the sole basis upon which a society legislates for or against the provision of particular medical procedures" (176). Reiterating traditional moral teaching, she asserts:

> In order to be moral, one's actions must be acts of autonomous choice—must be free from coercive force and from ignorance.... Only actions freely chosen, only decisions made in the face of real option can be considered to be within the realm of morality, with all the responsibilities this entails. (180)

The implications for Irish women facing problem pregnancies are clear. If they cannot freely choose to bear and raise their children, they are being coerced into accepting maternal responsibilities—and are thereby denied the opportunity to act as moral subjects by "accept[ing] the responsibilities of being born female" (184). Hogan thus implies that women are not fully autonomous citizens of a modern Ireland, a contention borne out by *Down by the River*.

Down by the River notably reflects upon the power of words to shape reality and their potential to harm the powerless. When Mary miscarries, for instance, the radical (even fundamentalist) Roisin verbally assaults Mary: "May you rot in hell ... You have murdered it ... You wanted that baby dead ... You willed it ... You'll pay for it every day of your life ... Women crying out for babies ... They'll curse you and God will curse you" (259). The host of a radio talk show segment devoted to discussing Mary's legal challenge characterizes the dilemma as "Magdalene versus the nation" (187), and a senior barrister describes Mary's flight to England for an abortion as "'Some little slut about to pour piss on the nation's breast'" (167). Anonymous letters intensify Mary's trauma: one writer attempts to scare her out of having an abortion: "The baby is always taken out alive. He will breathe, move and cry. The child is then butchered, head torn off, abdomen punctured with a sharp knife and left to die in a bucket. Read this nine times every hour and you will be saved" (236). Another tries to cajole her into carrying the pregnancy to term: "I hold your hand, believe me, I do. So many bigshots using your misfortune, loud-mouthing about you and your feelings. Don't listen to them. Be brave, Mary. May I call you Mary? Let the country be proud of you. Let us all stand up and cheer and say she won, she gave birth, she was good, she was great, she came through" (236). Mary is wounded by the words, perhaps almost as deeply wounded as she was by the incestuous rape. She experiences "antagonism ... from the pro-life women who pressure her to conform to their cause" (Slivka 121-22). She also, however, recognizes these words for what they are: "[Mary] thought that words were the thing people used to suit their purpose, to stuff up the holes in themselves, to live lies, and that one day those words would be sucked out of them and they would have to be their empty speechless selves at last" (O'Brien 184). In her introduction to *The Abortion Papers: Ireland*, Ailbhe Smyth exposes the power of words exerted over Irish women at the historical and fictional moment of the X case and in *Down by the River*: "What women are experiencing in Ireland at present is the literal and literally frightening power of language to constitute social reality. Language is used, in quite explicit and transparent ways, to construct or deny the contours and material substance of women's lives. Control through discourse is almost naïvely exposed in the present Irish controversy" (8). Throughout the novel, O'Brien explores the power of words to shape the realities of Irish women's lives, both through their vocalization and through their muting. Mary's inability to articulate James's incestuous abuse means that it is quite late in the novel before anyone knows—as opposed to suspects—who the father of her child is, and it is never quite clear whether anyone beyond her lawyers and the judges (i.e., the public and the prolife activists) knows his identity. The polyphony of voices means that all sides of the abortion debate are heard in *Down by the River*; it also means, though, that Mary's perspective is almost obliterated as the personal moral dilemma is eclipsed by the national one.

Mary's moral dilemma is the heart of the novel, albeit a deeply buried one. Speaking with Mona, a woman who befriended her at the English abortion clinic, Mary admits, "I don't know what to do" (232). Mona confirms for her that this truly is her personal journey: "'No one can tell you what to do ... Only yourself ... That's what's so hard ... That's what's so terrible about living,' and she puts her hand out, a smooth plump hand with a little array of rings, and they stood clasped, silent, listening quietly for the frightened things flailing their hearts" (232-33). This sentence is notable for its quiet acknowledgment of Mary's moral sovereignty. During a quiet conversation with Mrs. Fitz (one of Mary's court-appointed guardians during the court case), Mary faces the full horror of her situation and begins to assert her own will:

> "Do you hate him, Mary?He was the wrong father....[2] That's all."
> "And yet, you're you because of him.... That's one of life's strange mysteries."
> Maybe then, sitting on the bed as she drew on her stockings and looked down at her goose pimples and thought how ugly she was and how much uglier she would become, maybe then the little current of hope died in her. (235)

The narrative never makes explicit what this "little current of hope" is, but Mary's next words and actions imply she has a childish wish that the situation would simply resolve itself. The hope is killed, however, by the realization that her father, who has done this to her, may very well do it to her child as well; to save her child from her father's abuse demands that Mary not bear the baby. Again, O'Brien is understated here, giving simply the conversation tag "she said" without further description. Mary declares, "I don't want to have it and I don't want to kill it" (235) and then undertakes a run so violent that it scares Mrs. Fitz and her teenage sons, a clear attempt to induce a miscarriage. Mary pushes back against these anonymous attempts to define her by writing her own letter, a letter whose poignancy reveals Mary's moral maturity:

> I don't hate you, you know I don't. If only you were my sister or my brother but not my child. If you could be spirited out of me that would be all right, more than all right. It is just that I cannot bear you. I am asking your soul to fly off now and wait for the right mother. But I know that cannot be. (237, emphasis in original)

Although she cannot express her wishes this coherently to the adults assisting her, Mary can clearly reason through her dilemma; she identifies the optimal solution but is realistic enough to acknowledge that this is merely wishful thinking on her part. There is an unsensational pragmatism to her articulation that most of the other voices never manage to achieve, as they resort to either brimstone and hellfire rants or maudlin laments when speaking of Mary's tragedy. This sophisticated wish marks Mary's most maternal moment, and is the direct result of the insight she has gained from speaking with Mrs. Fitz.

Analysis of *Down by the River* demands that the reader consider why O'Brien has Mary miscarry the baby. There is the obvious factual factor—Miss X also miscarried—but since the historical details of the case have not in other instances constrained O'Brien, this narrative decision cannot be easily explained away in a novel that directly engages with Ireland's abortion laws. In her analysis of Irish postmortem traditions, Chiara Garattini posits the following:

> Traditionally, pregnancy, like birth, was covered in superstitions and secrecy in Ireland, and it is no surprise that also a pregnancy loss or a death at birth were muted in the discourse of the community and, sometimes, the family. Pregnancy loss seemed, up until a couple of decades ago, to be regarded by other members of the community as an event of little significance. (195)

Psychologically, in terms of Mary's character, Garattini's observations suggest that the spontaneous miscarriage is Mary's will controlling her body: miscarrying, particularly at the tense moment of her trial, can be read as her attempt to regain the privacy and insignificance that any other woman suffering a miscarriage would have. Garattini speaks of "a past in which the death of an infant or pregnancy loss were 'small things' in the overall struggle of daily life. People needed to 'get over it' and forget it as soon as possible" (203). Mothering in an era of globalization, however, precludes the privacy that enabled such stoicism. Throughout *Down by the River*, the reader sees Mary's desire to have her problem be this simple to solve, which allows her miscarriage to read as a desire to return to a simpler (though not necessarily kinder) past. Patricia Beattie Jung's observation regarding communal guilt illuminates this crucial moment. Jung discusses the community's responsibilities in cases of burdensome pregnancies: "Communities, ecclesial or civil, which seek to mandate childbearing only reinforce the powerlessness and violation many women have systematically experienced within those same communities" (297).

Miscarriage is also her body's way of forestalling a potential (and seemingly likely) miscarriage of justice. So long as she is pregnant, she is trapped in fulfilling the biological component of motherhood at the expense of the caring relationship—to frame this within the dichotomy of Chavkin's globalization of motherhood. The judges cannot give her permission to terminate the pregnancy precisely because it has been imbued with such significance for the national identity, an identity threatened by globalization forces. Ann Norton suggestively reads the miscarriage as instigated by the fetus. She labels it a "bitter loss of love, as if the child has seen the fight its existence caused and has chosen not to live in such a world, or as if it was murdered by the very people who sought ostensibly to protect its life" (91). The narration of the miscarriage hints at a hopeful ending to the novel. Traumatic as this experience is for Mary, two essential things happen during it. First, the baby fulfills her request: "I am asking your soul to fly off now and wait for the right mother" (237). Furthermore, although the moment of her miscarriage is painfully graphic, its explicitness is immediately indicative of a significant psychic shift in Mary. She now owns this experience: "It's ... It's ... It's coming out. Pouring out.... So small a creature to be able to wreak so much pain.... The pain is wild, there is vengeance in it. It is going now, going out of her, departing, a nebula out into nowhere" (257-58). Mary's ability to feel—deeply, physically—the pain of her miscarriage combines with her vision of the lost fetus as a "nebula out into nowhere" to signify that she has, through the assertion of her moral will, begun to develop her own subjectivity. She no longer needs to numb herself to the pain or to deny the reality of what is happening to her in order to survive; she has faced the most terrible outcome of her abuse and survived. And as a result, she no longer needs to cling to a fairy-tale wish that the fetus may be magically lifted from her and transplanted elsewhere. These factors hint that, on the personal level of Mary's life at least, O'Brien offers some hope in her ending. Mary opts out of state-imposed, enforced mothering precisely through her own ability to embrace the disaggregation of the physical and relational component of mothering that is the hallmark of motherhood in the age of globalization. This, in turn, effects a change in public attitudes toward mothering practices: when Mary sings karaoke, Norton suggests that "the Irish audience's 'innermost' selves, uncensored by social, political, or cultural rules and memories, recognize that Mary is more than an ill-educated country girl impregnated out of wedlock" (84). This could be, then, as a slight push back against the strictures imposed on mothering by globalization forces.

This hopefulness is not, however, unqualified. On a metatextual level, the narrative can be read as "raping" Mary yet again through the fictional changes that O'Brien implements. The major change that O'Brien makes in fictionalizing the case (and the one on which critics focus their attention) is the rapist's identity, to obvious effects. Miriam Mara contends in a representative argument that "O'Brien employs the obvious metaphor of rape for foreign invasion, but she reverses the traditional conception of England raping Ireland by representing an Irish man and/or Ireland as the rapist and by making England the place of redemption, of escape and freedom, rather than tyranny" (312-13). Linden Peach notes that "In what happens afterwards, Mary, like 'Miss X,' is seen as victimized twice, the second time by the way she is failed by the judicial system which is remote from her in geography, age, gender and understanding"

(76). In a very uncomfortable way—and disconcerting for feminist critics concerned with female autonomy—*Down by the River* itself seems to perpetrate a third "raping" of Miss X. To the best of my knowledge, no critical attention has been paid to the effect on the real figure behind this notorious case of its fictionalization by O'Brien. Does O'Brien use her tragedy for mere artistic fodder? Or is there a greater good accomplished by her (arguably sensationalist) appropriation of this painful episode?[3] This question has crucial implications for any consideration of the impact of globalization on mothering. Although attention to the constraints under which women mother has the potential to ameliorate these restrictions, it also (and simultaneously) serves to remind women that they mother under surveillance in the global era.

This is not merely an Irish problem. Globalization has highlighted the unequal access to reproductive justice across the globe and magnified the impact of reproductive labour on women's lives. Joanne Csete and Reilly Anne Willis assert that "Women's Rights, including women's reproductive rights, did not require a globalized world to be marginalized in national law and society" (205). They provocatively ask whether globalization has made it more difficult to apply a human rights discourse framework to counter "women's subordination as mothers, as workers, as members of households and as decision-makers about sex and reproduction" (205). In recent months, women (and their male allies) have publicly protested state control of their reproductive labour, from the Black Monday protests in ninety Polish cities against proposed new legislation that would criminalize abortion in all situations (current law only permits abortion in the case of a severe fetal anomaly, a threat to the mother's health and life, or a pregnancy from rape or incest) to the repeal the eighth marches in Dublin and twenty other world cities to the use of a drone to deliver abortion pills to women in Northern Ireland to Women on Waves, a Dutch nonprofit that provides medical abortions on board a ship in international waters. This is not just a European problem. Chile's president is working to change their abortion laws. Chile is one of six countries that currently ban abortion under any circumstance (as do Nicaragua, El Salvador, the Dominican Republic, the Vatican, and Malta). Chilean women who seek abortions are faced with the choice of an unsafe, illegal procedure or travelling abroad to countries such as Argentina, Cuba, or the United States. Similarly, Irish women travel to the UK and Polish women go to Germany or Slovakia. In a 1996 essay entitled, "We Are Ugly, But We Are Here," Edwidge Danticat laments the invisibility that erases women's stories:

> Watching the news reports, it is often hard to tell whether there are real living and breathing women in conflict-stricken places like Haiti. The evening news broadcasts only allow us a brief glimpse of presidential coups, rejected boat people, and sabotaged elections. The women's stories never manage to make the front page. However they do exist.

Down by the River explores the miracle of, in Danticat's words, "not only surviving exile but also triumphing in it" ("Interview" 198). The novel forces us to contend with the paradox that the outcome of the pregnancy is simultaneously a deeply personal matter for the pregnant woman and one that the public views as a matter of their business, thoroughly embodying the feminist motto, "the personal is the political."

Having undertaken a purely literary analysis of *Down by the River*, I ultimately find myself, too, needing to turn to the metatextual level, albeit through a radically different lens than those previously employed by O'Brien's critics. In the critical debate regarding O'Brien's novel and its accomplishments in terms of giving voice to the maternal voice, two Irish mothers' voices are conspicuously silenced. Sara Gerend persuasively argues that "O'Brien radically alters the facts of the actual case to implicate, and condemn as criminal, a patriarchal Irish legislature and its will to power" with the result that the novel "stresses that under current written anti-abortion legislation, mothers literally cannot speak" (43). Gerend thus can claim—and I completely concur with this assessment—that "Ultimately, O'Brien's fictional account of the X case brings to the fore the fact that Irish mothers are beings who want desperately to speak; despite the imposed cultural silence in the nation surrounding the topic of abortion, Irish mothers are searching for alternative ways to communicate their experiences" (49). Reading *Down by the River*, especially for the first time, is a deeply disturbing experience; knowing that the novel is based on the X case removes any possible refuge in the hope that Mary will not become pregnant while the horror is intensified by the fictional pose that the rapist is Mary's father. In my own subsequent readings, I find myself troubled by the question of how the real Miss X would read the novel. Fourteen at the time of her rape, pregnancy, and miscarriage, she was eighteen when the novel was published. I find the changes to her parents—her mother rendered nearly blind to her daughter's suffering and almost powerless to protect her, her father transformed from the avenger of the X case to the perpetrator of the Magdalene case—troublesome in the way they reinscribe the rape, this time for O'Brien's own ends (noble though they may be). This is particularly problematical in the context in which the novel is critically assessed: it is lauded for "giving voice to Ireland's mothers," an accomplishment it only reaches by appropriating the voice of one of Ireland's infamous mothers, the Magdalene of the X case, and silencing Miss X's mother by writing her out of the novel. With this reading, I am purposefully implying an ethical component to literature that may be generally considered to be an unfair expectation. In the case of a novel like *Down by the River*, however, focused as it is on probing at the impact of geopolitical and economic trends on women's mothering practices, it seems that the larger political motivations behind its composition also impose a greater degree of responsibility to those whose story it uses.

ENDNOTES

[1]Ann Lovett was fifteen years old when she gave birth beside a grotto; both she and her newborn son died, and the case entered the national conversation about out-of-wedlock births that was already under way. A few months later, a newborn boy was found stabbed to death on a beach in Kerry. A local woman who was misidentified as his mother was charged with and confessed to his murder; she later recanted that confession while admitting to killing her own son. The first child's identity was never determined.
[2]This sentence is an intriguing example of O'Brien's grammatically ambiguous sentences. Does Mary mean that he was the wrong

person to have fathered the child she is carrying or that he was the wrong father for Mary herself? Or both at once? Furthermore, the quiet dismissal of the tragedy—"That's all"—exemplifies O'Brien's restraint in her treatment of James MacNamara.

[3]Interestingly, in a 2002 *Irish Times* article, Fintan O'Toole argues that O'Brien crosses the "border territory between the real and the imagined" with her later 2002 novel, *In the Forest*, but not with *Down by the River* because "The family in the X case were and remain anonymous" (March 2, 2002).

WORKS CITED

Chavkin, Wendy. "The Globalization of Motherhood." *The Globalization of Motherhood: Deconstructions and Reconstructions of Biology and Care*, edited by JaneMaree Maher and Wendy Chavkin, Routledge, 2010, pp. 3-15.

Conrad, Kathryn A. *Locked in the Family Cell: Gender, Sexuality & Political Agency in Irish National Discourse*. University of Wisconsin Press, 2004.

Conroy, Pauline. "Maternity Confined—the Struggle for Fertility Control." *Motherhood in Ireland: Creation and Context*, edited by Patricia Kennedy, Mercier, 2004, pp. 127-138.

Csete, Joanne, and Reilly Anne Willis. "Rights as Recourse: Globalized Motherhood and Human Rights." *The Globalization of Motherhood: Deconstructions and Reconstructions of Biology and Care*, edited by JaneMaree Maher and Wendy Chavkin, Routledge, 2010, pp. 205-27.

Danticat, Edwidge. "An Interview with Edwidge Danticat." *Contemporary Literature*, by Bonnie Lyons, vol. 44, no. 2, 2003, pp. 183-98.

Danticat, Edwidge."We Are Ugly, But We Are Here." *The Caribbean Writer,* vol. 10, 1996, http://faculty.webster.edu/corbetre/haiti/literature/danticat-ugly.htm. Accessed 10 July 2009.

Dooley, Dolores. "Abortion and Moral Disagreement." *The Abortion Papers: Ireland*, ed. Ailbhe Smyth, Attic, 1992, pp. 166-74.

Dougherty, Jane Elizabeth. "'Never Tear the Linnet from the Leaf': The Feminist Intertextuality of Edna O'Brien's *Down by the River*." *Frontiers: A Journal of Women Studies*, vol. 31, no.

3, 2010, pp. 77-102.

Garattini, Chiara. “Creating Memories: Material Culture and Infantile Death in Contemporary Ireland.” *Mortality*, vol. 12, no. 2, 2007, pp. 193-206.

Gerend, Sara. “‘Magdalene versus the Nation’: Ireland as a Space of Compulsory Motherhood in Edna O’Brien’s *Down by the River*.” *Motherhood and Space: Configurations of the Maternal Through Politics, Home, and the Body*, edited by Sarah Hardy and Caroline Wiedmer, Palgrave Macmillan, 2005, pp. 35-53.

Fletcher, Ruth. “Post-colonial Fragments: Representations of Abortion in Irish Law and Politics.” *Journal of Law and Society*, vol. 28, no. 4, 2001, pp. 568–89.

Hogan, Linda. “Procreative Choice: A Feminist Theological Comment.” *The Abortion Papers: Ireland*, edited by Ailbhe Smyth, Attic, 1992, pp. 175-85.

Jung, Patricia Beattie. “Abortion and Organ Donation: Christian Reflections on Bodily Life Support.” *The Journal of Religious Ethics*, vol. 16, no. 2, 1988, pp. 273-305.

Norton, Ann. “From Eros to Agape: Edna O’Brien’s Epiphanies.” *Edna O’Brien: New Critical Perspectives*, edited by Kathryn Laing, et al., 2006, pp. 83-103.

O’Brien, Edna. *The Country Girls Trilogy and Epilogue*. 1960. Plume, 1987.

O’Brien, Edna. *The House of Splendid Isolation*. Plume, 1994.

O’Brien, Edna. *Down by the River*. Farrar, Straus, and Giroux, 1996.

O’Toole, Fintan. “A Fiction Too Far.” *The Irish Times*, 2 Mar. 2002, www.irishtimes.com/news/a-fiction-too-far-1.1052404. Accessed 22 Sept. 2017.

Peach, Linden. *Contemporary Irish and Welsh Women’s Fiction: Gender, Desire and Power*. University of Wales, 2007.

Slivka, Jennifer A. “Irishness and Exile in Edna O’Brien’s *Wild Decembers* and *In the Forest*.” *New Hibernia Review*, vol. 17, no. 1, 2013, pp. 115-31.

Smyth, Ailbhe. *The Abortion Papers: Ireland*. Attic, 1992.

van Elk, Martine. “Edna O’Brien.” *British Novelists Since 1960*, edited by Merritt Moseley, *Dictionary of Literary Biography*, vol. 231, Gale, 2001, pp. 176-91.

10.
Mothering (in) Which Nation?

Migration, Citizenship, and Motherhood of Filipino Immigrant Women Raising Japanese-Filipino Children

JOCELYN O. CELERO

IN THE MID-1980s, Japan's bubble economy stimulated a huge demand for sexualized and social reproductive labour, which resulted in the feminized migration of Filipinos. Thousands of Filipino migrant women arrived in Japan to either work for the booming entertainment industry across the country or to become brides to Japanese men in rural villages. A desire for economic security, self-autonomy, and freedom drove many Filipinas to seek a better life in Japan. Therefore, marriage became both the driver and the consequence of their previously short-term economic migration (Piper 458). In particular, the number of international marriages between Japanese men, and women from China, Korea, and the Philippines soared (Suzuki, "Women Imagined, Women Imaging" 142; "Between Two Shores" 431).

Filipinas (or Filipino women) constitute the second largest number of migrant spouses to Japanese nationals. Japanese and Filipino liaisons were formed either by Japanese men on business and Filipinas in the Philippines, or through personal meetings between Japanese men/women and Filipino men/women (Watanabe et al. qtd. in Bauzon 214; Suzuki, "Women Imagined, Women Imaging" 142; Jones and Shen 12; Celero, "Bicultural Parenting" 76). The latter best depicts the unions involving Japanese and overstaying Filipino entertainers so that the latter attains a legal status following Japan's restrictions on entertainers' entry in 1994 and 2005 (Anderson 3; Tutor 1; Celero, "Bicultural Parenting" 7). Japan's Ministry of Health, Labor and Welfare reports that from 1992 to 2012, Japanese men-Filipino women unions accounted for as high as 96 to 98 percent of the total number of Japanese-Filipino marriages. Since 2007, however, the number of Japanese-Filipino marriages has been decreasing, which reflects the falling demographic trends in the number of marriages in Japan. The number of divorces has been on decline as well. Japan reported a total of 3,920 Japanese-Filipino divorces in 2012, which accounted for 24 percent of the total number of divorces between international couples.

Despite these demographic changes, Japanese-Filipina marriages and families contribute to migrant settlement and population diversity in Japanese society. Filipinas come next to Chinese as the largest group to have received permanent resident status in Japan as spouses of Japanese citizens, with 115,857 getting status in 2014 (Ministry of Justice). This trend partly explains the growing tendency of Filipino migrant women to pursue settlement when rearing Japanese-Filipino children in Japan. The International Organization for Migration (IOM) estimates that about 100,000 to 200,000[1] Japanese-Filipino children are currently living in the Philippines and Japan, indicating the transnational nature of their childhood and family life.

Existing literature problematizes Filipino women's citizenship in relation to their status as migrant workers in the context of global migration (Rodríguez 342; Parreñas, *Servants* 95). Scholars view that state-given citizenship rights are no longer relevant in terms of rights and privileges in this era of globalization where migration flows tend to be rather short-term and temporary (Soysal 159; Sassen 7; Castles et al. 1-2). Women's marriage migration experiences impact on their citizenship choices. One study reveals that Filipinas in intermarriages often prefer the citizenship of their husband, not only to keep the union intact but also to access the socioeconomic benefits and rights that such legal membership bestows (Tibe-Bonifacio 144). Glenda Tibe-Bonifacio's discussion of the incentives of Australian citizenship shows that Filipino women in her study adopt Australian citizenship as a means to "empower themselves and compete equally in Australian society" (149). Tibe-Bonifacio's research focuses on Filipino marriage migrants' citizenship agenda, although it does not discuss the relationship between citizenship and motherhood.

This chapter explores the intersection between motherhood,

citizenship, and migration in the life narratives of Filipino women leading a transnational Japanese-Filipino family. Exploring Filipino mothers' strategies of raising Japanese-Filipino children and transnational migration as two key social phenomena, this chapter looks into how they live and negotiate multiple forms of national belonging through mothering. Motherhood is one of those practices through which women activate membership to a society. It consists of caring activities and seeking welfare for one's child. To focus on Filipino women's family and motherhood strategies is to analyze the sociological meaning of citizenship and to pay attention to the norms, practices, and identities constituting the experience of citizenship, rather than its political status that bestows rights and privileges upon individuals. Filipino migrant women are transborder citizens whose lives are influenced by legal pluralisms. As transborder citizens, they endeavour to connect to the states, laws, and cultural systems that legitimize, shape, and regulate their family lives (Glick Schiller 49). This chapter argues that Filipinos' strategies of motherhood indicate their ways of living transborder citizenship. These strategies enable them to construct a cohesive, unified, and settled family in Japan. The Filipino migrant women's transborder citizenship may be understood through (re)configuring the function of Japanese and Filipino citizenships, denizenship, and Japanese-Filipino transmigrant identity in a transnational family life.

RESEARCH METHODOLOGY

This chapter is based on the interviews conducted with seventy mothers living in Tokyo[2] and three focus group discussions with twenty-one Filipino women in Tokyo from 2013 to 2015. These respondents were sought through personal networks and snowball sampling techniques. Semistructured interviews were done using a mix of Japanese, English, and Filipino to elicit demographic data (age, education, length of residence in Japan, legal status, economic background, family size, frequency, and patterns of migration, etc.) as well as their life narratives, which focused on their legal membership and their strategies of raising a family in Japan (and in the Philippines). Interviews were fully transcribed and translated in English. In addition, this chapter incorporates some of the field notes taken from on-going research on the patterns of migration, integration, and social mobility of Japanese-Filipino families. The majority of the mother respondents belong to the forty to forty-nine years age group, and they have lived in Japan for twenty-one years or more. Many of them originally came to Japan to work as entertainers in the 1980s. Forty-one out of the seventy respondents have some university education, which indicates that Filipino migrant women in Japan are highly educated. Although most of them are former entertainers, they have gradually ventured into a broad band of economic activities in Japan, ranging from business owners to welfare dependents (Higuchi; Tenegra qtd. in Ito 63). In this study, twelve respondents are presently venturing into business either in Japan or the Philippines, ten respondents are living on subsidy support, whereas thirty-eight are working either in part-time or full-time job in Tokyo. These thirty-eight women are employed as company staff, assistant language teachers (ALT), caregivers, hotel and lodging chambermaids, and factory workers. In terms of legal status, fifty-four of them hold permanent residency, whereas fourteen are long-term residents, and only two have naturalized as Japanese. At the time of interview, thirty-three respondents had divorced their Japanese husbands, and twenty-nine were married. Pseudonyms were assigned to life accounts featured in this study to sustain confidentiality of data. The following sections describe Filipino mothers who engage in parenting practices as transborder citizens.

MOTHERHOOD AS ENACTING TRANSBORDER CITIZENSHIP: FILIPINO MIGRANTS' PATTERNS OF REARING JAPANESE-FILIPINO CHILDREN

Motherhood has historically and culturally been defined as the role of women in building nation-states and societies. According to Patricia Hill Collins, motherhood is a social practice consisting of three dimensions: 1) genetic, which pertains to mothers' reproductive or birth-giving role; 2) gestational, their duty to nurture children, and; 3) social motherhood, which involves embodying national culture vital for raising future citizens (qtd. in Yuval-Davis and Werbner 14). Carol Pateman suggests that these activities of producing future citizens of the state should be conceived of as the content of mothers' political citizenship (qtd. in Erel 16; Tibe-Bonifacio 148).

In Japan, the family serves as the pillar of Japanese identity and nationhood. Since the nineteenth century, the family has been regarded as the embodiment of "Japanese cultural ethos and the template of its social institutions" (Borovoy 68). Crucial to Japan's rapid transformation into a modern industrialized democracy during the post-World War II era was the dominant family structure's transformation from an extended "stem family" type to a nuclear, patriarchal one. This change dichotomized the family role with fathers as the earners and mothers as the caregivers (Holloway and Nagase 62; Holloway 196), which gave rise to the Japanese modern family. Despite experiencing fertility and population decline from as early as the 1970s (Ochiai, "Care Diamonds and Welfare Regimes" 61), Japan remains particularly distinct from other developed societies in the pervasiveness of familism as a social ideology (Ochiai, "The Ie (Family) in Global Perspective" 355). The prevalence of nuclear family as the normative structure has weakened the participation of relatives. Childcare and household production were bestowed into the hands of housewives and mothers (Ochiai, "The Ie (Family) in Global Perspective" 374-75; Holloway 96; Holloway and Nagase 62). The practice of motherhood is shaped by cultural models that Japanese families have adopted over the years.

The emergence of immigrant families, such as those of Filipino mothers, provides a context for examining motherhood as a negotiation of the prevailing cultural frames and ideals of family life in Japan. How Filipino women fulfill social reproduction for the productivity of either Japanese or Filipino society warrants an analysis of transborder citizenship, in which they participate in nurturing family life and belonging across societies. The next section discusses Filipino women's patterns of raising Japanese-Filipino children as their means for doing citizenship.

Assimilating

> My son has a Japanese father, and he was born here [in Japan] so that makes him Japanese. Japan has a safer en-

> vironment [compared to the Philippines]. There, it is hard to live without worrying about my child, whether he will get into drugs or gangsterism. Here, I am secured that my son will acquire adequate education and better employment in the future. (Janet, forty-seven, rears a fourteen-year-old child in Tokyo)

Assimilating pattern describes the parenting approach of a number of Filipino mothers who started a family in Japan and may be largely influenced by Japanese culture in rearing a family. Janet is an assimilating mother who finds security and wellbeing in raising her child in Japan. Knowing their child is of Japanese nationality, assimilating mothers refer to their children as the main constituents of the family. Their migrant status compels Filipino mothers to integrate into Japanese society to unify their household. They take pride in admitting themselves to the hospital prior to childbirth, either with or without the assistance of a working Japanese husband or Japanese in-laws. Adequate child- and healthcare facilities, as well as a safe social environment, convince assimilators like Janet that Japan is a better place to give birth and raise children. As most of them gave birth in Japan, assimilating mothers regard it as the home where the family should live and settle. Assimilating, thus, consists of mothering practices that enable Filipino women to integrate into Japanese society.

Assimilating mothers usually live a few years in Japan before giving birth and have invested in learning the Japanese language and cultural practices. As a part of raising children, assimilating parents try to become more visible in mainstream society. For instance, they send their children to a regular Japanese school where they participate in various activities with Japanese and non-Japanese parents. They form a social network with Japanese teachers, mothers, and neighbours in their respective community to forge solidarity with them and gain recognition as "virtuous citizens" (Ito 66). Unlike other migrant groups who reside with their co-ethnics in certain areas (Koreans in Shin-Okubo or Nikkei-Brazilians in Hamamatsu City), Filipina families live or co-reside with Japanese families, including their Japanese extended kin, in the greater Tokyo area (Fielding 105).

Filipinas employ assimilating strategies to generate shared self-identification as Japanese with their children; hence, they limit their observance of Filipino family practices. For instance, they prefer the Japanese language to Filipino or English when communicating daily with their children. They also use Japanese to emphasize the desirable features of Japan to their children. Anthropologist Masaaki Satake adds that even though Japanese husbands do not discourage Filipino wives from teaching their children the Filipino language, the former may put pressure on the latter to prioritize speaking Japanese to children (464).

Although Japanese-Filipino families strive to cohere with Japanese society, assimilating Filipino mothers do not break off their emotional ties in the Philippines. As a part of their family lifestyle, they occasionally bring their children to the Philippines to connect them to their extended kin. Mothers act as cultural brokers for their children, since the latter have limited Filipino language ability. Even though Japanese nationality is the primary basis of identity within assimilating families, Filipino mothers may continue to retain emotional links to their natal family in the Philippines, but they do not expect the same from their children. Thus, Filipino mothers' assimilation may be described as having stronger emotional linkage to Japanese society, to the home of their children, than their own homeland of the Philippines.

Maintaining

> Kota is only ten years old, so it is okay for us to stay in Japan for now. I want him to stay here ... until junior high school.... Then I would like him to go back to the Philippines. He will study in the university there. I would like him to return there, because I want him to reclaim his heart of a Filipino. His Filipino character has a weak foundation. Children [in Japan] could be really terrible; they easily lose respect for their mothers, and my son is picking that up. They [children] want to control their parents here, and my son thinks it is right. If he studies in the Philippines, I believe his character will improve. (Lea, forty-two, raising a ten-year-old child in Tokyo)

Maintaining consists of mothering practices oriented towards Filipino society and culture. It includes decisions to give birth and rear children in the Philippines in order to access caring support from one's natal family. Lea was one of Filipino respondents in this study who gave birth in the Philippines. Kota, her son, grew up there until the age of five; Lea decided to bring him to Japan to enter school in 2005. Maintaining mothers commonly agree that they do not feel obliged to adapt to Japanese culture to cope with everyday family life. Because they attach culture to the place of birth and socialization, they affirm being Filipino, whereas their children are Japanese. Filipinas draw from Filipino cultural practices as a basis for ensuring a cohesive family, owing to a lack of familiarity with Japanese culture. They prepare Filipino dishes more often than Japanese ones, teach children to pray before every meal, and teach them Filipino expressions to nurture emotional bond between them. Using the Filipino language, they also share their childhood stories with or describe the Philippines in detail to their children. Although children of maintaining mothers may go to Japanese schools in their formative years, some mothers like Lea would prefer them educated in the Philippines for its affordability and the opportunity to learn English. Many Japanese-Filipino children I interviewed moved to the Philippines to resume schooling in the middle part of elementary until secondary school. Maintaining mothers hold faith that studying in a Filipino school instills a Filipino character in their children, which they cannot inculcate alone in Japan. This notion of Filipino personhood inflects values of respect for and filial piety toward one's parents and the elderly. Thus, the maintaining approach adheres to the Filipino education system and values to better prepare a child for the future.

Maintaining Filipino mothers minimally participate in Japanese school events because of their poor language skills and inability to communicate with Japanese mothers. Some children occasionally act as cultural brokers for their mothers at school. The children often help with translating forms and informing their mothers of school or community activities that require parental involvement. Filipino mothers also incorporate religious practices in their children's socialization experience, taking them to church to hear mass, and raising them as churchgoers. Part of bolstering the significance of religious traditions to family life is taking the children to the Philippines as often as possible. Migration allows family reunions and enjoyment of religious practices, which connect Japanese-Filipino children to their extended kin in the Philippines. As a result, some Japanese-Filipino children grew up knowing and speaking the Filipino language, broken English, and/or a regional dialect. Hence, raising or sending children to the Philippines implies strengthening the children's ties toward their mother's homeland culture and, thus, toward the Filipino society. Recognizing their foreign status in Japan, maintaining Filipino mothers do not invest in learning Japanese culture. They feel that the burden of cultural adjustment lies on the shoulders of their children.

Switching

> Even if my children and I have decided to settle here [in Japan], it does not mean this is our only "home." Honestly, when I am in Japan, I spend more hours at work than with my children. In the Philippines, my children enjoy being there with my family ... Even if I am already a permanent resident here [in Japan], I can always travel with my children to the Philippines anytime.... My kids try to learn Filipino when they are in the Philippines, but because we only stay there for a while, they easily forget it [when they are in Japan], and remember it again when we come back. It is okay for now; they are still young ... they will learn it, eventually. (Linda, thirty-four, raising seven-year-old and five-year-old Japanese-Filipino kids in Tokyo)

Switching mothers like Linda claim that they may build a home in Japan and the Philippines, as their children are Japanese citizens who may develop a dual cultural orientation. Switching strategies function to instill in their children the importance of both Japanese and Filipino ethnic identification in their lives. It entails making them identify positively with being "*hafu*."[3] These Filipino mothers see that Japan and the Philippines have complementary functions in their children's socialization. Switching methods include decisions to raise children in Japan for its economic and social resources, and incorporate the Philippines as a place for instilling in their children Filipino character and cultural capital. Some children may spend several years of their childhood living in Japan as well as the Philippines. Sending children to the Philippines to learn Filipino and English balances learning experiences in Japan, and makes up a more holistic educational experience for their children.

Switching involves alternating the function of Japanese and Filipino cultures in the socialization experience of Japanese-Filipino children, and appropriating each culture while living in Japan or the Philippines. For instance, in Linda's aforementioned case, children learn Filipino faster while vacationing in the Philippines because they interact with their Filipino relatives, compared to some children who grew up in Japan and learned Filipino through their mothers' assistance. Meanwhile, mothers demonstrate competence in Japanese language in the community when interacting with other Japanese mothers, but they communicate with their children in Filipino at home. Interacting with the Japanese in their language aims to protect Filipino mothers and their children from cultural prejudice while making conversations in Filipino as a daily household practice intensifies the parent-child relationship. Even though they can become fluent in Japanese, Filipino mothers find it more natural to convey their inner thoughts and feelings in the Filipino language.

Filipino mothers express that nurturing ties with Japanese extended kin while in Japan is as valuable as maintaining emotional ties with their relatives in the Philippines through occasional visits. These regular annual visits have cultivated their children's appreciation for Filipino culture and language, which complements their acculturation experience in Japan. Compared to assimilating and maintaining mothers, switching mothers have raised children who are Japanese nationals with dual heritage, which they can appropriate according to the location and people around them. Acknowledging one's dual heritage is an outcome of several trips to the Philippines, with which children associate positive images and childhood memories.

Although the three patterns of mothering are distinct and ideal typical, their features tend to overlap as mothers employ one approach over another at a particular life stage, depending on the social setting, the family's economic resources, and the mother's social and cultural capital. Filipino mothers' switching strategies echo what Sharon Hays describes as "intensive parenting," which involves tremendous amount of time and care resources to manage emotional bonds across borders (qtd. in Parreñas, *The Force* 323). Over time, some Filipino mothers may combine these strategies to constitute their repertoire of parenting in a transnational space. Moreover, these strategies indicate that some Filipino women may build different orientations as mothers in relation to their children. Motherhood is a role that may encompass all other social identities, such as class, gender, age, ethnicity, and nationality. They may emphasize their foreign status in Japan, subjugate their Filipino nationality under the Japanese nationality of their children, or treat both Japanese and Filipino nationalities of equal importance to parenting and family life. Filipino mothers' decision-making and childrearing practices have been preconditioned by a range of aspirations for their children to become Japanese, bicultural Japanese, or transnational Japanese-Filipino. These diverse social identities indicate Filipino mothers' capacity to move and settle, manage, and negotiate motherhood in home and host societies. In activating transborder citizenship, they navigate social, cultural, and emotional landscapes across boundaries through multiple and differentiated family practices. Living transborder citizenship through raising children in dual social contexts enables them to be "quasi-civil servants" in Japan and the Philippines (Borovoy 143). What accounts for these rather diverse approaches to fulfilling motherhood?

WHAT IT TAKES TO MOTHER (IN) A NATION: FACTORS SHAPING FILIPINO WOMEN'S MOTHERING PRACTICES

Filipino women's national membership has compounded their role in social reproduction, which needs to be theorized adequately in relation to the prevailing family and transnational migration regimes. Beyond obtaining rights and obligations, scholars suggest analyzing motherhood as a role prescribed as women's national duty (Erel 696; Berkovitch 605; Yuval-Davis 6; Pyskir 50). As shown in the previous section, giving birth and nurturing future

Japanese citizens serve as the content of Filipino migrant women's transborder citizenship. The succeeding section discusses Filipino mothers' resources for citizenship—family structure, legal, social, and economic capital—that influence their capacity for motherhood.

Family Structure

> Giving quality education to the child is one thing, but what is more important is the formation which the mother should be able to do ... she should always be with the child. Even if parents here in Japan are mostly outside working, the mother should be with the child ... whatever the child does, reflects what the mother does. I think it is the mother, more than the father, who should be with the child. (Sara, fifty-two, mother of two Japanese-Filipinos in Japan)

The structure and composition of a family create a point of social difference among Filipino mothers in how they negotiate with the prevailing family norms and ideologies in Japanese society. Married mothers like Sara strive to conform to the normative social expectation to parent properly. Single, lower-class mothers strive to conform to the norm by gaining the right to stay and live with one's children. As Ayumi Sasagawa (qtd. in Borovoy 145) emphasizes, being a mother has become more than giving birth and attending to the material needs of one's child. As Japanese society has increasingly viewed motherhood as a fundamental social obligation of its female members, many Japanese as well as non-Japanese women prescriptively acquire education and cultivation. Hence, motherhood becomes the primary function of womanhood (Borovoy 160).

In dual-parent Japanese-Filipino families, physical togetherness between parents and children is appraised, and the mother bears the burden of assimilating to Japanese society through childcare. Following divorce, many single-parent Filipinas struggle to commit to a mothering role. In order to recuperate, they temporarily send children to the Philippines. In the Philippine context, familism also pervades Filipinos' strong attachment to one's extended family, which intensifies interdependence when carrying out family practices and obligations across generations (Alampay 107), and gender ideologies designate women into multiple domestic roles (Sobritchea 32). Committing to transnational parenting practice leads many migrant Filipinas to resume work in Japan upon giving birth in order to provide for the needs of the family, the extended kin takes care of their left-behind child in the Philippines. They send remittances in exchange for the extended kin's caring support to the left-behind child. Beyond compensating for their physical absence, this reciprocal practice demonstrates caring for natal family across the borders.

The greater reality is that not all Filipino women engage in transnational mothering. Many of them face difficulty balancing family and work life between Japan and the Philippines. The availability of divorce and remarriage in Japan causes some Filipinas to evaluate marriage and family relationships. They have come to view the former as an acceptable way to free oneself from an unhappy marriage, while the latter serves as an instrumental means to (re) build a family. Shifting notions of family linked to expanded repertoires for childrearing are consequences of their newfound social freedom and improved economic roles. Many assimilating single mothers tend to reconstruct the family as mainly consisting of them and their children. On the other hand, maintaining and switching methods may cause some Filipino mothers to incorporate extended kin caretakers in the Philippines into their idea of a cohesive family, who contribute to making transnational mothering and house holding possible.

Legal Status

Legal status is a factor that distinguishes documented from undocumented migrants. Japan's immigration law categorizes an immigrant's legal status in terms of residential status or marriage to a Japanese spouse. The former classifies migrants as either permanent or long-term residents, whereas the latter may aid foreign spouses in attaining permanent residency and even a working permit. A foreign spouse may lose the right to stay in Japan in the event of divorce. Thus, the Japanese government does not easily bestow legal rights upon every foreign spouse of a Japanese national, which is prerequisite to living together as a family.

Filipino migrant mothers' legal capital and national membership differ from their children, indicating that not all of them can lead a unified family life in Japan.

Of the seventy mothers interviewed in Tokyo, fifty-four have become denizens, fourteen hold a long-term resident status, and two have naturalized as Japanese. Denizenship denotes having permanent residence with some civil and social rights but lacking political rights (Hammar 15). Being a denizen enables married Filipinas to transition from possessing a spouse of a Japanese national visa to being legally secure without abandoning their Filipino nationality. Since denizenship permits freedom of mobility outside Japan, Filipino mothers may engage in switching and maintaining motherhood to regulate transnational family activities between Japan and the Philippines. Permanent resident status thus allows some assimilating single parent mothers to access social services from the local government in Japan. Migrant support networks and fictive kin caretakers also provide assistance to Filipinas who do not want to risk physical separation from their children, particularly when they are at a young age. Indeed, the legal position that migrant mothers hold determines the extent of caregiving arrangements and welfare services available to them and their family.

Some Filipino mothers, meanwhile, secure residential and mothering rights through long-term residency. Beginning in the 2000s, migrant women were granted the permission to stay in Japan to be with their child on the conditions that: "1) the child produced with a Japanese national has been in the care or under the guardianship of the person for a considerable period of time; 2) the person has parental authority (*shinken*) regarding the child and; 3) the child is recognized by a Japanese father to be his child" (Ishii). The long-term residency reinforces motherhood as a prerequisite for immigrant women to obtain the right to remain in Japan for their child's wellbeing rather than face deportation to the Philippines, which leads to separation from one's child. The provision for long-term residence implies that a migrant mother depends upon their child's Japanese citizenship to claim the right to settle in Japan on the condition that migrant women must prove their mothering capacity. The 2014 SMJ report cites cases where mothers lost child custody battles to their Japanese husband, and were denied access to long-term residency (7). Although local governments have made legal aid available to foreigners, such a resource may be unknown to migrant mothers lacking social networks. To rescue migrant families from eventual disintegration, a number of migrant support organizations have been founded since the late 1990s. Some of these networks have saved migrant women with undocumented status from separating from their children.

Marital life and familial commitments dictate the legal status of migrant women. Structural conditions such as immigrant regimes and policies may challenge their capacity to mother their child in Japan. The right to settle and raise a family in Japan is not equally distributed between documented and undocumented Filipinas. Even if the undocumented women secure a legal position, fulfilling family aspirations fully creates another challenge for them.

ECONOMIC AND CULTURAL CAPITAL

The different economic and cultural capital Filipino women obtain determines their mothering practices because it gauges the degree to which they can contribute to the development of Japanese and Filipino societies. Because the two social settings present distinctive conditions for a home space, safe environment, and child protection. Filipino mothers carve distinctive family life goals in each context. The desire for a better future—where childcare, food, education, and safety are perceived to be adequate—is central to Filipino women's motivations for migrating to and building families in Japan. Often, their family and personal aspirations are inextricably linked together. Emily, who has been living in Japan for twenty-five years, details what her migration to Japan means to her:

> It was here that I learned to earn from my own hard work. It was also here that I recovered from the pains of my marriage failure. It is not that I am bragging or something, because my ex-husband was quite well-off...but I really could not take the thought of being dependent on his money all my life. I want to earn from my own sweat. It was through (working in) Japan that I was able to fulfill

> my role as a mother, a daughter, and a sister. (Emily, fifty, divorced mother of a fifteen-year-old Japanese-Filipino)

Emily established a small retail business in Tokyo in which she sells Filipino food products, in addition to working as a part-time caregiver at a nearby hospice. During focus group discussions, many Filipino mother participants expressed that migrating to Japan empowered them. Emily's account shows that migration helped them overcome dependence on their husband in the Philippines and reclaim their worth as a woman. In the Philippines, existing cultural ideologies have restricted women to the domestic realm and denigrated their status and welfare (Sobritchea 41). Although a lot of women sought migration to Japan in the 1980s to fulfill the economic needs of their family, such a goal was likewise tied to a more individualized aspiration to gain economic autonomy over their husband as the family's breadwinner. Their expanded economic roles gave them a sense of agency to redefine the terms of contributing to the Filipino society. Indeed, migration has become the key to Filipino women's capacity to redistribute their emotional and reproductive labour in the care, formation, and sustenance of transnational households (Porio 211; Parreñas, *Children* 30).

Yet these claims of acquired autonomy and improved status in the Philippines seem paradoxical to the pervasiveness of negative images attached to being a Filipina in Japan. Because of their significant number[4] and concentration to the entertainment industry in the past, Filipinas have been stereotypically profiled as "*Japayuki*" (bound for Japan), a derogatory term for a sex worker. Moreover, the negative depiction of Filipinas as the "other" has buttressed the prevailing good-bad woman binary in Japanese society (Suzuki, "Women Imagined, Women Imaging" 142). The case of Filipinas in Japan validates what human geographer Jorge Carling has noted: migrant women's morality has been fundamentally gauged on the basis of sexuality and reproduction. Filipino women's negative identity has been exacerbated through media and public discourse, that their children are neglected of care and born out of failed Japanese-Filipino marriages. Yoshi, twenty-two, one of the Japanese-Filipino children interviewed, shared how Japanese-Filipino families tend to be perceived in Japan: "If a Filipino mother leads a family in Japan, the impression is that the children are often neglected, some of them stay away, because Filipinas are busy making money. I know that is not completely true because my mother took care of me" (Yoshi, twenty-two, born and raised in Japan). Growing up in a community and attending a school with other Japanese-Filipino children exposed Yoshi to the persisting negative stereotypes that discriminate not only against Filipino migrant women but also their children. Compared to that of local women, Filipinas' mothering is monitored (Ito 66). For instance, Filipino mothers on social welfare have been required to report their children's progress at school and their community involvement to their designated social worker (Celero, "In Fulfillment of Motherhood" 182).

Although divorce rates of international marriages are comparable to those of Japanese-Japanese marriages, there is a popular view that the former is more unstable (Satake 447). In 2011 and 2012, the divorce rate of Japanese and Filipino couples was 29.6 percent, and was 41 percent high in the previous decade. As a social risk group in Japan, single parent Filipinas take on the position of the breadwinner in the family. Even though they access government welfare support, many of them consider such assistance short term and prefer to work outside home (Celero, "In Fulfillment of Motherhood"188). About 80 percent of single mothers juggle odd jobs to augment family income. Against the normative structure of a patriarchal, nuclear family, Filipinas idealize and strive to do both childcare and paid work (Celero, "In Fulfillment of Motherhood"188).

Middle-class Japanese-Filipino families like Yoshi's affirm Japanese society's ideology of female domesticity, wherein Filipino mothers' worth is affirmed through their active role as a homemaker (Lock qtd. in Boling 179). Therefore, those "bad mother" Filipinas, based on Yoshi's description above, tend to prioritize paid work over the domestic role. This good and bad motherhood binary overlooks the middle ground, where many Filipinas manage a single-parent household in Japan and send remittances to their natal family in the Philippines, a role that distinguishes them from Japanese women.

The majority of Filipina respondents in this study perform maintaining and switching motherhood. Only a few Filipino women who manage a transnational household are indifferent to the persistent negative images of Filipinas in Japan. Internalizing marginality as a migrant is highlighted in their narratives by phrases such as "anywhere, discrimination happens," "discrimination is true for all foreigners, not only Filipinos," and "as foreigners, there is nothing we can do (about discrimination)." Filipinas' social discrimination, rooted in their ethnicity and migration history, cannot be easily overcome. Their actions to broaden their economic participation and intensify their local community involvement indicate that many Filipinas desire to gain positive social recognition in Japan.

Filipino women's migration often primarily aims to secure the wellbeing of their family over their own (Stivens 17; Yeoh et al. 309; Bauzon 222; Bauzon and Bauzon 301). Filipinas are migrant women who take charge of their own migration (Oishi 12), even though their movement may involve risks and generate unintended consequences. Susan represents one of those Filipino women who had to bear the repercussions of risks accompanied by their migration, such as discontent and false expectations:

> I was not happy with marrying a Japanese man at all. I was still pregnant when my husband was brought to jail. I have become the mother and the father to my child. Until his father died and I got divorced, I was not given a permanent visa. I am not complaining or self-pitying, but I will never marry a Japanese again. (Susan, forty-five, college graduate, hotel chambermaid)

Besides owning up the failure of their marriage and the burden of single parenting to themselves, Filipino women regard discrimination in Japan as a normative phase every migrant must endure as an "outsider" in the existing social order, which often situates migrants at the margins (Higuchi 111). Although there may be truth to the idea that most newcomer migrants in Japan and elsewhere must undergo sociocultural adaptation to gradually overcome marginalization, Filipino mothers constantly aspire to shed off the old image and tarnished reputation by switching to a different economic niche. The demographic challenges of an aging population, falling birthrates, and delayed marriage owing to the growing occupational mobility of women in Japan have been pivotal to Filipinas' changing economic position. The heightening demand for caregivers to provide elderly care as well as assistant language teachers to intensify English education as part of Japan's internationalization campaign has been highly advantageous for many Filipinas who earned some college education from the Philippines.

Acquiring the right to parent a child in Japan is one family aspiration of many Filipino mothers; becoming fit for motherhood is another. As motherhood involves transmitting the way of life to be passed on to succeeding generations, the educational attainment of mothers determines the kind of cultural capital and capacity for parenting a child in Japan. In this study, forty-eight out of seventy Filipino mothers had earned a college degree, which indicates educational attainment. However, distinct educational and linguistic resources earned in the Philippines proved to be difficult to use in Japan where Japanese language and culture are the prerequisites for cultural membership to Japanese society. Cultural difference makes educating children of immigrants in Japan problematic (Castro-Vázquez 236).

Responding differently to the pressures of integration to carry out their gestational and social motherhood has produced diverging childrearing patterns. Assimilating to Japanese society orients some mothers toward forming Japanese networks and studying the Japanese language as a way to realize their belief that the right social and cultural capital is essential for them and their children to gain inclusion to Japanese society. This maintaining method involves heavier reference to Filipino language and culture in building intimacy with their children, whereas the switching method indicates that a few Filipinas devote equal importance to Japanese and Filipino languages and cultures in socializing their children. Filipino mothers have created multiple ways of raising children whose social identity, belonging, and life possibilities have been drawn toward Japanese and Filipino societies. In this regard, they do not formulate their own future aspirations in isolation from Japanese-Filipino life possibilities.

CONCLUSION: THE CHALLENGES AND OPPORTUNITIES OF MOTHERING (IN) TWO NATIONS

This chapter explains the intersection between motherhood, migration, and citizenship through the case of Filipino migrant women in Japan. Their narratives have shown that citizenship beyond legal membership can be examined through the role of immigrant women (and their families) in this era of global migration and social reproduction crisis. The rising number of international families stimulates the need to understand the process of reproducing societies through the views and experiences of immigrant women. Giving birth and raising children in host societies prompt questions about which familial and social norms and frames should guide immigrant women's family life.

Reproducing future Japanese citizens is situated within larger debates of whether Japan will embrace its role as a migrant receiving society and who deserves to belong to Japan in the future (Kobayashi et al. 17). Questions about foreigners' belonging to a future Japan include how immigrant women desiring settlement into Japan, but engaging with transborder citizenship, may be accepted by mainstream Japanese populace. So far, assimilation seems to be the key mechanism through which Filipino migrant women and their children may integrate successfully as members, whereas the maintaining approach is marked by inadequate competence for mothering. Many Filipinas are aware that their migrant status creates a barrier toward inclusion to Japanese society. Although they have developed a range of strategies for parenting across borders, only a few mothers have been able to achieve a balance between migration and integration practices in leading a family through the switching motherhood pattern. Filipino mothers may have shared similar struggles in raising children in Japan, but they have activated their sense of agency differently. Diverse parenting practices have been contingent upon Filipino immigrants' different family structure, legal, economic, cultural, and social capital for motherhood.

This chapter also demonstrates that Filipinas are mothering two nations. Even though their strategies for aspiring for and forming a cohesive, unified, and settled family lean more toward Japan, most of them tend to maintain family commitments in their Filipino homeland. In engaging in motherhood across boundaries, they inevitably face dilemmas because of contradicting familial norms and expectations in Japanese and Filipino societies. Living with transborder citizenship, they are more likely to hold permanent residence in Japan and keep Filipino national membership. Naturalizing as Japanese may become an option for a few Filipinas. On the other hand, Filipino citizenship remains an essential component of their personhood, which keeps them emotionally tied to their natal family as well as to their homeland. The persistence of their strong ethno-nationalist feeling toward the Philippines further affirms that many Filipino migrant women do not necessarily envision full integration to Japanese society in the future.

Navigating through the functions of Japanese, Filipino, and Japanese-Filipino forms of membership in their individual and family lives, many Filipino mothers simultaneously pursue integration and citizenship in Japan and the Philippines. The concept of transborder citizenship helps explain how migrant women cultivate belonging to and participating actively in dual or multiple societies and family systems, through motherhood. It affirms the significance of sustaining multiple social connections among Filipino migrant women because a sense of identity, belonging, and inclusion are essential to their and their family's wellbeing. Immigrant women's citizenship may be understood as not only accruing rights and claims from the nation-state but also contributing to and negotiating membership in home and host societies.

ENDNOTES

[1]The Japanese-Filipino Children's Joint Statement released at the 2009 Conference for Japanese-Filipino Children held in Saitama City cited that there are at least 300,000 Japanese-Filipinos. However, there have been no consolidated statistical data on Japanese-Filipinos living in the Philippines and Japan (Japanese-Filipino Multi-sectoral Networking Project, IOM website).

[2]Most Filipino migrants reside in Kanto region.

[3]*Hafu*, the Japanese word for "half," is a more contemporary term, which is used to define individuals with dual cultural heritage in

general. Likewise, the prominence of hyphenated ethnic identities (Rumbaut 748) is also common, such as Japanese-Filipino, which refers to the offspring of Japanese and Filipinos.

[4]The highest recorded number of entertainer entrants to Japan was 50, 691 in 2004 (Ministry of Justice).

WORKS CITED

Alampay, Liane Peña. "Parenting in the Philippines." *Parenting Across Cultures*, edited by Helaine Selin, Springer, 2014, pp. 105-21.

Anderson, James. "Filipina Migration to Japan: Hostesses, House helpers, and Homemakers." *Filipinas*, No. 2, 1999, pp. 57-74.

Bauzon, Leslie E. "Filipino-Japanese Marriages." *Philippine Studies*, vol. 47, no. 2, 1999, pp. 206-23.

Bauzon, Leslie E., and Aurora F. Bauzon. "Childrearing Practices in the Philippines and Japan." *Philippine Studies*, vol. 48, no. 3, 2000, pp. 287-314.

Berkovitch, Nitza. "Motherhood as a National Mission: The Construction of Womanhood in the Legal Discourse in Israel." *Women's Studies International Forum*, vol. 20, no. 5, 1997, pp. 605- 09.

Borovoy, Amy. *The Too-Good Wife: Alcohol, Codependency, and the Politics of Nurturance in Postwar Japan*. University of California Press, 2005.

Bourdieu, Pierre. "The Field of Cultural Production, or: The Economic World Reversed." *Poetics*, vol. 12, no. 4, 1983, pp. 311-56.

Castles, Stephen, et al. *The Age of Migration: International Population Movements in the Modern World*. Macmillan, 1998.

Castro-Vázquez, Genaro. "The Educated Citizen: Cultural and Gender Capital in the Schooling of Latin American Children in Japan." *Journal of Research in International Education*, vol. 10, no. 3, 2011, pp. 244-60.

Celero, Jocelyn. "Bicultural Parenting in the Eyes of a Mother: Filipino Women's Politics of Mothering Japanese-Filipino Children." *Migration and a Multicultural Society*, edited by Lydia Yu-Jose and Johanna Zulueta, Ateneo de Manila University Press, 2014, pp. 80-90.

Celero, Jocelyn. "In Fulfillment of Motherhood: An Exploratory Study of Migrant Mothers on Welfare in Japan." *Journal on Global Social Welfare, Springer*, vol. 1, no. 4, 2014, pp. 179-89.

Celero, Jocelyn. "'Towards A Shared Future?': Transnational Identity and Belonging of Japanese-Filipino Families." *The Age of Asian Migration,* edited by Yuk Wah Chan, Heidi Fung, and Grazyna Szymanska Matusiewicz, Cambridge Scholars Publishing, 2015, Vol. 2, Chapter 3, pp. 67-94.

Collins, Patricia Hill. "African-American Women and Economic Justice: A Preliminary Analysis of Wealth, Family, and Black Social Class." *University of Cincinnati Law Review*, vol. 65, no. 3, 1997, pp. 825-52.

Erel, Umut. "Reframing Migrant Mothers as Citizens." *Citizenship Studies*, vol.15, nos. 6-7, 2011, pp. 695-709.

Hammar, Tomas. *Democracy and the Nation State: Aliens, Denizens and Citizens in a world of International Migration.* Aldershot, 1990.

Hays, Sharon. *The Cultural Contradictions of Motherhood.* Yale University Press, 1996.

Higuchi, Akihiko. "The Mechanisms of Social Exclusion in Modern Society: The Dilemma of Active Labor Market Policy." *International Journal of Japanese Sociology*, vol. 23, no.1, 2014, pp. 110-24.

Holloway, Susan D. *Women and Family in Contemporary Japan.* Cambridge University Press, 2010.

Holloway, Susan D., and Ayumi Nagase. "Child Rearing in Japan." *Parenting Across Cultures*, edited by Helaine Selin, Springer, 2014, pp. 59-76.

Ishii, Yuka. "The Residency and Lives of Migrants in Japan since the Mid-1990s." *Electronic Journal of Contemporary Japanese Studies*, 2005, www.japanesestudies.org.uk/articles/2005/Ishii.html. Accessed 25 June 2016.

Ito, Ruri. "Crafting Migrant Women's Citizenship in Japan: Taking 'Family' as a Vantage Point." *International Journal of Japanese Sociology*, vol. 14, no.1, 2005, pp. 52-69.

Jones, Gavin, and Hsiu-hua Shen. "International Marriage in East and Southeast Asia: Trends and Research Emphases." *Citizenship Studies*, vol. 12, no. 1, 2008, pp. 9-25.

Kobayashi, Tetsuro, et al. "Social Capital Online: Collective Use of the Internet and Reciprocity as Lubricants of Democracy." *Information, Community & Society*, vol. 9, no. 5, 2006, pp. 582-611.

Ministry of Health, Labor, and Welfare. "Kokuseki, Chiiki-betsu Zairyu Gaikokujin Su no Suii" ["Demography of Foreign Residents by Nationality and Region"]. Government of Japan, 2015.

Ministry of Internal Affairs and Communication. "Migrants in Japan by Prefecture." 2012.

Ministry of Justice. "Kokuseki (Syusshinchi) betsu Gaikokujin Toroku-sha Su no Suii" ["Demography of Registered Foreign Residents by Nationality"]. 2012.

Ministry of Justice. "Divorce Rates in Japan by Nationality." Government of Japan, 2012.

Ochiai, Emiko. "The Ie (family) in Global Perspective." *A Companion to the Anthropology of Japan*, edited by James Robertson, 2005, Blackwell Publishing Ltd, Chapter 22, pp. 355-79.

Ochiai, Emiko. "Care Diamonds and Welfare Regimes in East and South-East Asian Societies: Bridging Family and Welfare Sociology." *International Journal of Japanese Sociology*, vol. 18, no.1, 2009, pp. 60-78.

Oishi, Nana. *Women in Motion: Globalization, State Policies, and Labor Migration in Asia*. Stanford University Press, 2005.

Parreñas, Rhacel Salazar. *Children of Global Migration: Transnational Families and Gendered Woes*. Stanford University Press, 2005.

Parreñas, Rhacel Salazar.*The Force of Domesticity: Filipina Migrants and Globalization*. New York University Press, 2008.

Parreñas, Rhacel Salazar. *Servants of Globalization: Women, Migration and Domestic Work*. Stanford University Press, 2001.

Piper, Nicola. "Wife or Worker? Worker or Wife? Marriage and Cross-Border Migration in Contemporary Japan." *International Journal of Population Geography*, vol. 9, no. 6, 2003, pp. 457-69.

Pyskir, Bohdan. "Mothers for a fatherland: Ukranian statehood, motherhood, and national security", *The Journal of Slavic Military Studies*, vol. 7, no. 1, 1994, pp. 50-66.

Rodríguez, Robyn M. "Migrant Heroes: Nationalism, Citizenship and the Politics of Filipino Migrant Labor." *Citizenship Studies*, vol. 6, no.3, 2002, pp. 341-56.

Rumbaut, Ruben G. "The Crucible Within: Ethnic Identity, Self-Esteem, and Segmented Assimilation among Children of Immigrants." *International Migration Review,* vol. 28, no. 4, 1994, pp. 748-94.

Sassen, Saskia. *Losing Control?: Sovereignty in the Age of Globalization.* Columbia University Press, 1996.

Satake, Masaaki. "Filipina-Japanese Intermarriages: A Pathway to New Gender and Cross-Cultural Relations." *Asian and Pacific Migration Journal,* vol. 13, no.4, 2004, pp. 445-73.

Sobritchea, Carolyn Israel. "The Ideology of Female Domesticity: Its Impact on the Status of Filipino Women." *Review of Women's Studies,* vol. 1, no.1, 1990, pp. 26-41.

Soysal, Yasemin Nuhoglu. *Limits of Citizenship: Migrants and Postnational Membership in Europe.* University of Chicago Press, 1994.

Stivens, Maila. "Theorizing Gender, Power and Modernity in Affluent Asia." *Gender and Power in Affluent Asia,* 1998, pp. 1-34.

Stoler-Liss, Sachlav. "'Mothers Birth the Nation': The Social Construction of Zionist Motherhood in Wartime in Israeli Parents' Manuals." *Nashim: A Journal of Jewish Women's Studies & Gender Issues,* vol. 6, no.1, 2004, pp. 104-18.

Suzuki, Nobue. "Between Two shores: Transnational Projects and Filipina Wives in/from Japan." *Women's Studies International Forum. Pergamon,* vol. 23, no. 4, 2000, pp. 431-44.

Suzuki, Nobue. "Women Imagined, Women Imaging: Re/presentations of Filipinas in Japan since the 1980s." *US-Japan Women's Journal. English Supplement,* 2000, pp. 142-75.

Tenegra, Brenda. "Negotiating and Embedding Business in 'Social Circles': A Survival Strategy." *International Migration and the Reconfiguration of Gender Relations in Contemporary Japanese Society,* edited by Ruri Ito, Ochanomizu University Press, 2004, pp. 129-38.

Tibe-Bonifacio, Glenda Lynna Anne. *Filipino Women and their Citizenship in Australia: In Search of Political Space.* Dissertation School of History and Politics, Faculty of Arts, University of Wollongong, 2003.

Watanabe, Hiroyuki, et al. *The State of Internationalization and the*

Increase of International Marriages in Rural Areas, Department Research Institute Yearly Publication, 1993.
Werbner, Pnina, and Nira Yuval Davis, editors. *Women, Citizenship and Difference*. Zed, 1999.
Yuval-Davis, Nira. "Women, Citizenship and Difference." *Feminist Review*, vol. 57, no.1, 1997, pp. 4-27.

11.
A Motherhood Manifesto

Ivy Queen's *Vendetta*

CATHERINE MARSH KENNERLEY

A Santiago, Efra y Che.

> *Uno es tanta gente a la misma vez.*
> *(One is so many people at once).*
> *"El cuento de la mujer del mar,"*
> —Manuel Ramos Otero

IN HER RE-READING of Adrienne Rich's *Of Woman Born*, Andrea O'Reilly underlines the core contribution of the classic feminist text as making the distinction between the oppressive understanding of motherhood as an institution defined by patriarchy, and the experience of mothering seen from a nonpatriarchal stance, a source of empowerment for women. O'Reilly focuses on how Rich underscores the relationship between women claiming the power to redefine mothering, and feminist, antisexist childrearing. For daughters, this is important because the institution of motherhood dominates their relationships with their mothers. In other words, the freedom to be ourselves comes from rejecting the ethic of martyrdom that the traditional, patriarchal view of motherhood entails: what Rich terms "matrophobia." O'Reilly concludes that "mothering, that which invests mothers with agency, authority, authenticity, is better for children as well ... in being 'bad' mothers—outlaws from the institution of motherhood—we become better mothers for ourselves and for our children" (O'Reilly 72).

Ivy Queen (IQ), the most popular female reggaetón artist in both Puerto Rico and the diaspora, speaks frankly about the way she is raising her daughter; in her most recent video clip, the first since her daughter's birth, she appears with short hair, suspenders and a bowtie, singing her own composition, "Vendetta." In so doing, she reclaims the power to tell her story as a mother. In the video, amid images of her long career and her pregnancy, she blasts "the machistas toward the queen" who excluded her from the reggaetón scene, reminding them that they, too, echoing Adrienne Rich's words, are of women born. With this composition, IQ talks back to those who questioned her ability to perform while she was pregnant, and beyond them, to the institution of motherhood. She reaffirms something patriarchy would rather have us forget, our origins:

Como si no nacieron de una mujer
como si Adán por Eva no pecó en pleno Edén
como si no tuvieran hijas, hermanas o esposas
como si concebir a un un hijo fuera poca cosa

(As if they hadn't been born of a woman
As if Adam hadn't sinned for Eve in mid-Eden
As if they didn't have daughters, sisters or wives
As if conceiving a child was close to nothing)[1]

On the other hand, IQ sings as outlaw, a subversive mother, for various reasons besides her denunciation of institutionalized motherhood that bear careful consideration. First, it should be pointed out that IQ—known also as The Queen Mother, *la Reina del Reggaetón*, *la Caballota*, *la Potra*, *la Diva* or *La Maestra*, and as some reguetoneros have called her, the undisputed female voice of reggaetón—was a pioneer of what was at first called underground. In fact, IQ herself said of what later came to be known as reggaetón:

> *Yo escogí este género porque todo el mundo me decía que no era un género de mujer, que es de hombres y que era de atorrantes, y cuando a mí me dicen que no, ahí es que me pongo los pantalones en mi sitio y le meto mano.* (I choose this genre because everybody said that it wasn't for women, it was for men and hooligans and when they

> say no to me, then that's when I put my pants on the way I want them, and I throw down.) (Agencia AP)

She started her career with a song to which she referred in a CNN interview as her calling-card: "*Somos raperos pero no delicuentes*" ("We are rappers, not criminals"). In it, she answered attacks by the government, especially senator Velda González, who—incensed at images of scantily-clad women dancing *perreo*—had charged that reggaetón promoted violence and crime (Negrón Muntaner and Rivera). Writing about this early persecution, the keen-eyed Puerto Rican writer Ana Lydia Vega significantly called it "inquisition and paternalism" (Vega 96). Interestingly enough, a year later, the same senator, "flanked by reggaeton stars ... sporting tasteful makeup and a sweet, matronly smile, was lightly swinging her hips and tilting her head from side to side to a raucous reggaeton beat" (Negrón Muntaner and Rivera). This shows how from the start, reggaetón could be danced, as it still is, by mothers. From the outset, women in this genre challenged ideas of decency and respectability. In June Fernández's brilliant twist on Emma Goldman's feminist maxim, "*Si no puedo perrear, no es mi revolución*" (If I can't twerk, it's not my revolution"). As IQ put it, "Velda González gave us the best promotion, because she sparked the whole world's curiosity. We have to be grateful for that. She helped us commercialize the genre" (Negrón Muntaner).

Negrón Muntaner and Rivera understand that "in becoming the island's most important cultural export since Ricky Martin, reggaetón showcases how social groups written off by the state, educators, and the media have transformed a homegrown product from underground infamy to global popularity" or, as Juan Flores has called it, "the first transnational music in the full sense of the term" (x). Reggaetón comes from a mix of Dancehall Reggae and African American hip-hop, but also merengue, salsa, bachata, bomba, other Latin American and Caribbean rhythms, and today, even South Asian music (Báez; Lebrón). Even though this music went from being stigmatized to becoming a major commercial genre, it is still looked at askance, and even despised by some. IQ takes advantage of reggaetón's transnational circuit, and in constant negotiation with—and resistance to—the requirements of the male-dominated urban music industry, she manages to talk and sing about an uncomfortable subject: the institution of motherhood. Ivy Queen's strong voice resonates through only her music but tweets and interviews. Her public persona thus influences how motherhood is viewed and construed from Puerto Rico to Panamá, the Dominican Republic, Colombia, California, or New Jersey, and back to the national scene.

As a second outlaw element of her performance, it is crucial to understand how IQ has pushed the limits of reggaetón by focusing on gender. Scholar Zaire Dinzey-Flores, after reviewing a considerable number of reggaetón lyrics, observes that "the most popular themes in reggaetón songs are sex, dancing and partying, experiencing love, lyrical prowess, violence, and heartache ... the typical plot involves a guy really liking or even loving a woman, pursuing her by asking or demanding sex" (47). Moreover, she asserts that "only 12 of the 179 songs inverted the heteronormative spectacle and put males under the gaze." Most of those songs were IQ's (65). A quick review of IQ's oldest hits reveals how her songs question or transform reggaetón's usual themes. In "*Yo Quiero Bailar*," the woman is in charge of her sexuality: "Because I call the shots, I'm the one that decides when we get down." In "*Que Lloren*," she questions the masculinist norm that men should not express their emotions, asking them to cry and suggesting that it would improve their relationships. The video clip shows IQ interrupting a gathering of men in which a guru says excitedly that men do not cry; she contradicts him, pushes men, and establishes herself as the authority covering the symbol of the fist with a poster of IQ's sentimiento (feeling). And in her most recent album, *The Vendetta Project*, the song "*Soy Libre*" ("I Am Free") proposes a relationship that has freedom as its premise: she refuses to be controlled. On the same album, "*Dime A Mi Quién*" stands out because with IQ's powerful voice she claims her rightful place and tells how they wanted to take her down: "*tumbarla*." She also calls herself the "Mother of this genre," and stresses her years in the industry. Then she modulates her voice and sings "*bien, yo lo hago bien, yo soy libre, piénsalo bien, dime a mí quién me va a vencer*." ("Well I do it well, I am free, think it over, tell me who's going to defeat me?")

IQ genders reggaetón; in fact, no reggaetón artist before her has written and sung lyrics about motherhood in this hypermasculine scene which, in Alexandra T. Vázquez's words, suffers from a "rampant misogyny" and "allots little to no space for women's voices" (304). As IQ notes, her pregnancy cost her work opportunities, as she was locked out of the reggaetón scene: only at Calibash in Los Ángeles and Santo Domingo was she able to perform while visibly pregnant. Concerning the origin of the title cut of her thirty-two-song album *Vendetta*, composed seven months after her daughter was born, IQ states:

> pure, pure, pure Ivy Queen, pure rage, pure soul.... The reason why the song Vendetta was born is a very special reason for me: the birth of my daughter Naiovy, my years in the industry, the frustration of being locked-up for eight months straight without being able to go onstage just because I was pregnant ... All I could do was the Calibash in Los Angeles and Santo Domingo, those were the only shows I did, and anger was consuming me, I couldn't keep quiet any longer, then when I hear this beep, what I felt was rage. I was venting about the fact that because one is a woman, it doesn't mean that by becoming a mother one dies, it doesn't mean that when one is a mother one has to leave behind one's dreams because now the kids are there ... I wanted to vent about attacks that were being made against me, for being pregnant and wearing heels ... not all women are the same. If you generalize, it's really that you're fucked up and you're closing all your doors. (Vflow cruz)

It is worth emphasizing here that IQ is speaking against the traditional imperative and standards that govern women, especially mothers—the biological capacity of a woman's body, as Sylvia Tubert argues, that has become the univocal definition of the feminine. When she talks and sings about motherhood, she denounces the impossibility of the traditional paradigm for motherhood because it is unreachable, shot through with archetypes that do not allow women to be conceived of in the complexity of who they are, of their subjectivity. Those archetypes also do violence to identities and generate further violence and exclusion.

Thus "Vendetta," which serves as the title cut for four different albums that include it—one hip-hop, one salsa, one urban, and one bachata—underscores the anger in IQ's return after giving birth.[2] The album's black cover features a big, red letter V (evocative not only of the word "vendetta" but also of the vagina, the origin of the world) and an image of IQ's eyes. Together with the accompanying video ("Ivy Queen en el Monólogo de la Vagina"), this album can be read as a powerful transnational manifesto in which IQ reclaims and asserts her power as a mother.

At the beginning of the "Vendetta" video, IQ appears surrounded by microphones and images of her preparing in her dressing room. Tellingly, there is no makeup, only a microphone (covered with "bling bling" rhinestones) and a razor. She stands the microphone among the other ones, her red lips and Chanel earring set off against the black and white background. As Dinzey-Flores explains, "'bling' is as much about being poor and threatening as it is about being successful, rich and legal" (55). She starts singing, alluding to her street origins: "Because I don't believe in anybody, because I grew up on the street"; she asserts that the reference to the street validates the singer's authenticity (45). Images of her career flash past (particularly one scene of her boxing), emphasizing her long trajectory, a theme that recurs in many of her other songs. Ivy Queen is claiming her place as an artist in her own right, as she denounces the music industry's falsehood and hypocrisy. But beyond that, she is legitimating her voice as a mother, beyond the limits of the patriarchal institution of motherhood.

She speaks ironically of the way the media referred to her pregnancy, the disrespect to which she was subjected, which she calls morbid fascination in her song, and the way that the industry excluded her because she was pregnant. She also questions how pregnant women are viewed and treated. By referring singing to the oxygen that people in the music industry tried to take from her, she illustrates a strong image of the violent—and at times literally asphyxiating—nature of gender norms. In addition, she contests the woman-mother dichotomy, the reduction of her subjectivity to motherhood.

Recuerdo bien el día de la gran noticia
la reina embarazada, que clase de primicia
y a mis espaldas yo solo escuchaba
mejor contrato a otro, la tipa esta apagada

No podemos traerla, tampoco invitarla
como si yo tuviera un virus o estuviera muerta
que clase de infelices, yo nací para cantar
este es mi oxígeno y así me lo querían quitar

(I remember well the day of the big news
The pregnant queen, what a scoop
And behind my back all I heard was
Better hire somebody else this woman's out

We can't bring her, can't invite her
As if I had a virus, or was dead
What pathetic losers, I was born to sing.
This is my oxygen, and they wanted to take it from me
like that)

As she sings the subsequent part of the song, the image of her unmistakably pregnant body taking centre stage at Calibash appears: one of the two places where she was allowed to perform while pregnant, as mentioned before. And at the end of the chorus, she holds out her middle finger, a gesture that can be read as part of her "Vendetta," but also as a flaunting of the conventions of decent and of respectable motherhood.

Es mi manera para yo poder ganarme el pan
machistas con la reina, se los voy a recordar
si se creían que su rostro se me va a olvidar
este es mi tema y mi Vendetta solo va a empezar

(It's my way of earning my bread
Sexists toward the queen, I'm going to remind them
If they thought I was going to forget their face
This is my song, and my Vendetta's just beginning)

The song also makes it clear that she is positioning herself as a mother. She is also rebutting the attacks on her appearance based on sexist aesthetics; this rebuttal might seem heteronormative were it not for the part in which she emphasizes that she does not discriminate.

> *Mi certificado, dice femenino*
> *igual que el de mi hija, más yo no discrimino*
> *la única vez que quisiera cambiar de sexo*
> *es para darme par de golpes, con todos estos insectos*
>
> (My certificate says Female
> Just like my daughter's, but I don't discriminate
> The only time I've wanted a sex change
> Is to throw down hard with all those insects)

It is important to pause to remember that the comments she received about her appearance during her pregnancy were not new; she has been the object of such attacks since she started in the music industry. Along these lines, critic Jillian Báez points out the "contradictions" she sees in her change of appearance and her crossover to the U.S.:

> her physical aesthetics have shifted and contradicted some of her lyrics. For example, during her early career she dressed in baggy jeans—a signifier of hip hop masculinity—and now she dresses in much more hyper-sexual, hyper-feminine dress, conforming to norms for female Latin American and U.S. artists. As such, her lyrics may provide a counterhegemonic site, but her shift in a physical aesthetics may construct IQ as an overall less subversive icon. (70)

Báez does concede that though "her self representations may be problematic, she continues to provide a counterhegemonic site of female empowerment when compared to her male counterparts" (75). Although I understand her critique of the music industry's standards and requirements for women, I would argue that IQ's "problematic" appearance, with the apparent "contradictions"

Báez points out, makes her critical stance in "Vendetta" more meaningful. After all, considering the complexity of Manuel Ramos Otero's words quoted at the beginning of this chapter, what does a good mother looks like?

On the other hand, as Petra Rivera-Rideau explains, IQ's transformation of her body—the whitening the U.S. music industry requires of Latinas—was not met with the same "approval" as that of Jennifer López or Shakira (100-111). In other words, rather than being seen as the desirable Latina, she has been perceived as masculine, a transgender woman, or a lesbian. Rivera-Rideau points out that this perception of IQ, together with her own strong voice and masculine self-presentation, enables her to inhabit the world of reggaetón. She goes on to point out the "excess" in IQ's appearance, and, drawing from Frances Negrón Muntaner, she compares her to the great salsa singer Celia Cruz, who was also crowned as queen of her equally male-dominated genre (112). Negrón Muntaner rightly argues that as reggaetón has become more global, the following has occurred:

> Ivy Queen has been exposed to more discriminatory eyes and has nurtured a differently gendered persona similar to the Cuban queen's. On the one hand, Ivy Queen reminds fans that she is a "real" woman through a "flaming" style that includes high heels, long hair, nails up to four inches long, platinum accessories and plastic surgery to enhance bust size. On the other hand, given the perception that she is not a conventionally attractive woman, she insists that "in contrast to other divas she does not come to sell her nalgas [buttocks] but her lyrics." (108)

Negrón Muntaner reminds us that, like Celia Cruz, IQ combines an "excessive style" while "singing like a man" (109); like Celia, IQ also welcomes drag queens imitating her: a key, Negrón Muntaner says, to being remembered. It is no coincidence that when IQ went on stage at the 2005 Latin Grammys, the only woman among twelve reguetoneros claiming the legacy of the salseros who were wearing t-shirts featuring salsa stars like Héctor Lavoe and Ismael Rivera, it was Celia Cruz's image on IQ's chest, over jeans and a short golden skirt. Nor is it coincidental that the Vendetta project includes homage to Celia Cruz, IQ's feminine (perhaps matrilineal) musical ancestor: her rendition of Celia's "*Quimbara, quimbara... Ee! Mamá*!" can be interpreted as a kinship claim. In fact, Rivera-Rideau also reminds us that IQ's lyrics, performance style, and emphasis on *sentimiento* (feeling) "builds from the work of La Lupe, Guillot, and other boleristas and filin artists by using lyrics about love and suffering to make a larger call for the recognition of the humanity of reggaeton women" (121).

Additionally, IQ confronts the racist overtones of the criticisms of her appearance. Rivera-Rideau points out that the excess in her performance challenges and rethinks discourses of racial democracy in Puerto Rico that can resonate across borders:

> Dominant constructions of black womanhood thus rely on the objectification of the black female body—something that is simultaneously desirable and reviled because it defies the (white) "norm." Since black women are depicted as the bearers of the island's population in narratives that describe Puerto Rico's histories of race mixture, Puerto Rican racial democracy requires a continuous renunciation of the humanity of black womanhood in order to distance the population from this blackness, and to sustain the association between Puerto Ricanness and whiteness. As a result, reducing the black woman to an object—that is, not human—negates her capacity for not only reason, but also any emotions or feelings beyond the instinctual, rendering her the opposite of the notions of respectability that underlie dominant constructions of Puerto Rican identity. In contrast, Ivy Queen demands respect and recognition for all people through her music and performance, thus exposing these inconsistencies within dominant discourses of racial democracy. (108)

Mayra Santos Febres, an Afro-Puerto Rican writer, reflects on this excess in a mostly autobiographical essay, titled "Confesiones de una mujer lucía" ("Confessions of a Show-Off Woman"). For Santos Febres, the woman who does not abide by the rules of modesty, who wants to wear red lipstick and a short skirt, transgresses and is perceived as an outlaw. She adds, "The presence of a *mujer lucía* destabilizes the sexual roles assigned by society" (10). The "*mujer lucía*" needs a lot of courage to go out into the world and also to contest a certain puritanism that lingers in some strands of feminism. Santos Febres feels that "the audacity of the *mujer lucía* is necessary to imagine a different world, where there is space to dance on top of billiard tables, free at last" (13). This is precisely the way IQ presents herself to the world. She flaunts discourses of respectability that are part and parcel of race and class hierarchies, and this is what makes her overall performance transgressive.

IQ's performance also destabilizes traditional notions of motherhood: by speaking and singing about motherhood, she positions herself in a crucial space for questioning notions of identity, race, gender, and culture. Although IQ does not identify as Afro-Puerto Rican, Afroboricua or black, Rivera-Rideau affirms that her music and public persona are almost inseparable from "reggaetón, a genre linked to both local constructions of blackness and African diasporic practices." "Thus," Rivera-Rideau continues, "her performance implicitly joins in conversation with larger dialogues about blackness and Puerto Rican racial democracy, even if she herself does not identify as black" (109). By grounding her latest work in motherhood, IQ deeply questions notions of respectability, gender, and race that reverberate transnationally. As Marta Cruz-Janzen explains:

> Mothers are important in Latino cultures and are visible proof of matrilineal racial lines that cannot be concealed. Motherhood is also a paramount value within doctrines of nationalism, patriotism, and racialism endorsed by most Latino nations.... In Spanish, country of origin becomes madre patria ... nationalism and patriotism, without diminishing national patriarchy, legitimize women as bearers and nurturers of powerful men and nations. A complete national identity requires a mother. However, this powerful national icon cannot be black/African American woman. (177)

IQ also valorizes maternal bodies—specifically, those bodies treated with violence as a result of racism. In "Vendetta," in particular, she underlines the body, her own disrespected, criticized, marginalized maternal body, as she asserts and humanizes it as the vehicle to bring her daughter into the world.

Por eso este mundo está mal dividido
esta equivocado y está mal repartido
para traer mi hija yo fue su vehículo
y para mantenerla canto, no sean ridículos

(That's why this world is badly divided
It's wrong and badly distributed
To bring my daughter I was her vehicle
And I sing to support her, don't be ridiculous)

Her insistence is particularly important in the Puerto Rican context: poor mothers are commonly maligned in many ways, the most recent being the term "*yal*," aimed at poor, young, black women (in the U.S. context, "ratchet" is a terribly similar term). Anti-*yal* Facebook pages have sprouted in recent years (repeating the meme, *No más yales en Puerto Rico*); one talentless Puerto Rican actress has become known for her tasteless parody of poor mothers, even calling herself "*la caballota*" in clear reference to IQ. Teresa Córdova has rightly called this out as being a sexist and classist Blackface, and Katsí Rodríguez agrees:

> While it would be incorrect to say that they are black women, because from looking at them it is evident that they are not necessarily dark-skinned, it could be said that yales are almost black because they're so cafre, almost black because they're so poor, almost black because they're such whores. That is to say that the imaginaries and expectations attributed to black bodies in a white-supremacist context like ours are the same ones with which yales are punished for failing to act/want to be/look like white women, so they need to be eliminated. Because they degrade gender. Today they represent everything the nation had and still

> has to leave behind in order to be modern. That is why so much time and energy is invested in reinforcing the yal stereotype, so as to invalidate and silence the depth of the violence to which they are subjected, made into a joke and you're expected to laugh, we're expected to laugh so nothing will change.

They are outsiders, outlaws. For Rodríguez, this scorn is

> punishment for the eroticism and sexual agency with which they charge their bodies, as well as their rupturing of the ideal traditional family, and their non-observance of the parameters of decency, modesty and respectability which, through the mandate of gender, the nation imposes upon them as a requirement for proving itself to be advanced, civilized and on the road to progress.

This is about control: who can reproduce, which women should become mothers. State, religious, and even popular discourses establish maternities that are out of place.

As "Vendetta" travels its transnational circuit, Ivy Queen's song can be read as a powerful manifesto on behalf of every mother who does not fit the ideal of "respectable" and "decent" motherhood. She denounces, claims, and performs subversions, holding out a different model of motherhood for those imprisoned mothers in Vega Alta (the only penal institution—at the time—for women in Puerto Rico, where she herself was once incarcerated). Dancing mothers with their toddlers at an IQ concert in Panamá open unconventional readings of reggaetón, as Alexandra Vazquez reminds us (302), and wherever IQ performs, she calls out all those outlaw mothers powerfully for recognition and dignity.

As reggaetón continues defying national borders, Puerto Ricans not only can question ideas about racial democracy in Puerto Rico but can also make Afro diasporic connections beyond the simple labeling of "Latino." Rivera-Rideau, following Mark D. Perry's ideas about hip-hop, argues that "while many people may consider reggaetón as yet another genre encapsulated by the Latin music category, its associations with hip-hop and urban culture bring to mind specific ties to blackness that extend beyond the race mixture that presumably forms the basis of all things 'Latino'" (328). The same may be true of IQ's songs; as they travel, so does her message to mothers, her protests, and her claims that she stakes in *Vendetta*. IQ emphasizes that her power derives from words, "*Porque estoy de pie, no voy para atrás, porque soy leal y traigo letras.*" ("Because I'm standing up, I'm not going backwards, because I'm loyal, and I've got lyrics.")

Many people still seem to dismiss reggaetón as monolithically sexist and in bad taste. Another questionable Facebook page, originating in Puerto Rico, urges its visitors to "Support our local products, but not reggaetón, not that." Creators of the page draw a line around what they consider "real Puerto Rican culture," which tends to follow the officialist discourse of cultural nationalism: that Puerto Ricans are a mixture of three races, Taíno, Spanish, and African, but with the Spanish privileged as the basis of our national identity. Raquel Rivera rightly adds that "the colonial government has at times been the most influential promoter of the dominant strand of cultural nationalism, with all its racist, classist, xenophobic, patriarchal, and homophobic shortcomings" (218). Still, reggaetón is a transnational cultural and economic force. Although commodified by the music industry, it still manages to subvert and transgress more than elite notions of propriety and good taste. For Dinzey-Flores, reggaetón brings to the forefront "the image of urban poor, violent and disillusioned Puerto Rico and gives Puerto Rico's urban poor a resounding voice with a marked local, and even international, range" (61). On the other hand, Báez explains that "reggaetón functions as an exchange of cultural production between Puerto Ricans on the island, Puerto Ricans on the U.S. mainland, other Latin Americans and Latina/os, African Americans, and other peoples of the Caribbean" (64). Reggaetón brings the issues of poverty, violence, the urban experience, race, identity, sexuality, and gender to a global stage (Báez; Dinzey-Flores). As IQ travels, so do her continuous challenges to traditional views on motherhood, and even reggaetón. On her journey, she proposes new identities. IQ constructs a strong transversal motherhood manifesto, as she embodies her claims: her body cannot be ignored. She invites us, in her interviews and with her music, to talk back to oppressive views of motherhood, to defy containment, and to practice solidarity. She encourages us to bring forward our experience as mothers without losing ourselves, and she does it within the male-supremacist world of reggaetón: definitely no small feat.

I wish to thank James Seale Collazo for his generous help in translating and editing this article (including the lyrics). I also wish to thank Katsí Yarí Rodríguez for her insightful conversation on gender, race, and reggaetón.

ENDNOTES

[1] All translations were done by James Seale Collazo.

[2] Regarding this production, IQ explained to *Billboard* that she wanted to do something powerful with *Vendetta*: "As an artist and as a writer, I write different types of music, I am not only writing urban music, hip hop music, reguetón music, I am also a salsa writer ... so I took my chance to do these four albums ... because I wanted to show people my potential as an artist because I am tired of people of putting me in this box. It is important. In my perspective as a woman I don't like to look the same, either in the look or in the music. I do everything against the current ... it's about my evolution as woman, you stand in front of the mirror and you have the courage to make the changes that you want, not the ones the music industry may put on you" ("Ivy Queen Interview").

WORKS CITED

Agencia AP. "Ivy Queen cuenta su historia de superación." *Telemetro*. 28 Apr. 2008, telemetro.com/entretenimiento/Ivy-Queen-cuenta-historia-superacion_0_35396474.html. Accessed 23 Sept. 2017.

Báez, Jillian M. "'En mi imperio': Competing Discourses of Agency in Ivy Queen's Reggaetón." *Centro Journal*, vol. 18, no. 11, 2006, pp. 63-81.

Cruz-Janzen, Marta I. "Latinegras: Desired Women—Undesirable Mothers, Daughters, Sisters, and Wives." *The Afro-Latin@*

Reader: History and Culture in the United States, edited by Miriam Jiménez Román and Juan Flores, Duke University Press, 2010, pp. 282-95.

Dinzey-Flores, Zaire Zenit. "De la Disco al caserío: Urban Spatial Aesthetics and Policy to the Beat of Reggaetón." *Centro Journal*, vol. 20, no. 2, 2008, pp. 35-69.

Fernández, Suzette. "Ivy Queen Gets Her Revenge." *Billboard*, 30 Jan. 2015, www.billboard.com/articles/columns/latin-notas/6458082/ivy-queen-interview. Accessed 14 Dec. 2016.

Flores, Juan. "What's All the Noise About?" *Reggaeton*, edited by Raquel Rivera et al., Duke University Press, 2009, pp. ix-xi.

"Ivy Queen en el Monólogo de la Vagina hablando del tema 'La Vagina Furiosa'." *YouTube*, uploaded by Datkiddjean23, 1 Mar. 2012, gaming.youtube.com/ watch?v=rhYQuYYIohU&list=FLz_ BCI03ENRpXYTLQFwf3xA. Accessed 14 Dec. 2016.

"Ivy Queen Interview: The Word 'Diva,' Her Four New Albums & How She'll Spend Mother's Day." *YouTube,* uploaded by *Billboard,* 29 Apr. 2015, www.youtube.com/watch?v=yI_B8qP7xUI. Accessed 14 Dec. 2016.

"Ivy Queen-*Vendetta*." *YouTube*, uploaded by IvyQueenVevo, 13 June 2015, www.youtube.com/watch?v=fljU5MccE9Y.

Kazetari, Mari [June Fernández] "Si no puedo perrear, no es mi revolución." *Periodismo de gafas violeta*, 24 July 2013, gentedigital.es/comunidad/june/2013/07/24/si-no-puedo-perrear-no-es-mi-revolucion/. Accessed 14 Dec. 2016.

Lebrón, Marisol. "Con un Flow Natural": Sonic Affinities and Reggaeton Nationalism." *Women and Performance: A Journal of Feminist Theory*, vol. 21, no. 2, 2011, pp. 219-33.

"Los 12 Discípulos Live from the Grammys." *YouTube*, uploaded by Diamond Music Casa Productora Urbana Artist System, 27 June 2007, www.youtube.com/watch?v=uq1m6S32InU. Accessed 23 Sept. 2017.

Negrón-Muntaner, Frances. "Celia's Shoes." *From Bananas to Buttocks: The Latina Body in Popular Film and Culture*, edited by Myra Mendible, University of Texas Press, 2007, pp. 94-116.

O'Reilly, Andrea. "'We Were Conspirators, Outlaws from the Institution of Motherhood': Mothering against Motherhood and the Possibility of Empowered Maternity for Mothers and

Their Children." *Mother Outlaws: Theories and Practices of Empowered Mothering*, edited by Andrea O'Reilly, Women's Press, 2004, pp. 59-73.

Queen, Ivy. Interview by Ismael Cala. *CNN*, 12 March 2015, edition.cnn.com/videos/spanish/2015/03/12/cnnee-cala-ivy-queen.cnn. Accessed 14 Dec. 2017

Queen, Ivy. "Yo quiero bailar." *Diva Platinum Edition*, Universal Music Latino, 2003.

Queen, Ivy. "Que lloren." *Sentimiento*, Univision, 2007.

Queen, Ivy. *Vendetta*. Siente Music, 2015.

Queen, Ivy. "Vendetta." *Vendetta* Siente Music, 2015.

Ramos Otero, Manuel. "El cuento de la mujer del mar." *Tálamos y tumbas. Prosa y verso de Manuel Ramos Otero*, edited by Lilliana Ramos Collado and Dionisio Cañas, Universidad de Guadalajara, 1998, pp. 161-194.

Rich, Adrienne. *Of Woman Born: Motherhood as Experience and Institution*. Norton, 1976.

Rivera-Rideau, Petra. *Remixing Reggaetón: The Cultural Politics of Race in Puerto Rico*, Duke University Press, 2015.

Rivera, Raquel. "Will the "Real" Puerto Rican Culture Please Stand Up? Thoughts on Cultural Nationalism." *None of the Above: Puerto Ricans in the Global Era*, edited by Frances Negrón Muntaner, Palgrave Macmillan, 2007, pp. 217-231.

Rodríguez, Katsí Yarí. "Degradando a la yal: racialización y violencia de mujeres pobres en Puerto Rico."unpublished paper, San Juan, 2015.

Santos Febres, Mayra. *Sobre piel y papel*, Ediciones Callejón, 2005.

Tubert, Silvia. *Figuras de la madre*. Ediciones Cátedra, 1996.

Vázquez, Alexandra T. "Salon Philosophers: Ivy Queen and Surprise Guests take Reggaetón Aside." *Reggaeton*, edited by Raquel Rivera et al., Duke University Press, 2009, pp. 300-311.

Vega, Ana Lydia. *Mirada de doble filo*, Editorial de la Universidad de Puerto Rico, 2008.

Vflow cruz. "Ivy Queen_Vendetta_Dvd Full_Album Informercial_2014." *Youtube*, uploaded by Vflow Victory Productions, 29 Dec. 2014, www.youtube.com/watch?v=y2e8uJL2YmA. Accessed 29 Dec. 2016.

12. Mothering Beyond Transnational Borders

Trajectories of Zimbabwean Migrant Women in South Africa

KEZIA BATISAI

GLOBALIZATION IN THE twenty-first century has been characterized by the increased movement of people, goods, services, technology, and capital—processes that have produced an interconnected world. Labour markets and forms of gendered work that emerged out of these global processes have prompted the migration of women predominantly from the global South to the global North (Batisai 165). Over the years, scholars have concentrated on transnational migration; the gendered (mothering) experiences of noncitizens of the recipient countries in the global North (Fonkem 40; Gamburd 35; George 144; McGregor 805; Oishi 4; Parreñas 560; Pasura 143; Sassen 254; Tinarwo and Pasura 521); and the impact of such on children left in the global South (Boccagni 261; Kufakurinani et al. 114; Madziva and Zontini 429; Ukwatta 107). These scholars often explore questions of gender and transnational mothering under the ambit of "the transfer of care from the global South to the global North" (Madziva and Zontini 429; Parreñas 561). Where scholars have explored South-South encounters, the focus has been on gender, mothering, agency, (domestic) work, and migration between and within Asian countries (Deshingkar et al. 9). Broadening the scope of transnational migration beyond the global North and Asian bias noted above, this chapter maps and profiles the gendered realities of globalization and transnational mothering within and between African countries.

I begin with a brief overview of how scholars (Batisai, "Pushing the Limits of Motherhood"; Jeannes and Shefer; Nzegwu; Oyewumi; Stephens) have broadly theorized and analyzed motherhood in

Africa. Scholars on the continent reiterate how central motherhood is to women's lives (Stephens 1) and to African cultures and societies at large (Mills 1; Nzegwu 1; Oyewumi 1). For instance, Oyeronke Oyewumi acknowledges that mothers are the very foundation in which society, social relationships, and identities are built (1). Scholarly engagement with motherhood in Africa includes the analysis of how older women push the limits of motherhood in rural Zimbabwe (Batisai, "Pushing the Limits of Motherhood") and how women in South Africa negotiate their "traditional positioning as mothers" (Daniels 1) in light of the contextual sociopolitical and cultural realities (Magwaza 1).

Building on this growing body of literature on motherhood, I look at how globalization shapes the life and work realities of mothers in South Africa from a sociocultural and economic perspective. It is noteworthy that South Africa is increasingly a major transnational destination for migrants from different African countries—a development scholars attribute to the ever-evolving sociopolitical and economic crisis on the continent (Kufakurinani et al. 122; Batisai, "Transnational" 167; Batisai, "National Belonging, Difference and Xenophobia" 121). The growing presence of foreign nationals in different pockets of Johannesburg points to a need to understand women's diverse and complex experiences of mothering in this changing landscape.

To explore the interplay between mothering and globalization, I use a feminist standpoint to analyze data that emerged from six months of fieldwork with Zimbabwean migrant women in Johannesburg. In particular, this chapter explores the interplay between transnational mothering and (re)productive engagements in the context of globalization through subjective narratives of three categories of Zimbabwean migrant women in South Africa. The first two categories are migrant women whose realities either allow or do not allow them to live with their children in a foreign country. I unpack how migrant women experience mothering within a context foreign to them and the subsequent meaning they assign to transnational mothering experiences deeply embedded in the sociocultural, political, legal, and economic landscapes of both countries. The analytic processes of these mothers are heavily informed by narratives of work vis-à-vis relationships that develop between them and their children, as evidenced by their references to intimacy, separation, moral degeneration, and bewilderment.

The third category of Zimbabwean migrant women in South Africa explores how globalization has sustained a career-oriented class of women who postpone mothering—a category with which I identify. Narratives are drawn from single Zimbabwean women whose career paths are shaped by globalization in order to deconstruct and transform longstanding reductionist cultural constructions of women as objects of reproduction. Analyzing how these women exercise agency and pursue their professional choices before becoming mothers furthers our understanding of why they defer or postpone having children. Overall, these women's narratives illuminate the complex ways in which the transnational mothering of Zimbabwean migrant mothers responds to shifting historical, sociocultural, political, and economic terrains in the context of globalization.

METHODOLOGICAL ISSUES

This study takes a qualitative approach to explore the experiences of Zimbabwean women and the meaning they attach to mothering in and from transnational contexts. The decision to engage with Zimbabwean migrant women in Johannesburg, South Africa, was both subjective and purposive. As a feminist scholar, I was heavily influenced by my subjective positionality—a Zimbabwean woman who permanently resides in South Africa. Apart from my subjective positionality, the idea flowed from Mazars et al., who among other scholars, frame Zimbabweans as "the largest group of non-nationals residing in South Africa" (13).[1] As mentioned earlier, the heavy presence of Zimbabweans in South Africa is attributed to the drastic political and economic crisis that has over the years turned Zimbabwe "from an immigrant receiving to a migrant-sending country" (Crush et al. 4). As JoAnn McGregor and Dominic Pasura suggest, "Zimbabwe [is] a country which now has a diverse transnational diaspora of professionals, labour migrants, asylum seekers, refugees and others following the exodus from the late 1990s that involved as much as three million people, or a quarter of the population" (2). The influx of "skilled and unskilled, men and women, married and unmarried" Zimbabweans into South Africa (Crush et al. 4) reveals the agency many citizens have exercised to capitalize on transnational opportunities presented by migration and globalization. A myriad of studies on Zimbabwean migrants that emerged subsequent to this influx document:

> irregular migration; the brain drain of skilled professionals; the living and working conditions of migrants in South Africa; remitting behavior and remittance flows; the xenophobic treatment and human rights abuse of migrants; migrant identity; prospects for diaspora engagement; and the confused policy responses of the South African authorities. (Crush et al. 4)

Clearly missing from the topics above are questions to do with transnational mothering among Zimbabwean migrants residing in South Africa—questions previously explored by Roda Madziva and Elisabetta Zontini in the context of forced migration in the United Kingdom (UK).

Driven by both subjective and purposive judgments, and restricting the number of interviewees to a manageable sample of twelve, I embarked on a six-month fieldwork journey in 2015 aimed at gaining in-depth insight into Zimbabwean migrant women's mothering experiences in South Africa. Over and above their gender, the twelve interviewees were purposively selected based on marital status, number of children, and occupation in order to arrive at a sample representative of the three categories of women (four women living with their children; four women not living with their children; and four who do not yet have children). I accessed these women through personal and previous research contacts who then introduced me to women in their sphere of influence with whom I established rapport and generated a snowball sample of possible research participants.

Fieldwork was an exploration of these twelve women's migratory trajectories through in-depth interview questions around "mothering beyond national borders." In addition to in-depth interviews, my insider (Zimbabwean) and outsider (foreigner) positionalities created space for me to observe on a daily basis and hear stories about mothering among Zimbabwean women living in Johannesburg. These observations and migratory stories were invaluable to my data analysis process.

The narratives[2] of mothering presented and analyzed in this chapter draw on Zimbabwean migrant women's everyday existential and residential circumstances, as well as their work realities in this foreign space. Although these analyses are drawn from a small sample of Zimbabwean women located in South Africa, the findings are of great significance to studies of globalization and transnational mothering in other contexts beyond the boundaries of these two geographical spaces.

ZIMBABWEAN MIGRANT WOMEN IN SOUTH AFRICA

A critical mapping of Zimbabwe's migration trends points at the historically gendered nature of mobility, characterized by the migration of men to regional and international destinations (Bloch 1; Madziva and Zontini 432). As a result of the more recent volatile economic and political landscapes alluded to earlier, however, these migration patterns have shifted, resulting in the emigration of Zimbabweans of all genders, marital statuses, age groups, and diverse professional backgrounds (Crush et al. 4)—an exodus McGregor and Pasura trace back to the late 1990s (2). The twelve Zimbabwean migrant women I interviewed (Pamela, Ruth, Sekai, Bertha, Tracy, Kelly, Thandeka, Candy, Anne, Claire, Rudairo, and Esther) came to South Africa between 2000 and 2014, with their families or alone.

The twelve women reside in low- and high-density suburbs of Johannesburg and earn a living from diverse formal and informal sector activities, including nursing, teaching and/or lecturing, accounting, domestic work, and hairdressing. These employment realities significantly shape the experiences and narratives of mothering in Johannesburg. Unlike their counterparts in the informal sector, interviewees working in the formal sector can often afford to live with all their children. The subsequent thematic sections explore the narratives of these interviewees and the meanings they assign to their experiences of mothering, either within the boundaries of South Africa or from outside the borders of their homeland.

MOTHERING WITHIN THE BOUNDARIES OF SOUTH AFRICA

The analysis in this section is drawn from the interviewees' experiences of mothering within South Africa—a context foreign to them. Pamela, Ruth, Sekai, and Bertha—who in response to the drastic socioeconomic and political shifts in Zimbabwe migrated to South Africa to pursue better living and working conditions—constitute the first category of women whose narratives are explored here. As professional women, they followed proper immigration procedures when they relocated to South Africa with their husbands and children. These women feel that the work that they do and the salaries that they (and their husbands) earn are in line with their academic credentials and previous work experience. It is against this backdrop that Pamela, Ruth, Sekai, and Bertha note that their stable monthly cash flows allow them to live with their families in Sandton, Morningside, Rivonia, and Bryanston — some of the affluent suburbs north of Johannesburg.

Experiences of mothering in a foreign space further bring these four women together, which creates conditions challenging their roles as mothers and compromise the mother-child relationship. Pamela, aged fifty, says the following:

> My family does not struggle financially ... we are very liquid. We can provide for our three teenage children [two sons and a daughter] ... but we have failed as parents to raise them according to our culture from home. A mother has to know that South Africa is a foreign space where sociocultural landscapes governing life, gender and sexuality in particular, are different. What worries me is that my children have assimilated. They lead a very fast life to the extent that my daughter has assumed a new sexual identity that is contrary to our values as Zimbabweans. It hurts so bad to watch your teenagers grow astray ... it is every mother's worst nightmare.

The excerpt above exposes the extent to which Pamela's transnational mothering experience is shaped by the economic and sociocultural realities of the context in which she is located. Mothering in this transnational space is about negotiating between the opportunities and challenges stemming from such context. On the one hand, Pamela enjoys her immigration status in South Africa and the benefits of further economic emancipation that come with transnational labour migration, but on the other, she battles with her children's loss of moral standing. Hence, the bewilderment evident in her narrative: "Mothering in South Africa is never the same as in Zimbabwe…it is a constant battle with your emotions. I guess that is the price we pay for living in the diaspora … I don't know … what can I say?"

Ruth, aged forty-eight, who also has to deal with similar emotional dilemmas, attributes her mothering challenges to the upward class mobility she experienced when she migrated to South Africa. She acknowledges that the mother-child relationship is under threat as children adopt new behaviours at affluent schools, which many Zimbabwean mothers find very difficult to deal with at home:

> Our household income changed significantly when we moved to Johannesburg … we have a decent life … way better than in Zimbabwe. Two of my four boys, who were in their late teens when we relocated, have always had access to disposable cash. I thought since my two sons had spent the greater part of their teenage life in Zimbabwe, they were not going to struggle with adolescence issues … I was so wrong … they are now rude, they backchat … they experiment a lot … with anything that you can think of … they have lost the plot.

Furthermore, Ruth argues that the affluent school that she sends her other two sons has high rates of physical and cyber bullying. As a mother, she finds any form of bullying in the absence of corporal punishment in South Africa very problematic because she has to deal with the emotional effects on her children who now feel unmotivated to go to school:

> Bullying is really worrisome especially in South Africa, a country that battles with violence … even in schools … there are reports of students who stab each other and their

> teachers as well. It is a big concern but there is very little that a mother can do to stop it. You cannot smack your child because of the rights discourse that protects children in South Africa ... I feel powerless as a mother.

Over and above the shift in behaviour and the notions of violence, Ruth's narrative below suggests that mothering in a transnational context raises issues of cultural homogenization and hybridization that threaten one's cultural identity: "My children are snobbish ... they do not want to speak Shona anymore ... and they think it is cool ... my young adults have really lost their identity ... they have assumed new cultures. I do not think all this was going to happen if were in Zimbabwe ... we were rooted in our culture as a family." Sekai, aged fifty-five, affirms Simon Turner's observation that transnational settings have produced "a space of indeterminacy where ... some institutions—such as the family—are put under pressure and forced to change" (1052). Speaking as a mother who represents the family institution, Sekai argues that the way her children resist her counsel somewhat destabilizes motherhood as an institution, and contributes to family degeneration:

> These children challenge me as an individual and as a mother. The tension leaves me with strong feelings of separation ... we live together physically but we are separated emotionally ... and this is really a pain for me as a mother ... I strongly feel that I should have control over the fruit of my womb ... but not in South Africa ... life is very fast down here compared to Zimbabwe ... that's the diaspora for you ... I have come to understand that you win some ... you lose some ... it is gambling I believe.

Although she equally struggles to advise and maintain a sound relationship with her children, Bertha, aged forty, has an unwavering standpoint, which somewhat challenges Turner's observation that "the family institution in the context of globalization is forced to change" (1052). Her narrative below suggests that Bertha has found ways of negotiating the complexities of mothering in the diaspora:

> I know that many Zimbabwean mothers in South Africa battle with sociocultural challenges but they should find ways of preserving our cultural identity beyond our national borders. For me, this often means serving my teenage children Zimbabwean dishes in South Africa ... speaking in vernacular [Shona] ... frequenting home during public holidays ... irrespective of the resistance I face from the children ... yes, home is Zimbabwe ... I am just here to make ends meet ... it is a well-calculated financial move.

Contrary to their children who struggle with the politics of identity in South Africa, home and Zimbabwean identity are in every cell of these transnational mothers' blood. Their children's identity crisis partly stems from questions around whom they are when they are growing up among strangers in a transnational space where some have the liberty to acquire new ways of life, and others learn and speak languages foreign to them. Pamela, Ruth, Sekai, and Bertha concur that children in the diaspora construct their resistance narrative against their mothers' expectation that they will adhere to sociocultural prescriptions when they have lost touch with a country which they seldom visit or identify with. The mothering approaches these women adopt nonetheless speak to Gloria Anzaldúa's notion of "carrying home on her back": "Yet in leaving home I did not lose touch with my origins because lo mexicano is in my system. I am a turtle, wherever I go I carry 'home' on my back" (43).

It is against this background that Paula, Ruth, Sekai, and Bertha constantly draw on norms and values that are core to their home identity, and try to enforce these on their children despite the resistance. The women's experiences signal the need for further conceptualizations of mothering alert to the sociocultural, legal, and economic conditions shaping the lives of Zimbabwean migrant women in South Africa, and their subsequent effects on the mother-child relationship in the diaspora.

MOTHERING FROM OUTSIDE ONE'S NATIONAL BORDERS

The multifaceted economic and political crisis in Zimbabwe saw many parents migrating alone and leaving their children behind, resulting in prolonged periods of separation or even permanent separation (Madziva 70). Like those in the first category of interviewees, the second group of Zimbabwean women—Tracy, Kelly, Thandeka, and Candy—migrated to South Africa in an attempt to escape the economic and sociopolitical strain weighing heavily on citizens with limited (if any) sources of income. What distinguishes these two groups is the fact that Tracy, Kelly, Thandeka, and Candy are single mothers who battled with the dilemma of leaving their children in Zimbabwe when they got the opportunity to migrate to South Africa. Furthermore, they do not have postsecondary education qualifications, and when they migrated to South Africa, they did not acquire the proper immigration documents. As a result, they have the right neither to live nor to work in South Africa. Tracy, aged forty-six and a lower-end domestic worker in the north of Johannesburg, states:

> Desperate times call for desperate measures ... I came to Johannesburg in 2005, without any documentation ... I do not have any formal training, and I have worked as a nanny all my life ... The salary that I earn in Johannesburg is barely enough to sustain my two daughters who are in their early teens. I cannot live with them in Tembisa because I rent a small shack ... and the conditions are not habitable, especially for my children ... I just endure this shack life for the sake of my children ... that is what I call motherhood.

Unlike Tracy, Kelly, aged thirty-eight, works as a live-in maid for a family in one of the affluent suburbs north of Johannesburg. She does not have transport costs as she does not have to commute to work. What connects these two women is the fact that their working and living conditions do not allow them to live with their children in South Africa, and as a result, their children are cared for by members of the extended family in Harare, Zimbabwe. Kelly relays:

> I am a single mother of four [two sons and two daughters]

> … I came to Johannesburg in 2007 when life in Zimbabwe got really tough. I left my children under the guardian of my ailing mother who died in 2008. Upon her death, my children hopped from my cousin to another distant cousin who is barely managing … and often complains about 'the erratic remittances' from South Africa … irrespective of the fact that the money is coming from a position of sacrifice … I send the bulk of my earnings home.

Kelly's narrative bears a resemblance to "the traditional African practice of child fostering" (Madziva 71), through which some Zimbabwean migrants to the UK left their children under the guardianship of family members and friends. What is strikingly similar about Kelly's experience and that of the Zimbabwean migrants in the UK is the way her children were constantly moved from one caregiver to another with or without their consent. Likewise, Roda Madziva attributes this volatility to either the death of the caregiver or to the existing economic terrain, which often renders child fostering within the family and among friends unstable and unsatisfactory (71). Kelly, like Madziva, observes how these manifestations often strain relationships between transnational family members because of the lack of trust: "My heart bleeds when I think about them, especially the ill-treatment … I do not have control over this because I am not physically there for my children. Despite the distance, what keeps me going is the material support … at least they are clothed, they have food on the table and they are going to school." Mothering for Kelly and Tracy becomes transnational, as they parent and nurture their children left in Zimbabwe from South Africa. Experiences of transnational mothering for this pair are about how they negotiate the realities of being absent mothers who are only connected to their children through remittances. This is echoed by Thandeka, aged thirty and a divorced mother of two. Since 2000, she has lived in Alexandra Township and doubles as a hairdresser and a domestic worker in the northern suburbs. She says:

> The only thing that brings me close to my children in Zimbabwe is the money … the remittances I send them

> on a monthly basis. I skip going home because I do not have a work visa ... it is too risky ... and I also feel that it is better and cheaper for me to remit the money than to incur transport costs and other financial demands that emerge as you visit family and friends ... but this decision is emotionally costly ... I lose [the] physical bond with my children.

Thandeka's education background and immigration status affect the kind of job she can obtain and the salary she earns on a monthly basis. These circumstances, similar to those of Tracy, Kelly, and Candy, limit her ability to live with her children or even visit them in Zimbabwe. According to Thandeka, the emotional costs outweigh the economic gains. Candy, aged thirty-five concurs. She complains about lack of physical nurturing and control over her children, who are being raised by the extended family beyond the borders of South Africa: "I was not there when my daughters had their first menstrual period ... daughters need their mothers ... for guidance and motherly support during that time of the month ... especially in the early days. They also have to be controlled throughout puberty or adolescence confusion and beyond ... I feel bad ... guilty as a mother."

Tracy, Kelly, Thandeka, and Candy feel that their mothering roles are challenged because they are absent mothers who cannot adequately support their children financially. Failure to fulfill their mothering roles weakens these four women's sense of self, and, subsequently, they feel and frame themselves as inadequate mothers. Their experiences contradict positive narratives of "material mothering" observed among Sri Lankan women who use money they remit home to compensate for their absence (Gamburd 200). In essence, they challenge conceptualizations that mothering can operate without physical proximity (Madziva and Zontini 428), and love can be expressed in more material forms. Often, these four migrant women feel guilty about neglecting their own children, as the money they earn is not enough to support their children in Zimbabwe beyond school fees and basic groceries. This echoes the experiences of Zimbabwean mothers in the UK documented by Madziva and Zontini, who explore "the obstacles to family life caused by separation" (429). These experiences also resonate with a sense of loss rooted in the absence of physical interaction between mothers and their children recorded by Paolo Boccagni among Ecuadorian mothers in Italy (265-66). Yet the Zimbabwean migrant women acknowledge that social networking platforms such as WhatsApp have in recent years increased their level of interaction with their children back home. Nevertheless, the women agree that nothing is worth more than being with your family and children.

AGENCY, PROFESSIONALISM, AND DEFERRED MOTHERING

This section explores ways in which the third category of interviewees, a career-oriented class of single and married Zimbabwean women, postpone or defer mothering upon migrating to transnational spaces. Anne, Claire, Rudairo, and Esther are professional women who live in Illovo, Rosebank, Hyde Park, and Parkmore, north of Johannesburg. These women exercise agency and pursue their professional choices before engaging in motherhood. Anne, aged twenty-nine, illuminates the meaning some single Zimbabwean women living in South Africa assign to their professional choices and trajectories. "I came to Johannesburg, South Africa in 2007 to pursue further studies. I did my undergrad at Wits [Witwatersrand] and finished in 2010. By 2013, I was already done with my honours and master's and I moved straight into PhD studies in 2014. I do not have children and I am not planning to have any in the near future. My academic/career is my first born."

Mothering for professional women who live beyond the national borders of their homeland is conceptualized in relation to the drastic economic shifts in Zimbabwe. Rudairo, aged thirty-six, defers mothering because she feels that if she has children now, she would likely plunge into financial despair. Hence, she needs to shape her career first so that she can, in the near future, contribute toward household income. She declares, "Given the economic turmoil in Zimbabwe, I will only become a real mother after I am satisfied that I have made a financial impact on my family [parents and siblings] in Zimbabwe ... and when I am in a position to make meaningful financial contribution to my own family whenever I decide to have children."

Similarly, Claire, aged forty and a single Zimbabwean woman, opts not to have children so that she can both study and work. Her reasons are informed by her belief that transnationalism creates a space for women's emancipation and upward mobility, but simultaneously limits these professionals' chances of meeting potential suitors from home. Claire shares the following:

> I am focusing on my career and as I do that I have very limited time to mix with people, and when I do so, chances of hooking up with a desirable Zimbabwean man are very slim ... the market is dry. This has shifted how I perceive and approach marriage ... and impacted on mothering as well. I am sure you are smart enough to discern why I am not married and without children yet ... no pressure at all.

Claire, Anne, and Rudairo use their careers to introduce and define who they are in a way that, on one hand, suggests that their careers are of great significance to them and, on the other, somewhat trivializes mothering. Furthermore, the career paths and choices that they have made transform longstanding reductionist cultural constructions of women as mere objects of reproduction. Further analysis of the excerpts above also suggests that these professional migrant women challenge traditional beliefs and expectations to which a woman is morally bound. Findings from previous research locate these beliefs—which frame marriage as the ultimate societal expectation that often prevails over career choices—in the idea that a woman should eventually get married to avoid losing her morals and values (Batisai, "Body Politics"). Mothering in this context is read through notions of respectability that women earn through marriage and childbirth.

For Esther, who is thirty-eight and in the academy, deferred mothering is informed by the need to strike a balance between two conflicting identities—academic and a mother. Academic mothers, as noted by Venitha Pillay, are conceived in intellectual spaces as "rational, unemotional and logical" (1). However, being a mother also comes with "nurturing, loving, emotions and sensitivity" (1). In light of these binary positionalities, Esther is pursuing her professional choices before she becomes a mother. She elaborates:

> I am not a mother; I am very single and happy. When I was doing my PhD, my personal theory was: 'a PhD is a lot of things in one ... it is a child, or even children, a husband, in-laws ... you name it.' Now I am an academic ... the workload is just too much ... it is equivalent to all these people ... I cannot imagine adding real people to the workload. Clearly, I am not talking from experience because I am neither a mother nor a wife/daughter-in-law ... but I have seen and observed those who walked that road ... and I am not ready for this.

Clearly discernable from this excerpt is a narrative of fear rooted in the "perceived strain of mothering" on one's career. This fear takes us to the following question: "So how do these two identities inhabit a being and how are they played out in daily life, at home and work?" posed by Mesthire in her review of Venitha Pillay's *Academic Mothers* (2007) (127) . Although the review challenges the way Pillay renders the pursuit of a balance between motherhood and an academic career futile (128), Mesthire acknowledges that the book "opens debate over motherhood in academia" (129)—issues that are beyond those raised in this chapter but warrant further exploration.

CONCLUDING REMARKS

The migratory trajectories of Zimbabwean women analyzed in this chapter reveal subjective knowledge about mothers, mothering, and globalization, and illuminate how the mother role is performed differently depending on one's intersecting multiple positionalities. Zimbabwean migrant women's experiences and abilities to fulfill their motherly roles are shaped and controlled by the realities specific to the (transnational) context in which they are located. These women's narratives offer a more nuanced understanding of transnational mothering that is cognizant of the diverse experiences of mothers located in the global South—Africa to be specific—which is often invisible within the existing research. This chapter has addressed this gap with an analysis that goes beyond narratives of women's resilience and adaptability

(Madziva and Zontini 429), often rooted in the global North. Contrary to Ushehwedu Kufakurinani et al.—who only explore "the emotional consequences of parents' spatial mobility on middle class families where material resources maybe ample" (114-15)—I have looked at the effects of transnational mothering on both middle- and working-class migrant mothers located in South Africa.

Expanding the definition of separation that has been explored and interrogated by many scholars (Boccagni 264; Kufakurinani et al. 117; Madziva and Zontini 430) enables us to explore the experiences of mothers who physically live with their children but feel emotionally separated. The narrative of separation and moral degeneration concurs with how Lisa Jeannes and Tamara Shefer challenge "the myth of the Perfect Mother," especially the expectation that a mother must be the one who understands her children (1). The women I interviewed struggle to understand their children, since they have acquired new ways of life and developed new identities in foreign spaces.

Middle-class migrant women mothering within the boundaries of South Africa deal with these emerging transnational realities constantly by reconnecting to a past they once shared with their families in Zimbabwe. This strategy, according to Jill Richardson, "allows them to forge new fluid identities and to create new concepts of home that work within a transnational and Diaspora framework" (2). The migrant women also infer that diasporic spaces challenge their roles as mothers. This signals the need to reconceptualize transnational mothering by taking into account the negative impact of upward class mobility and increased disposable income on the mother-child relationship.

Beyond the benefits of labour migration and middle-class migrant women's experiences of separation from their children in South Africa, the chapter also analyzes narratives of struggle among mothers who battle to raise their children in Zimbabwe from the borders of another African context. In essence, the narratives encompass separation, distress, and bewilderment emerging out of experiences of mothering children left in Zimbabwe. These narratives are shaped by the limited resources working-class Zimbabwean migrant women erratically remit home. Family members (mothers and their children) are forced to survive on meagre resources, which weakens these women's sense of self. Since they do not have the resources and time to physically nurture, guide, and support their children, these Zimbabwean migrant women often feel inadequate about their roles as mothers. Their narratives add value to ongoing "moral debates over cultures of parenting and broader social change provoked through emigration in the context of Zimbabwe's politico-economic crisis" (Kufakurinani et al. 117)—especially the fact that migrant mothers, in the absence of physical interaction, often cannot guide their children through the confusion of adolescence.

The narratives of migrant women in the third category not only reflect the practice of deferred mothering, but also reinforce earlier findings by Joan Ferrante et al. on how gender equality increased rates of female education and downplayed constructions of motherhood as women's primary responsibility (qtd. in Ziehl 28-29). Indeed, Zimbabwean migrant women's narratives of mothering illuminate the ways in which complex dynamics of transnational mothering respond to shifting historical, sociocultural, political and economic terrains and structures.

In all, the analyses in this chapter draw on migratory trajectories of Zimbabwean women in ways that better our understanding of experiences of mothering in South Africa and Zimbabwe among other global South (African) contexts with similar historical, legal, economic, political, and sociocultural landscapes. The women's experiences significantly contribute to conceptualizations of mothering that are alert to how these landscapes shape the lives of migrant women in the global South, especially regarding the meanings they assign to their experiences of mothering from outside the borders of their homeland and their subsequent effect on the mother-child relationship. These analyses open space for further research on the diverse realities impacting the mothering experiences of women who occupy both high and low ends of the migration hierarchy in different African contexts and beyond.

ENDNOTES

[1]This assertion is fully alert to contestations over the exact number

of Zimbabweans living in South Africa because of the prevalence of undocumented migrants in the country.

[2]All the narratives of the twelve interviewees are published under the shield of pseudonyms.

WORKS CITED

Anzaldúa, Gloria. *Borderlands/La Frontera: The New Mestiza.* Aunt LuteBooks, 1987.

Batisai, Kezia. "Pushing the Limits of Motherhood: Narratives of Older Women in Rural Zimbabwe." *African Studies*, vol. 76, no.1, 2017, pp. 44-63. *Taylor and Francis Online*, doi.org/10.1080/00020184.2017.1285667. Accessed 17 Feb. 2017.

Batisai, Kezia. "Interrogating Questions of National Belonging, Difference and Xenophobia in South Africa." *Agenda*, vol. 30, no. 2, 2016, pp. 119-130. *Taylor and Francis Online*, doi.org/10.1080/10130950.2016.1223971. Accessed 22 Aug. 2016.

Batisai, Kezia. "Transnational Labour Migration, Intimacy and Relationships: How Zimbabwean Women Navigate the Diaspora." *Diaspora Studies*, vol. 9, no. 2, 2016, pp. 165-78. *Taylor and Francis Online*, doi.org/10.1080/09739572.2016.1185236. Accessed 23 May 2016.

Batisai, Kezia. *Body Politics: An Illumination of the Landscape of Sexuality and Nationhood? Re-seeing Zimbabwe through Elderly Women's Representations of Their Sexual and Gendered Lives.* Dissertation, U of Cape Town, 2013. https://open.uct.ac.za/handle/11427/3598. Accessed 17 Apr. 2014.

Bloch, Alice. "The Development Potentials of Zimbabweans in the Diaspora. A Survey of Zimbabweans Living in the UK and South Africa." International Organization for Migration, 2005. Migration Research Series no. 17.

Boccagni, Paolo. "Practising Motherhood at a Distance: Retention and Loss in Ecuadorian Transnational Families." *Journal of Ethnic and Migration Studies*, vol. 38, no. 2, 2012, pp. 261-77. *Taylor and Francis Online*, doi.org/10.1080/1369183X.2012.646421. Accessed 1 Nov. 2015.

Crush, Jonathan, et al. "The Third Wave: Mixed Migration from Zimbabwe to South Africa." Southern African Research Centre,

Queen's University, Canada, and the Open Society Initiative for Southern Africa, 2012. Migration Policy Series no. 59.

Daniels, Doria. "They Need to Know Where They Came from to Appreciate Where They Are Going to—Visual Commentary of Informal Settlement Women on Motherhood." *JENDA: A Journal of Culture and African Women Studies. Motherhood*, no. 5, 2004, pp. 1-9, africaknowledgeproject.org/index.php/jenda/article/view/97. Accessed 18 Jan. 2016.

Deshingkar, Priya, et al. "Does Migration for Domestic Work Reduce Poverty? A Review of the Literature and an Agenda for Research." Migrating out of Poverty Research Programme Consortium, May 2014, Working Paper 15.

Fonkem, Achankeng. "Gender Roles and Conflict among Lebialem Immigrant Families in the USA." *Diaspora Studies*, vol. 6, no. 1, 2013, pp. 40-49. *Taylor and Francis Online*, doi.org/10.1080/09739572.2013.843291. Accessed 1 June 2015.

Gamburd, Michele Ruth. *The Kitchen Spoon's Handle: Transnationalism and Sri Lanka's Migrant Housemaids.* Cornell University Press, 2000.

George, M. Sheba "Dirty Nurses and Men Who Play: Gender and Class in Transnational Migration." *Global Ethnography: Forces, Connections and Imaginations in a Postmodern World*, edited by Michael Burawoy, et al, University of California Press, 2000, pp. 144-74.

Jeannes, Lisa, and Tamara Shefer. "Discourses of Motherhood among a Group of South African Mothers." *JENDA: A Journal of Culture and African Women Studies. Motherhood*, no. 5, 2004, pp. 1-16, africaknowledgeproject.org/index.php/jenda/article/view/98. Accessed 18 Jan. 2016.

Kufakurinani, Ushehwedu et al. "Transnational Parenting and the Emergence of 'Diaspora Orphans' in Zimbabwe." *African Diaspora. The Difference that Crisis Makes: Diasporic Entanglements with Home and the Case of Zimbabwe*, vol. 7, no. 1, 2014, pp. 114-38.

Madziva, Roda. "Living Death: Separation in the UK." *Forced Migration Review*, no. 34, 2010, pp. 70-71, www.fmreview.org/urban-displacement.html. Accessed 2 Nov. 2015.

Madziva, Roda, and Elisabetta Zontini. "Transnational Mothering and Forced Migration: Understanding the Experiences of Zimbabwean Mothers in the UK." *European Journal of Women's Studies*, vol. 19, no. 4, 2012, pp. 428-43, http://ejw.sagepub.com/content/19/4/428. Accessed 2 Nov. 2015.

Magwaza, Thenjiwe. "Perceptions and Experiences of Motherhood: A Study of Black and White Mothers of Durban, South Africa." *JENDA: A Journal of Culture and African Women Studies. Motherhood*, vol. 4, no. 1, 2003, pp. 1-18, africaknowledgeproject.org/index.php/jenda/article/view/84. Accessed 18 Jan. 2016.

Mazars, Céline, et al. "The Well Being of Economic Migrants in South Africa: Health, Gender and Development." Working Paper for the World Migration Report. International Organization for Migration, 2013.

McGregor, JoAnn. "Joining the BBC (British Bottom Cleaners): Zimbabwean migrants and the UK care industry." *Journal of Ethnic and Migration Studies*, vol. 33, no. 5, 2007, pp. 801-24. *Taylor and Francis Online*, doi.org/10.1080/13691830701359249. Accessed 1 May 2015.

McGregor, JoAnn, and Dominic Pasura. Introduction. "Frameworks for Analyzing Conflict Diasporas and the Case of Zimbabwe." *African Diaspora*, vol. 7, 2014, pp. 1-13. eprints.gla.ac.uk/109140/, doi:10.1163/18725465-00701001. Accessed 1 May 2015.

Mesthire, Uma Dhupelia. "A Review of *Academic Mothers*." *Feminist Africa, Rethinking African Universities II*, no. 9, 2009, pp. 127-29, http://agi.ac.za/journal/feminist-africa-issue-9-2007-rethinking-universities-ii. Accessed 20 Feb. 2015.

Mills, Shereen W. "Mothers in the Corridors of the South African Legal System: An Assessment of the Johannesburg Family Court Pilot Project." *JENDA: A Journal of Culture and African Women Studies. Motherhood*, vol. 4, no. 1, 2003, pp. 1-34, africaknowledgeproject.org/index.php/jenda/article/view/85. Accessed 18 Jan. 2016.

Nzegwu, Nkiru. "Cultural Epistemologies of Motherhood." *JENDA: A Journal of Culture and African Women Studies. Motherhood*, no. 5, 2004, pp. 1-4, africaknowledgeproject.org/index.php/jenda/article/view/92. Accessed 18 Jan. 2016.

Oishi, Nana. *Women in Motion: Globalization, State Policies, and Labour Migration in Asia*. Stanford University Press, 2005.

Oyewumi, Oyeronke. "Abiyamo: Theorizing African Motherhood." *JENDA: A Journal of Culture and African Women Studies. Motherhood*, vol. 4, no. 1, 2003, pp. 1-7, africaknowledgeproject.org/index.php/jenda/article/view/79. Accessed 18 Jan. 2016.

Parreñas, Rhacel Salazar. "Migrant Filipina Domestic Workers and the International Division of Reproductive Labor." *Gender and Society*, vol. 14, no. 4, 2000, pp. 560-80, www.jstor.org/stable/190302. Accessed 5 May 2015.

Pasura, Dominic "A Fractured Transnational Diaspora: The Case of Zimbabweans in Britain." *International Migration*, vol. 50, no. 1, 2012, pp. 143-61. *Wiley Online Library*, doi/10.1111/j.1468-2435.2010.00675.x. Accessed 6 Apr. 2015.

Pillay, Venitha. *Academic Mothers*. Unisa and Trentham Books, 2007.

Richardson, Jill Toliver. "Gendered Migrations: The Migratory Experience in Loida Maritza Pérez's *Geographies of Home*." *Label Me Latina/o*. vol. 1, 2011, pp. 1-24, http://labelmelatin.com/?cat=9. Accessed 5 May. 2015.

Sassen, Saskia. "Global Cities and Survival Circuits." *Global Woman: Nannies, Maids and Sex Workers in the New Economy*, edited by Barbara Ehrenreich and Arlie Hochschild, Metropolitan Books, 2003, pp. 254-74.

Stephens, Rhiannon. *A History of African Motherhood. The Case of Uganda, 700-1900*, Cambridge University Press, 2013.

Tinarwo, Tandeka Moreblessing, and Dominic Pasura. "Negotiating and Contesting Gendered and Sexual Identities in the Zimbabwean Diaspora." *Journal of Southern African Studies*, vol. 40, no. 3, 2014, pp. 521-38. *Taylor and Francis Online*, doi.org/10.1080/03057070.2014.909258. Accessed 28 Jan. 2015.

Turner, Simon. "Studying the Tensions of Transnational Engagement: From the Nuclear Family to the World-Wide Web." *Journal of Ethnic and Migration Studies*, vol. 34, no. 7, 2008, pp. 1049-56. *Taylor and Francis Online*, doi.org/10.1080/13691830802230323. Accessed 3 Nov. 2015.

Ukwatta, Swarna. "Sri Lankan Female Domestic Workers Overseas: Mothering Their Children from a Distance." *Journal of Population Research*, vol. 27, no. 2, 2010, pp. 107-31, archive.cmb.

ac.lk:8080/research/handle/70130/2740. Accessed 11 Mar. 2015.
Ziehl, Susan. *Population Studies: Introduction to Sociology*, Oxford University Press, 2002.

13.
Positive Engagements with Globalization

Lessons from Maternal Activists in Transnational Women's Groups during the Liberian Civil War

CRYSTAL M. WHETSTONE

GLOBALIZATION, BROADLY UNDERSTOOD as the "expansion and intensification of all kinds of social relations across borders" (Sørensen 410-411), is driven by governments, corporations, and civil society organizations in ways that shape not only international relations between states but also the everyday lives of ordinary people (Sørensen 410-411). In this case study, I use Margaret Keck and Kathryn Sikkink's theory of transnational advocacy networks (TANs)—which they define as networks of activists that build links between civil society, government, and international organizations in ways that transform national sovereignty and enact social change—to analyze the maternal activism of the Mano River Women's Peace Network (MARWOPNET) and the Women in Peacebuilding (WIPNET) Network. TANs are associated with international and domestic nongovernmental organizations (NGOs), but they are also linked to social movements, foundations, the media, churches, trade unions, consumer organizations, intellectuals, and even parts of regional and international intergovernmental organizations and national governments (Keck and Sikkink 8-9). The efforts of MARWOPNET and WIPNET during the Liberian civil war highlight the uniting role that motherhood can play in transnational women's activism.

THE LIBERIAN CIVIL WAR

From its founding in the mid-1800s, Liberia was ruled by descendants of African Americans, known as Americo-Liberians, who discriminated against Indigenous ethnic groups (Akpan 218-219, 221, 225-236; Badmus 813). Americo-Liberian dominance ended in 1980 when an Indigenous Liberian, Samuel Doe, launched a coup d'état. Without Americo-Liberians as a common enemy, ethnic friction among Indigenous Liberians escalated until Charles Taylor of the National Patriotic Front of Liberia (NPFL) militia launched a civil war against Doe in 1989. An uneasy peace was reached in 1996 (Badmus 814-815; "Liberia—UNIOMIL Background"). Although Taylor was elected president in 1997, the war did not end as Taylor became increasingly autocratic and used the state's armed forces as his own personal security (Harris 437-440; Birikorang 294, 297). By 1999, a new militia, the Liberians United for Reconciliation and Democracy (LURD), and later a splinter of LURD, challenged Taylor's forces. Fighting continued until women activists forced all sides to sit down to peace talks in Accra, Ghana, in June 2003, which eventually led to the war's conclusion in October 2003 (Birikorang 294-295; Sewell 17-19).

TRANSNATIONAL ADVOCACY NETWORKS IN LIBERIA

Keck and Sikkink reveal how TANs challenge both Westphalian understandings of national sovereignty and the notion that the international system functions separately from domestic systems (4, 12-15, 32-37). In cases such as Liberia, where domestic avenues to political change are blocked by oppressive rulers, TANs provide a space in which both domestic and international actors can challenge sovereign governments through the international community. Keck and Sikkink describe this as a "boomerang" effect, in which domestic actors reach out to international allies, who, in turn, put pressure on autocratic governments to enact positive changes that cannot otherwise be achieved through domestic channels. TANs accomplish this task through information, symbolic, leverage, and accountability politics that attract the attention of the media and the international community, where even the most oppressive of dictators still require some approval from the international community (12-16, 106-109). In Liberia, MARWOPNET and WIPNET employed these politics of information, symbolic, leverage, and accountability by creating impactful information about the war for domestic and international audiences. They used stories to symbolize the difficulties of the war, and they relied on the persuasive abilities of powerful individuals within the government, militias, and their own CSOs to hold Charles Taylor and rebel generals accountable; all of this culminated in an end to the war (Keck and Sikkink 16, 18-25; African Women Peace and Support Group 48-52). A key aspect of this work was MARWOPNET's and WIPNET's use of maternal framing, which allowed women to use their informal powers as mothers in politically persuasive ways (Moran and Pitcher 508, 513-514; Bauer 198).

MANO RIVER WOMEN'S PEACE NETWORK

MARWOPNET was founded in May 2000 in Abuja, Nigeria, to coordinate the efforts of women from the countries around the Mano River who were working to bring conflict resolution to Guinea, Liberia, and Sierra Leone. Organizers with the Femmes Africa Solidarité (FAS), a Swiss-based NGO, brought together the women who would go on to form MARWOPNET (African Women Peace and Support Group 42-46). TANs bring new resources to domestic actors and social movements, and FAS's stated purpose is to support women on the continent of Africa working at the grassroots level to end conflicts, ensure human security, and uphold women's rights (Keck and Sikkink *x*, 1; "Objectives"). Once activists in the Mano River region received the outside support of FAS, they were able to come together through MARWOPNET, which served as an umbrella organization for development-focused women's groups in the area. MARWOPNET was headquartered in Freetown, Sierra Leone, and although its members came from varying ethnic and socioeconomic backgrounds, all members used their status as wives and mothers in their efforts to end the conflicts in the region (Moran and Pitcher 508, 513-514; African Women and Peace Support Group 45; Sewell 17-19; Johnson 68; "Profile of the Mano River").

A major project undertaken by MARWOPNET, which ran June through August 2001, worked to bring the presidents of Guinea, Sierra Leone, and Liberia together to address the respective civil wars in Liberia and Sierra Leone ("Profile of the Mano River").

After successfully convincing Charles Taylor and then Sierra Leonean president Ahmad Tejan Kabbah to meet with one another, a MARWOPNET delegation of Liberian, Sierra Leonean, and Guinean women encountered difficulties with then Guinean president Lansana Conté, who refused to meet with Taylor. Emphasizing their status as mothers, the delegation reported to Conté that the mothers and children in the Mano River region were suffering terribly in the ongoing armed conflicts (Sewell 16-17). One Liberian woman named Mary Brownell informed Conté that he had no choice but to meet with Taylor and she would lock the two together in a room and sit on the key until the men worked out a plan to end the fighting (Fleshman). In March 2002 in Rabat, Morocco, Conté indeed met with Taylor and Kabbah as MARWOPNET had insisted (African Women Peace and Support Group 45-46). Conté has since stated that the demanding manner in which the women addressed him and forced him to talk with Taylor and Kabbah would have been unacceptable to him coming from men. Conté reportedly said, "Only a woman could do such a thing and get away with it" (qtd. in Fleshman). As a result of the 2002 meeting, the three heads of state agreed, at least in theory, to begin peace talks, reopen the borders between the three countries, work to decrease the availability of small arms, and find ways to increase economic development in the Mano River region (Femmes Africa Solidarité 588-589). Although the fighting in Liberia would continue for another year, the women not only were successful in persuading the three leaders to meet, they saw signs of hope as these governments began to at least rhetorically outline steps to address the human security needs in the Mano River countries. Following the convening of the three presidents in Rabat, the male minister of internal affairs of Sierra Leone stated that the MARWOPNET activists had "excelled as mothers where fathers had failed" (qtd. in Moran and Pitcher 508). This decisive event illustrates the significant role that MARWOPNET's maternal activism played in their transnational peace work.

WOMEN IN PEACEBUILDING NETWORK

In November 2001, members of the West African Network for

Peace-building (WANEP), a CSO founded in 1998 to end conflicts in West Africa, created a new branch that sought to increase peace-building through women's activism—the Women in Peacebuilding Network (WIPNET) (Ekiyor and Gbowee 134; "About Us, West Africa Network;" "WIPNET: Women in Peacebuilding"). It was designed not simply to work to end conflicts within West Africa but also to address violations of women's social and cultural rights believed to be caused by the lack of women's participation in civic and political institutions (Ekiyor and Gbowee 134).

In April of 2003, as LURD fighters marched from the countryside toward the capital Monrovia, Liberian WIPNET members instituted an organizing effort that they called the Mass Action for Peace (*Pray the Devil Back*; Ekiyor and Gbowee 135). This movement had its roots in the personal experience of WIPNET activist Leymah Gbowee who in June 2002 felt called upon to gather the women in her church to pray for peace. Gbowee visited churches throughout Monrovia to recruit women to pray for peace, eventually forming the Christian Women Peace Initiative. A Muslim woman named Asatu Bah Kenneth learned of Gbowee's effort and was inspired to create a parallel collective within the Monrovian Muslim community, which she called the Liberian Muslim Women's Organization. Under the umbrella of WIPNET, Gbowee and Kenneth united forces to show Liberian women's solidarity. In March 2003, when it became apparent that LURD leaders were planning a large scale attack on the civilian population, the women developed a plan to call for an end to the violence (*Pray the Devil Back*). On 11 April, 2003, approximately one thousand members of WIPNET, dressed in all white, began to meet daily at Monrovia's main fish market, which was located in a central area along a road that President Taylor passed daily. Openly defying government restrictions against protests, WIPNET activists demanded Taylor's recognition of their petition, which requested an immediate ceasefire from all factions and the start of an official dialogue between the warring parties to be monitored by a third party (African Women and Peace Support Group 49; *Pray the Devil Back*).

When Taylor ignored them, the women decided on a second tactic. In addition to their street protests, the women began a sex strike: they refused to have sexual relations with their husbands or boyfriends until the fighting stopped. WIPNET hoped that this would persuade the men to press for a ceasefire. Vaiba Flomo, leader of the Christian Women Peace Initiative, explained that part of a woman's power lies in denying her husband access to her body (*Pray the Devil Back*). The sex strike coupled with the daily protests in Monrovia's fish market attracted major attention from local and international media and the general public (Ekiyor and Gbowee 134-135; Witter; *Pray the Devil Back*; Gbowee). During their demonstrations, WIPNET activists carried placards demanding an end to the fighting and sang songs denouncing violence. At one point, over 2,500 women participated in the daily protests—women who represented all aspects of Liberian society religiously, ethnically, and socioeconomically (Ekiyor and Gbowee 135-136; *Pray the Devil Back*).

Through this skillful use of the international media, members of the Liberian branch of WIPNET were eventually able to pressure Charles Taylor to meet with them that very month, in April 2003 (Ekiyor and Gbowee 135-137; *Pray the Devil Back*). During this meeting with Taylor and representatives of his administration, WIPNET activists demanded that Taylor develop an immediate ceasefire with the leaders of the rebel factions. Gbowee made the official statement to Taylor in which she stressed that a major concern of WIPNET was the future of their children if the war continued (*Pray the Devil Back*). Taylor did not submit to the activists' demands in April. However, due to the women's unceasing daily protests and their participation in demonstrations outside of the U.S. embassy, the parliament, and other government buildings, activists kept international interest in the situation high, and by June 2003, international pressure compelled Taylor to submit to negotiations in Accra, Ghana (*Pray the Devil Back*; Ekiyor and Gbowee 137).

When peace talks began on 4 June, 2003, delegations from several women's groups attended the conference, although they were not actually invited and had to lobby for access to the hall where negotiations were taking place. Through persuasive arguing, female activists secured a place at the peace table with two representatives and two observers who were present throughout the talks. WIPNET sent a delegation to Accra to continue their Mass Action for Peace effort and eight members of MARWOPNET's Liberian branch, led by Ruth Sando Perry, officially represented all of the women's groups at the negotiations (Ekiyor and Gbowee 136; Sewell 17; *Pray the Devil Back*). The media captured images of the women activists weeping and pleading for peace. Scholars have traced this form of protest to the roles played by women in West African funeral traditions, in which women's collective weeping has been a prominent feature of the funeral rite (Tripp et al. 207). Gbowee stated to reporters that the women were at the peace talks to serve as the men's conscience (*Pray the Devil Back*).

When negotiations appeared to stall, members of the women's groups decided on more extreme tactics (Ekiyor and Gbowee 137). The breaking point came on 21 June, 2003, following a bombing of the US Embassy by LURD forces in which a community of internally displaced persons staying within the embassy's walls was killed. Activists began recruiting more women to join them outside of the negotiation room (*Pray the Devil Back*). Once gathered, the female activists—now numbering over two hundred and holding signs that read "Killers of our people. No impunity this time!" and "How many babies do you intend to slaughter?"—barricaded the door to the negotiation room to prevent the leaders of the warring factions from leaving (Ekiyor and Gbowee 137; Sewell 17-19; Gbowee). For two hours, the activists refused to relent until security guards were called, and one of WIPNET's leaders, Leymah Gbowee, was threatened with arrest for "obstructing justice" (*Pray the Devil Back*; Gbowee). In response to the guards, Gbowee began to strip off her clothing—a shocking action in this context in which it is considered both a taboo and a curse throughout most West African societies for a man to see his mother naked. Importantly, in Liberian society, men view all women older than themselves as their mothers. For these all-male security guards, it appeared as if their mother was ready to curse them (*Pray the Devil Back*; Lederach and Lederach 31; Steady 105). Filomina Steady describes Gbowee's defiant act as a "weapon symbolizing the power of motherhood," meant to shame the men trying to arrest her (105). Gbowee's actions caused a massive uproar in the hallway in front of the negotiation room, and succeeded as the agitated guards failed to arrest her. In this excitement, a LURD general saw his chance to escape, but the women pushed him back into the negotiating room as if they were sending a misbehaving child back to his room for a time out. One of the official mediators, Nigerian president General Abulsalami Abubakar, scolded the militia generals and representatives from Taylor's government, and told them that if they were "real" men, the women would not have to treat them like boys (*Pray the Devil Back*).

After the uproar over the near arrest, the women felt that they had made their point and agreed to let the men leave. However, the activists threatened that if progress was not made within two weeks, they would again lock the men in the negotiating room (*Pray the Devil Back*). The women issued three ultimatums: first, that the delegates representing the warring parties attend all further negotiation sessions; second, that the men refrain from insulting the women; and, lastly, that all parties sign onto a final peace accord within two weeks (Gbowee 51). Significantly, the media was attracted to the great commotion caused by the women's sit-in, which provided yet another reason for the men to resume talks: mounting international pressure to end the war (Ekiyor and Gbowee 137). With the world watching, the mood of the negotiations altered. Prior to the women's effort, the leaders of the warring factions refused to compromise and appeared to relish to attention that they were accorded in the high level talks. Now, a sobering weight fell upon them (*Pray the Devil Back*).

Many analysts cite the women's demonstration as the singular event that put enough pressure on rebel leaders and Taylor to sign the Comprehensive Peace Agreement that ended the fourteen-year civil war (Sewell 18-19; Gbowee; Badmus 827-828, 832-835; African Women Peace and Support Group 48-52). However, it is important to note that MARWOPNET and WIPNET were neither the first Liberian groups to adopt maternal framing in their political organizing, nor the first to engage in transnational activism with the aim of peace. During the 1990s, the Liberian Women's Initiative (LWI) was at the forefront of maternalist peace activism, and many other groups engaged in transnational advocacy work. Indeed, these earlier CSOs set the stage for the later actions of MARWOPNET and WIPNET, and, in fact, many women involved with LWI joined forces with MARWOPNET and WIPNET (African Women and Peace Support Group, 17, 22, 43-50).

MATERNAL FRAMING

Keck and Sikkink emphasize the importance of framing, or symbolic politics, in TANs, since the boomerang effect requires that the international community be concerned enough to take action to pressure a domestic regime. TANs must work to present their issues in a way that sparks enough interest to emotionally move people (10, 17, 19, 23-24). MARWOPNET's and WIPNET's decision to emphasize their identities as mothers allowed them to reach both domestic and international audiences who resonated with the women's concern for their children (Sewell 17-19; *Pray the Devil Back*). Scholars such as Andrea O'Reilly argue that motherhood can be a politicizing and radicalizing experience (28-30). In addition to raising women's activist consciousness, motherhood can provide women with political cover, since maternal activists appear to adhere to traditional gender roles by embracing their identities as mothers, which obscures the political nature of their actions (Neuman 65). Most importantly in the context of TANs, women politically mobilized as mothers receive ample media attention because of their seemingly nonthreatening status. Moreover, it can be difficult for adversaries to attack maternal activists because their motivations appear to be pure and selfless, as they are working on behalf of others rather than themselves (Hilhorst and van Leeuwen 98, 101-102; Hammami 162-163, 165-166, 168). This has well served women organizing against autocratic regimes who employ motherhood as a cover for their activities (Waylen 336, 338-340; Moran and Pitcher 508, 513-514; Bauer, 198). Cynthia Stavrianos fittingly calls maternal activists "wolves in sheep clothing," since their political intentions are often hidden by their roles as mothers (7).

To both domestic and international audiences, motherhood was a tool that allowed Liberian activists to present their issues in a way that made their own maternal suffering and the suffering of their families the centre of attention. People could relate intimately to MARWOPNET's and WIPNET's wartime suffering and concern for loved ones in a way that simultaneously disguised much of what was political in the women's activism. In 2001, the presidents of Liberia, Sierra Leone, and Guinea found it impossible to ignore the MARWOPNET women who emphasized their status as mothers and demanded that leaders meet to resolve their differences. Later, Charles Taylor found it equally impossible to ignore the women protesting at Monrovia's fish market, dressed as they were in all white and singing for peace. The symbolic use of white as both the colour of peace and the colour of purity emphasized Liberian women's status as moral mothers. Taylor was unable to enforce his own decree against political protests because a crackdown on mothers would have been unfitting even for an autocratic ruler. Liberian women used their status as mothers to pressure domestic political leaders to resolve the armed conflict. Equally important, the symbolic use of mothering appealed to international audiences who related to the all-encompassing selflessness of a mother's love that led to the international pressure, which ultimately forced Taylor and LURD to commit to peace. As Leymah Gbowee puts it, it was the women of Liberia who created a "peaceful, feminine havoc" that brought an end to the war.

MOTHERHOOD IN TRANSNATIONAL ADVOCACY NETWORKS

Traditionally, women in Liberia have been seen as outsiders to political processes. Jacqui Bauer believes that a number of structural factors, combined with the multitude of women's organizations and intensive women's grassroots organizing during the war, increased female participation in politics since the war ended in 2003. Bauer directly ties women's peacebuilding, which was rooted in women's status as mothers, to their participation in the 2005 election that brought Africa's first democratically elected female president into office (198, 209-210). According to Oyeronke Oyewumi, in Africa, it is not sisterhood but rather motherhood that unites women (11-13, 22). Indeed, the literature is clear that motherhood is a significant concept in Liberia and sub-Saharan African generally, regardless of religious, ethnic, or socioeconomic background. Motherhood plays a role in cultural understandings of women's leadership capabilities (Tripp et al.,

25-28; Steady, 13, 30-35, 116-117, 150, 239, 241). Both MARWOPNET and WIPNET are located within larger CSOs, and women's connection to motherhood may have played a part in uniting women within these TANs during the war. Activist Leymah Gbowee agrees that the focus on motherhood was a unifying force even if class tensions and other divisions did flare up during their organizing for peace (Gbowee 144-145). What women accomplished in the Liberian civil war is similar to what human rights groups in Argentina's Dirty War achieved in overthrowing a military junta in the 1980s, much of it done through the maternal framing of the group the Mothers of Plaza de Mayo (Fisher, 32, chapter 2 more generally; Keck and Sikkink, 16-17). Along with scholars such as Oyeronke Oyewumi and Andrea O'Reilly, I speculate that motherhood may be a unifying force because of its inclusive nature, which holds the potential of empowering women and getting them politically engaged (Oyewumi, 11-13; O'Reilly, 28-30). Based on this, I believe that using maternal framing in TANs could prove particularly useful in combating negative aspects of globalization, such as the new wars, like Liberia's, that are rooted in social and identity divisions, which Mary Kaldor traces to globalization processes (1-8).

CONCLUSION

The maternal activism performed by women situated within TANs undeniably changed the course of events in Liberia. Certainly, globalization has wrought devastation upon women around the world, particularly in regard to socioeconomic issues and war. However, globalization has positively led to the development of certain TANs that have empowered women, implemented environmental protections, and increased the human security of many around the world (Keck and Sikkink ix, see chapters 3-5). In Liberia, women's use of maternal framing helped turn the tables on Charles Taylor and rebel forces through the use of symbolic politics, and it helped women break into political activism. Combating the ills of globalization requires a transnational approach, and as Liberia indicates, motherhood may serve as a more inclusive factor around which to mobilize women. Nevertheless, the use of maternal framing in the context of TANs is not always successful. For example, Kurdish women with Turkey's Saturday Mothers have attempted to use maternal framing to bring domestic and international attention to the plight of their missing sons, husbands, and brothers, who were captured by the state in the 1990s. Yet outside desire to help Turkey's Kurds remains minimal, and today the situation of disappeared Kurdish men is more dangerous than ever, with new illegal detentions on the rise (Gokpinar; Carreon and Moghadam 22; Kirişci; Sevinin). There are further issues with the very notion of maternal framing in the context of peace activism, which problematically naturalizes links between women, motherhood, and peace that in the long-term may limit women to the home "where they belong" (Charlesworth, "Are Women Peaceful?" 348; "Feminist Methods" 387). Future research is needed to investigate not only under what conditions the maternal frame operates effectively, but also its long-term consequences on women's political participation.

WORKS CITED

"About Us." *West Africa Network for Peacebuilding*, www.wanep.org/wanep/index.php? option=com_content&view=category&layout=blog&id=7&Itemid=11. Accessed 21 Apr. 2017.

African Women and Peace Support Group. *Liberian Women Peacemakers: Fighting for the Right to be Seen, Heard, and Counted.* Africa World Press, 2004.

Akpan, M.B. "Black Imperialism: Americo-Liberian Rule over the African Peoples of Liberia, 1841-1964." *Canadian Journal of African Studies,* vol. 7, no. 2, 1973, pp. 217-36.

Badmus, Isiaka Alani. "Explaining Women's Roles in the West African Tragic Triplet: Sierra Leone, Liberia, and Côte D'Ivoire in Comparative Perspective." *Journal of Alternative Perspectives in the Social Sciences*, vol. 1, no. 3, 2009, pp. 808-39.

Bauer, Jacqui. "Women and the 2005 Election in Liberia." *Journal of Modern African Studies*, vol. 47, no. 2, 2009, pp. 193-211.

Birikorang, Emma A. "Ecowas and the Second Liberian War." *South African Yearbook of International Affairs*, 2003/2004, pp. 293-302.

Carreon, Michelle E., and Valentine M. Moghadam. "'Resistance is Fertile': Revisiting Maternalist Frames Across Cases of Women's Mobilization." *Women's Studies International Forum,* vol. 51, 2015, pp. 19-30.

Charlesworth, Hilary. "Are Women Peaceful? Reflections on the Role of Women in Peace Building." *Feminist Legal Studies*, vol. 16, 2008, pp. 347-61.

Charlesworth, Hilary. "Feminist Methods in International Law." *The American Journal of International Law*, vol. 93, no. 2, 1999, pp. 379-94.

Ekiyor, Thelma Aremiebi, and Leymah Roberta Gbowee. "Women's Peace Activism in West Africa: The WIPNET Experience." *People Building Peace II: Successful Stories of Civil Society,* edited by Paul van Tongeren, et al., Lynne Rienner Publishers, 2005, pp. 133-40.

Femmes Africa Solidarité. "Engendering the Peace Processes in West Africa: The Mano River Women's Peace Network." *People Building Peace II: Successful Stories of Civil Society,* edited by Paul van Tongeren, et al., Lynne Rienner, 2005, pp. 588-93.

Fisher, Jo. *Mothers of the Disappeared.* South Press End, 1989.

Fleshman, Michael. "African Women Struggle for a Seat at the Table." *African Renewal,* vol. 16, no. 4, 2003, http://www.un.org/en/africarenewal/vol16no4/164wm1.htm. Accessed 25 Sept. 2017.

Gbowee, Leymah. "Effecting Change through Women's Activism in Liberia." *Institute of Development Studies (IDS) Bulletin,* vol. 40, no. 2, 2009, pp. 50-53.

Gokpinar, Ali. "The Saturday Mothers." *Open Democracy*, www.opendemocracy.net/ali-gokpinar/saturday-mothers. Accessed 21 Apr. 2017.

Hammami, Rema. "Palestinian Motherhood and Political Activism on the West Bank and Gaza Strip." *The Politics of Motherhood: Activist Voices from Left to Right*, edited by Alexis Jetter et al., University Press of New England, pp. 161-68.

Harris, David. "From 'Warlord' to 'Democratic' President: How Charles Taylor Won the 1997 Liberian Elections." *The Journal of Modern African Studies,* vol. 37, no. 3, 1999, pp. 431-55.

Hilhorst, Dorothea, and van Leeuwen, Mathijs. "Local Peace

Builders and Local Conflict: The Feminization of Peace in Southern Sudan." *The Gender Question in Globalization: Changing Perspectives and Practices (Gender in a Global/Local World)*, edited by Tine Davids and Francien Van Driel, Ashgate, 2007, pp. 93-108.

Johnson, Stephanie Anne. "Women, Shared Leadership, and Policy: The Mano River Women's Peace Network Case Study." *The Journal of Pan African Studies*, vol. 4, no. 8, 2011, pp. 59-69.

Kaldor, Mary. *New and Old Wars: Organized Violence in a Global Era*. Stanford University Press, 1999.

Keck, Margaret E., and Kathryn Sikkink. *Activists beyond Borders: Advocacy Networks in International Politics*. Cornell University Press, 1998.

Kirişci, Kemal. "Turkey: Getting Worse Before It Gets Better." *Brookings Institute*, www.brookings.edu/blog/order-from-chaos/2016/11/01/turkey-getting-worse-before-it-gets-better/. Accessed 11 May 2017.

Lederach, Jill Angela, and John Paul Lederach. *When Blood and Bones Cry Out: Journeys through the Soundscape of Healing and Reconciliation*. Oxford University Press, 2010.

"Liberia—UNOMIL Background." *United Nations*, http://www.un.org/en/peacekeeping/missions/past/unomilFT.htm. Accessed 21 Apr. 2017.

Moran, Mary H., and M. Anne Pitcher. "The 'Basket Case' and the 'Poster Child': Explaining the End of Civil Conflicts in Liberia and Mozambique." *Third World Quarterly*, vol. 25, no. 3, 2004, pp. 501-19.

Neuman, Tamara. "Maternal Anti-Politics in the Formation of Hebron's Jewish Enclave." *Journal of Palestinian Studies*, vol. 33, no. 2, 2004, 51-70.

"Objectives." *Femmes Africa Solidarité*, www.fasngo.org/objectives.html. Accessed 21 Apr. 2017.

O'Reilly, Andrea. "Introduction: Maternal Activism as Matricentric Feminism: The History, Ideological Frameworks, Political Strategies and Activist Practices of the 21st Century Motherhood Movement." *The 21st Century Motherhood Movement: Mothers Speak Out on Why We Need to Change the World and How to Do It*, edited by Andrea O'Reilly, Demeter Press, 2011, pp. 1-33.

Oyewumi, Oyeronke. "Introduction: Feminism, Sisterhood, and Other Foreign Relations." *African Women and Feminism: Reflecting on the Politics of Sisterhood,* edited by Oyèrónké Oyewumi, Africa World Press, 2003, pp. 1-24.

Pray the Devil Back to Hell. Directed by Gini Reicker, performances by Leymah Gbowee, Etweda, Sugars, Cooper, and Vaiba Flomo. Passion River Films, 2008.

"Profile on the Mano River Women's Peace Network." *World Movement for Democracy*, www.wmd.org/resources/whats-being-done/ngo-participation-peace-negotiations/profile-mano-river-womens-peace-netw. Accessed 21 Apr. 2017.

Sevinin, Eda. "Politics of Truth-Seeking and the Saturday Mothers of Turkey." *Research Turkey: Centre for Policy and Research on Turkey,* http://researchturkey.org/politics-of-truth-seeking-and-the-saturday-mothers-of-turkey/. Accessed 21 Apr. 2017.

Sewell, Erica K. "Women Building Peace: The Liberian Women's Peace Movement." *Critical Half: Bi-Annual Journal of Women for Women International,* vol. 5, no. 2, 2007, pp. 14-19, http://wfwmarketingimages.womenforwomen.org/news-women-for-women/assets/files/critical-half/CH_december07_final%20file.pdf. Accessed 21 Apr. 2017.

Sørensen, Georg. "Globalization and the Nation-State." *Comparative Politics.* 3rd ed., edited by Daniele Caramani. Oxford University Press, 2014, pp. 407-20.

Stavrianos, Cynthia. *The Political Uses of Motherhood in America.* Routledge, 2014.

Steady, Filomina Chioma. *Women and Leadership in West Africa: Mothering the Nation and Humanizing the State.* Palgrave Macmillian, 2011.

nhgTripp, Aili Marie, et al. *African Women's Movements: Transforming Political Landscapes.* Cambridge University Press, 2009.

Waylen, Georgina. "Women and Democratization: Conceptualizing Gender Relations in Transition Politics." *World Politics,* vol. 46, no. 3, 1994, pp. 327-54.

"WIPNET: Women in Peacebuilding (WIPNET)." *West Africa Network for Peacebuilding,* http://www.wanep.org/wanep/index.php? option=com_content&view=category&layout=blog&id=10&Itemid=20. Accessed 21 Apr. 2017.

Witter, Lisa. "Sex Strike for Peace?" *Huffington Post*, 25 May 2011, www.huffingtonpost.com/lisa-witter/sex-strike-for-peace_b_98742.html. Accessed 21 Apr. 2017.

14. Transnational Mothering and Trauma in Edwidge Danticat's *Breath, Eyes, Memory*

DORSÍA SMITH SILVA

IN THEIR PIONEERING ARTICLE "'I'm Here, but I'm There': The Meanings of Latina Transnational Motherhood," Pierrette Hondagneu-Sotelo and Ernestine Avila coin the term "transnational motherhood" to reflect the experience of mothers who live and work in different countries from those of their children (548). In examining the contexts of this migration, scholars have examined the multiple impacts of transnational mothering on mothers and their families.[1] In exploring the social, political, economic, and cultural frameworks of motherhood, questions unfold about whether the practice enables immigrant mothers to provide for the wellbeing of their children more than if they had remained in their homeland. Incorporating this standpoint from multiple standpoints, transnational mothers have greater access to financial means and, therefore, can send remittances back to their homeland. In doing so, their children often have better opportunities to receive schooling, basic goods, shelter, clothing, and medical services. At the same time, however, transnational mothers and their children may experience social and emotional hardships. Since they are geographically separated from their children, transnational mothers may worry about their children's emotional and physical care when left in the hands of family members or "othermothers."[2] As Melanie Nicholson states in her study on transnational migrant women, "transnational mothers are living a particularly difficult form of shared mothering, a form dictated by their arduous journeys, their long separations from their children, and their relegation to the lowest rungs of the economic and social ladder" (14). In addition, they may experience guilt that they had to leave their children behind and feel pressure that they are mothering at a distance—a form of mothering that is complicated by the oppressive patriarchal construction that good mothers take care of their own children's emotional and physical needs. For the children of transnational mothers, tensions may arise from being separated from their mothers, particularly in regard to depriving them from "that primary maternal-child bond" (Levitt 76). Although they acknowledge the receipt of goods and opportunities from their transnational mother's hard work and sacrifice, these children often miss their mothers and may experience loss, guilt, anger, and depression.

In *The Pleasures of Exile*, George Lamming indicates that migration is "a site of both alienation and reconnection" (135). A part of this perspective—which forms the framework for examining Edwidge Danticat's novel *Breath, Eyes, Memory* (1994)—is exploring the migration of transnational mothers as encompassing several economic advantages and emotional costs. Within this context, transnational mothering demonstrates a contradictory process, especially regarding how these mothers and their children address the realities of transnational experiences and navigate the trauma within the transnational process. It is this conceptualization of trauma of transnational mothers and their children that I examine in this chapter; particularly, the emotional, social, and physical trauma of having to migrate, of mothering from across geographical boundaries, and of (re)negotiating the familial relationship when children reunite with their transnational mothers. By trauma, I refer to the emotional and/or physical pain or wound caused by conflict, tension, or friction:

> Medically, trauma refers to serious or critical bodily injury, wound, or shock. Psychologically, it refers to a direct or indirect (e.g. witnessing) experience that is sudden, perceived to be dangerous, emotionally painful distressing, or shocking. Trauma often involves physical manifestations and may result in *lasting* mental and physical effects. A parsimonious definition equates mental trauma with the persistence of disabling distress, dysfunction, or vulnerabil-

> ity after danger is over and adversity subsides. (Klingman and Cohen 17, emphasis in original)

In the context of the novel, the trauma within transnational mothering is tied to certain painful historical events in Haiti. In examining the legacy of trauma for transnational mothers and their children, I illustrate how transnational mothering incorporates the painful reality of enduring emotional burdens. Furthermore, I highlight the possibilities of empowerment for transnational mothers and their children as they regard the ways in which they can transform their distressing situations.

MIGRATION, TRAUMA, AND TRANSNATIONAL MOTHERING IN *BREATH, EYES, MEMORY*

As Ann Cvetkovich argues in her essay "Transnational Trauma," "the presence of geographical dislocation in a range of trauma histories suggests the intersections of trauma and migration" (120). Danticat explicitly ties the migration of women to the atrocities perpetuated under the Duvaliers in Haiti—a time in which Haiti had suffered widespread violence caused by the corrupt rule of its former President Francois "Papa Doc" Duvalier who won the presidency in 1957 and changed the constitution in 1964 to declare himself "president for life" (Hillman and D'Agostino 119). Upon "Papa Doc's" death in 1971, Jean Claude "Baby Doc" Duvalier used the threatening volunteer policemen known as the Tonton Macoutes to maintain his hold on power:

> This militia ... was ruthlessly used to smother dissent and terrorize and murder opponents. The Tonton Macoutes were granted automatic amnesty through Duvalier's powers for any crime they committed. The name Tonton Macoute (literally translated as "Uncle Gunnysack") originated from Haitian Creole folklore. It was the name of the bogeyman that walked the streets after dark kidnapping children who stayed out too late and stowing them away in his burlap sack never to be seen again. Similar to the climate of Stalinist Russia, those who dared to speak out against

> Duvalier would disappear at night and risked their own abduction. (Perper and Cina 129)

"Baby Doc's" damaging legacy continued until he was exiled to France in 1986. According to John Scanlon and Gilbert Loescher, legal and illegal migration from Haiti to the United States increased significantly with the rise of power of the Duvaliers ("Papa Doc" and "Baby Doc"). According to some estimates, as many as 300,000 Haitians migrated illegally in the 1980s to escape the repression and poverty of Haiti (Perper and Cina 313). Danticat explores in the text how Haitians—especially the women who were raped by the Tonton Macoutes—were frequently haunted by rampant political violence and abusive acts. Their migration becomes linked to wanting to physically and psychologically distance themselves from the terror of dictators and the concrete experiences of rape; typical reactions to the trauma spiral into feelings of pain, violation, fear, and loss. Their efforts to escape from these horrors force them to migrate in search of spaces where the political and personal body may find some safety and heal.

Breath, Eyes, Memory tells the story of the twelve-year-old Sophie Caco, who lives in the impoverished countryside in Haiti. Although she enjoys her caring and friendly neighbours, Sophie must also endure the harshness of living in a village stricken by poverty, brutality, and illiteracy. In particular, many of the villagers are uneducated and are forced to work in the rough cane fields to earn a meagre living. In order for Sophie to acquire a "solid" education and be free from the violence and oppression entrenched in Haiti, her Tante Atie and her Grandmè Ifé agree to send her to live with her mother in New York. Even though she has been told that "in this country, there are many good reasons for mothers to abandon their children" (20) and she would like to see her mother, Sophie fears the idea of permanently living with her. She says, "Besides the care packages and letters, I only knew my mother from the picture on the night table by Tante Atie's pillow. She waved from inside the frame with a wide grin on her face and a large flower in her hair" (8). And when she tries to give her Aunt a handmade Mother's Day card, Sophie is surprised that her Aunt insists that she give it to her "biological" mother. She tells her, "When it is Aunt's Day, you can make me one" (9). Her Aunt also tries to reassure Sophie that living with her mother in New York will be "the best thing that is ever going to happen to [her]" (14) and they "have no right to be sad" (17) because her mother is sending for her.

Sociologists Marjorie Faulstich Orellana et al. invoke the complex set of changes in the family that are interwoven into the transnational experience. In addition, they state that this process leaves transnational children vulnerable to the shifting negotiations of familial roles and responsibilities: "leaving children behind frames children as dependents. Their care depends on the willingness of kin to provide for them and on the financial support that families are able to send back" (580). Thus, the children of transnational mothers usually depend on the care of extended relatives or women in the community that are known are "othermothers." In *Breath, Eyes, Memory*, Sophie's birth mother Martine leaves Haiti for New York soon after she is born. Leaving her in the care of Tante Atie, Martine mainly becomes known to Sophie through the remittances and recorded tapes that she sends and her photograph. Consequently, in addition to having a physical and emotional separation with her mother, Sophie recognizes Tante Atie as her caregiver and othermother and has little desire to be reunited with her mother. This deep attachment to the othermother, according to researcher Umut Erel, is fairly typical, since children see their othermother as the primary caregiver (126). In this context, Sophie's hesitation to be reunited with Martine is tied to her losing the only maternal figure that she knows and represents the unraveling of her mother-daughter dyad with Tante Atie.

As previously stated, the loving mother-child relationship between Tante Atie and Sophie is illustrated at the beginning of the novel when Sophie makes a Mother's Day card for Tante Atie. Navigating through the multiple meaning of being Sophie's "othermother," Atie repeats to Sophie that the card is "for a mother, your mother" (Danticat 9). These words are perhaps shocking to Sophie, since she has given a Mother's Day card to her aunt every year, and she views her aunt as her maternal figure. Within their relationship, Tante Atie's conflicting emotions reflect the complexity of her role. Although she accepts Sophie as her child, telling her years later, "You were my child (173)," Tantie Atie nevertheless reinforces the strict biological motherhood construction that she is not Sophie's real mother because she did not give birth to her. In doing so, she necessitates the emotional and physical separation of Sophie from her and advocates for a reintegration of Sophie as being Martine's daughter. Nevertheless, Sophie finds it difficult to embrace these abrupt changes. In an attempt to reinforce their relationship, she folds the Mother's Day card under Tantie Atie's pillow while she sleeps (17).

The process of Sophie joining her mother is further complicated by the escalating violence in Haiti. Although she protests leaving her aunt, Sophie realizes that Tante Atie has a clear understanding of the deep-seated dangers of living in Haiti. From a realistic standpoint, she acknowledges that she should go to New York and live with her mother on her way to the airport. There she witnesses soldiers shooting students who are protesting against the government: "Some of the students fell and rolled down the hill. They screamed at the soldiers that they were once again betraying the people. One girl rushed down the hill and grabbed one of the soldiers by the arm. He raised his pistol and pounded it on top of her head. She fell to the ground, her face covered with her own blood" (34). As one character mentions, "There is always some trouble here [in Haiti]" (33). This significant "push factor," as pointed out by Javiera Cienfuegos Illanes, is one of the reasons for women to migrate (205). In regard to Sophie's migration, the matter becomes more complex as she must reconcile her construction of motherhood with her estrangement from Martine: "Welcome to New York, this face seemed to be saying. Accept your new life. I greeted the challenge, like one greets a new day. As my mother's daughter and Tante Atie's child" (49). For Sophie, her journey becomes interwoven with the heavily accentuated burden of reestablishing this mother-daughter relationship—a challenging process that must be understood in the context of her confrontation of the traumas of transnational migration.

Danticat links Sophie's escape from Haiti's social, political, and economic unrest to her mother's migration to New York—a migration linked to a violent history and emotional trauma. Martine left Haiti after being raped by an unknown man, likely a member of the Tonton Macoutes. Fearing that "he [the rapist] would creep out of the night and kill her in her sleep" (139), Martine migrated to New York after giving birth to Sophie. While in New York, Martine feels safe and has the financial means to provide for her daughter and family back in Haiti. Yet the psychological trauma Martine endured in Haiti resurfaces when she reconnects with Sophie in New York. Reconnected, Martine sees Sophie's physical resemblance to her rapist father for the first time, and she maps Sophie as a physical and emotional reminder of the violence and shame of having a child out of wedlock. She says: "But now when I look at your face I think it is true what they say. A child out of wedlock always looks like its father" (61). She also begins to envision "the rapist everywhere" (199) and to suffer from nightmares, which Sophie often witnesses. Sophie says, "I would hear her [Martine] screaming for someone to leave her alone. I would run over and shake her as she thrashed about" (81). As she begins to emotionally withdraw from Sophie, Martine realizes that this promise of a better life in the United States also comes with the memory of violence and trauma. To further contextualize the understanding of the emotional toils transnational mothers like Martine unavoidably encounter, Sarah Horton argues that they frequently have "long-standing legacies of hurt, mistrust and trauma" (25) and "suffer from *nervios* [anxiety] and other somatic symptoms due to the structural violence of poverty and trauma, compounded by long-standing conditions of political violence" (27). Furthermore, she contends that "transnational separations strain the bond between mother and child, as mothers' relative immobility reverberates throughout a family stretched across borders" (31).

The tensions and emotional divide between Sophie and her mother also manifest when Sophie starts to have nightmares and becomes fixated with the identification of her father and her mother's rape:

> My father might have been a Macoute. He was a stranger who, when my mother was sixteen years old, grabbed her on the way back from school. He dragged her into the cane fields, pinned her down on the ground. He had a black bandanna over his face so she never saw anything but his

> hair, which was the color of eggplants. He kept pounding her until she was too stunned to make a sound. When he was done, he made her keep her face in the dirt, threatening to shoot her if she looked up. (139)

The scars soon transfer onto Sophie, and her nightmares mirror Martine's; they become dreams "about the same thing: a man with no face, pounding a life into a helpless young girl" (193). They undergo this mental anguish because of the oppressive treatment of women by the Tonton Macoutes: "When they [the Macoutes] entered a house, they asked to be fed, demanded the woman of the house, and forced her into her own bedroom. Then all you heard was screams until it was her daughter's turn. If a mother refused, they would make her sleep with her son and brother or even her own father" (139). According to Donette A. Francis in "'Silences Too Horrific to Disturb,'" the Tonton Macoutes used rape as a "notorious method of maintaining their power" and wielding terror among Haitians (80). Rape survivors feared further retaliation from the Tonton Macoutes, and the remaining targets worried about their potential subjection to sexual violations. Hence, the unreported sexual assaults remained "invisible," and Duvalier's regime used these unspoken stories to quell any future narratives of rape and sexual misconduct by the Tonton Macoutes. As they recognize that they cannot escape the painful memories associated with their experiences in Haiti, Martine and Sophie understand the paradox of their transnational journeys; they have greater access to more resources and financial means, but the lingering memories of the heightened violence against women in Haiti coupled with the emotional grief of Martine's separation from Sophie take a major toll on their identities and relationships. The weight of which, Horton finds, has the ability to reverberate through their "worlds reshaped by trauma" (28).

Despite the numerous adversities, transnational mothers like Martine migrate to escape acts of violence and provide financially for their families. In an attempt to comprehend the distressing demands Martine faced as a transnational mother, Sophie recognizes that her mother's emotional trauma from her unpunished rape bears a similarity to the power of the Tonton Macoutes in fairy tales. In children's stories, Sophie recalls, "the Tonton Macoute was a bogeyman, a scarecrow with human flesh. He wore denim overalls and ... always had scraps of naughty children, whom he dismembered to eat as snacks" (138). Children hide from the mythological bogeymen because they are told, "If you don't respect your elders, then the Tonton Macoute will take you away" (138). Like the children in the fairy tales, women flee when they see the dangerous Tonton Macoutes. They know that the Macoutes can sexually abuse women and then use their authority to keep these acts hidden. Furthermore, they use their control to intimidate women into leaving Haiti. The end result is a society where transnational mothers exist out of the basic necessity of survival. For these mothers, they are forced to flee their homelands because their current realities bring considerable peril. Moreover, they must also abandon the Haitian government, especially since it refuses to address the sexual violence committed against women and dismisses women's tales of mistreatment as unreal. In "Challenging Violence: Haitian Women Unite Women's Rights and Human Rights," literary scholar and critic Anne Fuller also blames the Tonton Macoutes' acts of violence on the lack of rights and protections women have under Haitian law. In particular, she states that "rape was never defined in the law, but was classified as among crimes against morals" (41). Moreover, "medical certificates were required to prove rape and were difficult to impossible for most women to obtain" (41). With laws that discouraged and encumbered the reporting of rapes, women became again subjected to a framework that supported their cruel and unequal treatment. In an attempt to succeed not only economically but with their rights intact, Haitian transnational mothers consider the dimensions of migration to address the importance of preserving their psyche, valorizing their identities and bodies, and upholding their equality of political, social, and economic treatment.

Martine's inability to convey her experience of sexual violence leads to more psychological trauma. Because Haitian culture dictates that a raped woman loses her purity and opportunity to marry a respectable man, Martine obsesses that Sophie will have what the Tonton Macoutes stole from her—chastity and a marriage to a successful man. As Carolle Charles mentions in "Gender and Politics in Contemporary Haiti: The Duvalierist State, Transnationalism, and the Emergence of a New Feminism (1980-1990)," for "most women cross culturally, in Haiti, marriage often determines or solidifies a woman's class position and not exceptionally, the majority of elite Haitian women gain or maintain their class position through marriage" (142). In order to ensure Sophie's purity and respectability for marriage, Martine performs "tests" to check for an unbroken hymen.[3] During this test, a mother inserts a finger into her daughter's vagina to see if her hymen is still intact. She explains to Sophie that "a mother is supposed to do that to her daughter until the daughter is married. It is her responsibility to keep her pure" (61). Testing is a process that has been passed down through generations of women. Martine's mother tested both her and Atie, and when Sophie becomes interested in an older man, Joseph, the tradition is passed to her. According to Myriam Chancy, testing in Haiti is "born out of necessity and out of the legacy of African social formations" (127). Clare Counihan further adds that "the logic of testing provides a fiction in which women exert a degree of sexual agency: by remaining within the boundaries of sexual propriety testing defines, women can (supposedly) forestall imminent rape" (40). In the end, it reinforces the trauma of transnational mothers and their children. In New York, Martine reinvents "testing" to protect and deter Sophie from what she knows to be the "dangers of men" and to ensure that she have a chance at social mobility through marriage if she stays a virgin. Hence, from Martine's perspective mothers test their daughters in hope of providing them with a better life. For Sophie, the tests are an attempt to control her sexuality and a violation of her body, which mimic the effects of rape: "I closed my eyes upon the images of my mother slipping her hand under the sheets and poking her pinky at a void, hoping that it would go no further than the length of her fingernail" (155). The "testing" symbolically transfers all the differentiated affects her mother experienced during and after her rape—anger, fear, frustration, and shame—to Sophie in a continuous archive of trauma.

To cope with the testing, Sophie learns to "double" by disconnecting her mind from her body and thinking of "pleasant things" (155). Her dissociative episodes give her "a means of mental escape at the moment when no other escape is possible" (Herman 239) and a strategy of denying her sexual victimization at the hands of her mother. In an attempt to regain control over her body and end the weekly tests, Sophie decides to take a pestle and force it into her vaginal area to break her hymen: "My flesh ripped apart as I pressed the pestle into it. I could see the blood slowly dripping onto the bed sheet ... [I] took the pestle and the bloody sheet and stuffed them into a bag. It was gone, the veil that always held my mother's finger back every time she tested me" (88). Sophie succeeds in failing the next chastity test, but she is forced by Martine to leave the household: "My mother grabbed me by the hand and pulled me off the bed. She was calm now, resigned to her anger. 'Go,' she said with tears running down her face. She seized my books and clothes and threw them at me. 'You go to him and see what he can do for you'" (188). Although she seeks solace in a hasty marriage to her boyfriend, Sophie still ensures a framework of trauma. In particular, her memories of sexual abuse plague her marriage and generate negative associations of her body image and sexual contact. Like Martine, she is silenced into denying the history of sexual violations and overlooking her abusers.

Sophie and Martine's relationship also becomes strained when Sophie realizes that Haitians face daily ridicule in New York. While attending a French-English bilingual school where most of the instruction is in French, she fears interacting with the other students because of the stories she hears:

> A lot of other mothers from the nursing home where she [Martine] worked had told her that their children were getting into fights in school because they were accused of having HBO—Haitian Body Odor. Many of the American kids even accused Haitians of having AIDS because they had heard on television that only the 'four Hs' got AIDS—Heroin addicts, Hemophiliacs, Homosexuals, and Haitians. (51)

Even outside of the school, Sophie faces ridicule for being a Haitian. She says, "We were 'the Frenchies' ... called ... 'boat people' and 'stinking Haitians'" (66). According to Richard S. Hillman and Thomas J. D'Agostino, there is "a strong anti-Haitian social stigma" in the United States (232). Because of this viewpoint, Sophie is subjected to stereotyping and classified as "unacceptable ... what does not [belong] ... the 'Other'" and pushed "into symbolic exile [as a member of] 'the Others'" (Hall 258). By having her ethnicity negatively portrayed as "a nasty West Indian" (67), Sophie is alienated in a space separated from Haiti and the terrain of extended family. These racial incidents cause her to question her life with her mother and whether life as an outsider—away from her homeland and extended family—is worth this promise of a better existence in the United States and the emotional cost of being a transnational family.

In her article "Voices of Hope: Hearing and Caring for Haitian Adolescents," Jessie M. Colin explains the psychological effects of Haitian adolescents migrating to the United States. She states these adolescents face various forms of discrimination and are at risk of social isolation:

> Haitian adolescents are unique as a cultural group because they are Black, and they come from the only Caribbean island where Creole is spoken by all its citizens (the other main language is French), which does not help in communicating with Americans. Their inability to communicate in English, as is the norm in the United States, accentuates the adolescents' difficulties and increases their feeling of loss of identity ... they are not welcomed by their host country like other immigrant groups ... Because of the primacy of race in American society, Haitians generally are faced with fewer options in the determination of their identity. They are automatically classified as Black without regard to their ethnicity and cultural background. (188)

Colin also comments that some Haitian adolescents feel pressure to repress their ethnic identity or go to the extent of claiming another ethnic identity, such as Bahamian. With the great degree of prejudice against Haitians, these immigrants like Sophie experience trauma and cultural isolation when trying to adapt to life in the United States. Compounded with these multiple oppressions, they present a nuanced picture of the often paradoxical transnational experience.

Although the trauma Martine and Sophie suffer is generational, it is not a part of the cycle regarding how Sophie raises her own daughter, Brigitte. In fact, Sophie is determined that Brigitte never cross the boundary of trauma associated with separation and geographical displacement: "It was up to me to make sure that my daughter never slept with ghosts, never lived with nightmares, and never had her name burnt in the flames" (203). This desire to protect Brigitte also recentres Sophie's maternal obligation, as her duty replaces the preservation of Brigitte's chastity through testing with the development of Brigitte's self-identity, autonomy, and liberation. Thus, Sophie ends the trap of trauma and victimization with the powerful and fundamental understanding that her daughter will not suffer in the future and become a reproduced extension of the painful transnational experience.

Toward the end of the novel, Danticat returns to the messages about the circulation of trauma in Martine's life. Eventually, Martine's mental state unravels to the point that she commits suicide in the family's bathroom by stabbing herself in the stomach when she learns that she is pregnant, as the pregnancy causes her to imagine her child as her tormentor: "Everywhere I go, I hear it. I hear him [the unborn child] saying things to me.... He calls me a filthy whore.... This child, I will never look into its face" (217). Sophie understands her mother's trauma by piecing together her story. As she recognizes that her mother's custom of testing is embedded in safeguarding Sophie's purity and adherence to maternal obligation, Sophie reveals her mother's pain of being a victim of the testing, losing her virginity, and being raped: "'I did it,' she [Martine] said, 'because my mother had done it to me. I have no greater excuse. I realize standing here that the two greatest pains of my life are very much related. The one good thing about being raped was that it made the testing stop. The testing and the rape. I live both every day'" (170). Through the interrogation of her relationship with Martine, Sophie also stresses how the trauma of transnational migration continuously haunted her mother. As a transnational mother who had migrated from the silence of violence and shame, Martine could only relieve such tensions by inflicting harm to her own and to Sophie's mind and body: erasing their sexuality and harming and even at times destroying their physical selves. This ritual, according to Sophie, must never be repeated. In order for her to overcome the compounded traumas associated with migration, Sophie returns to Haiti to face a "place where nightmares are passed on through generation like heirlooms" (234) and goes to the cane field where Martine was raped. Her grandmother and aunt watch her catharsis in the field and acknowledge Sophie's liberation from the psychological trauma of sexual violence and migration. They both call out, "'*Ou libéré'*—Are you free?" (234). Before Sophie can answer their question, her grandmother puts her fingers over Sophie's lips and tells her, "Now, you will know how to answer," meaning that Sophie can voice her pain and refigure Haiti as departure and homeland, while recreating her transnational experience as a site of healing (234).

CONCLUSION

Breath, Eyes, Memory explores the painful journey of transnational families. These narratives of grief are magnified by the trauma inflicted by the violence in Haiti, separation of Martine and Sophie, emotional distress when Martine and Sophie are reunited, and layers of discriminations borne by Martine and Sophie across geographical boundaries. As they shoulder these burdens, they must assuage their feelings of loss, guilt, and anxiety. In order to do this however, both Martine and Sophie must attempt to understand the trauma associated with their transnational processes. Martine's embodied distress leads to her suicide and thus she becomes a part of the continuous loop of succumbing to the multiple toils that may emerge from transnationalism. Sophie, on the other hand, dismantles the feedback cycle and offers hope of surpassing the severe emotional grief inflicted upon transnational children. In doing so, Danticat illustrates how the transnational experience can be reconfigured into a construction of agency and empowerment.

ENDNOTES

[1]These scholars include Wendy Chavkin, Jocelyn Fenton Stitt, Jane-

Maree Maher, Melanie Nicholson, R.S. Parreñas, Silvia Pedraza, Geraldine Pratt, and Esther Suurmond among others.

[2]For a discussion on "othermothers" as women who raise children that are not biologically their own, see Sharon Abbey and Andrea O'Reilly, Simone A. James Alexander, Susan E. Chase and Mary F. Rogers, and Patricia Hill Collins.

[3]For a discussion on testing in *Breath, Eyes, Memory*, see Brooks Bouson and Cooke.

WORKS CITED

Abbey, Sharon, and Andrea O'Reilly, editors. *Redefining Motherhood: Changing Identities and Patterns*. Second Story, 1998.

Alexander, Simone A. James. *Mother Imagery in the Novels of Afro-Caribbean Women*. University of Missouri Press, 2001.

Brooks Bouson, J. *Embodied Shame: Uncovering Female Shame in Contemporary Women's Writings*. SUNY Press, 2009.

Chase, Susan E., and Mary F. Rogers. *Mothers and Children: Feminist Analyses and Personal Narratives*. Rutgers University Press, 2001.

Charles, Carolle. "Gender and Politics in Contemporary Haiti: The Duvalierist State, Transnationalism, and the Emergence of a New Feminism (1980-1990)." *Feminist Studies*, vol. 21, no.1, 1995, pp. 135-64.

Colin, Jessie M. "Voices of Hope: Hearing and Caring for Haitian Adolescents." *Journal of Holistic Nursing*, vol. 19, no. 2, 2001, pp. 187-211.

Collins, Patricia Hill. *Black Feminist Thought: Knowledge, Consciousness, and the Politics of Empowerment*. Routledge. 1991.

Cooke, Jennifer, editor. *Scenes of Intimacy: Reading, Writing and Theorizing Contemporary Literature*. Bloomsbury, 2013.

Counihan, Clare. "Desiring Diaspora: 'Testing' the Boundaries of National Identity in Edwidge Danticat's *Breath, Eyes, Memory*." *Small Axe: A Caribbean Journal of Criticism*, vol. 16, no. 1,2012, pp. 36-52.

Cvetkovich, Ann. *An Archive of Feelings: Trauma, Sexuality, and Lesbian Public Cultures*. Duke University Press, 2003 .

Danticat, Edwidge. *Breath, Eyes, Memory*. Vintage, 1994.

Erel, Umut. *Migrant Women Transforming Citizenship: Life-Stories from Britain and Germany*. Routledge, 2009.

Francis, Donette A. "**Silences** Too Horrific to Disturb": Writing Sexual Histories in Edwidge Danticat's *Breath, Eyes, Memory*." *Research in African Literatures,* vol. 35, no. 2., Summer 2004, pp. 75-90.

Fuller, Anne. "Challenging Violence: Haitian Women Unite Women's Rights and Human Rights." *Association of Concerned African Scholars Bulletin*, vol. 55-56, Spring/Summer 1999, pp. 39-48.

Hall, Stuart, editor. *Representations: Cultural Representations and Signifying Practices*. Sage, 1997.

Herman, Judith. *Trauma and Recovery: The Aftermath of Violence—From Domestic Abuse to Political Terror*. Basic, 1992.

Hillman, Richard S., and Thomas J. D'Agostino, editors. *Understanding the Contemporary Caribbean*. Lynne Rienner, 2003.

Hondagneu-Sotelo, Pierrette, and Ernestine Avila. "'I'm Here, but I'm There': The Meanings of Latina Transnational Motherhood." *Gender and Society,* vol. 11, no. 5, 1997, pp. 548-571.

Horton, Sarah. "A Mother's Heart is Weighed Down with Stones: A Phenomenological Approach to the Experience of Transnational Motherhood." *Culture, Medicine & Psychiatry*, vol. 33, no. 1, 2009, pp. 21-40.

Illanes, Javier Cienfuegos. "Migrant Mothers and Divided Homes: Perceptions of Immigrant Peruvian Women about Motherhood." *Journal of Comparative Family Studies*, vol. 41, no. 2, 2010, pp. 205-24.

Klingman, Avigdor, and Esther Cohen. *School-Based Multisystemic Intercentions for Mass Trauma*. Kluwer Academic/Plenum Publishers, 2004.

Lamming, George. *The Pleasures of Exile*. University of Michigan Press, 1991.

Levitt, Peggy. *The Transnational Villagers*. University of California Press, 2001.

Maher, JaneMaree, and Wendy Chavkin, editors. *The Globalization of Motherhood: Deconsructions and Reconstructions of Biology and Care*. Routledge, 2010.

Nicholson, Melanie. "Without Their Children. Rethinking Motherhood among Transnational Migrant Women." *Social Text*, vol., 24, no. 3, 2006, pp. 13-33.

Orellana, Faulstich Marjorie, et al. "Transnational Childhoods: The Participation of Children in Processes of Family Migration." *Social Problems*, vol. 48, no. 4, 2001, pp. 572-91.

Parreñas, Rhacel Salazar. *Children of Global Migration: Transnational Families and Gendered Woes*. Stanford University Press, 2005.

Pedraza, Silvia. "Women and Migration: The Social Consequences of Gender." *Annual Review of Sociology*, vol. 17, no. 1, 1991, pp. 303-325.

Perper, Joshua A., and Stephen J. Cina. *When Doctors Kill Who, Why, and How*. Copernicus Books, 2010.

Pratt, Geraldine. *Families Apart: Migrant Mothers and the Conflicts of Labour and Love*. University of Minnesota Press, 2012.

Scanlon, John, and Gilbert Loescher. "Human Rights, U.S. Foreign Policy, and Haitian Refugees." *Journal of Interamerican Studies and World Affairs*, vol. 26, no. 3, 1984, pp. 313-56.

Stitt, Jocelyn Fenton. "Globalization and Mothering." *Encyclopedia of Motherhood*, edited by Andrea O'Reilly, Sage, 2010, pp. 457-61.

Suurmond, Esther. "Good Motherhood and the Need for a Transnational Perspective." *Journal of Social Intervention*, vol. 19, no. 4, 2010, pp. 100-111.

About the Contributors

Jessica Adams is an assistant professor of English at the University of Puerto Rico—Río Piedras. She is the author of *Wounds of Returning: Race, Memory, and Property on the Post-Slavery Plantation* (University of North Carolina Press, 2007), and co-editor of a number of volumes, including *Guantánamo and American Empire: The Humanities Respond* (Palgrave, 2016). Her fiction and creative nonfiction have appeared in a variety of journals.

Dwayne Avery is Assistant Professor and Program Director of the Communication Studies Program at Memorial University of Newfoundland. He is the author of *Unhomely Cinema: Home and Place in Global Cinema*. His research explores the "place of motherhood," especially ways in which motherhood ideologies are tied to specific geographical locations, from the domestic home to the urban apartment.

Kezia Batisai is a senior lecturer in sociology at the University of Johannesburg who holds a PhD in gender studies from the University of Cape Town. She has conducted research on gender, sexuality, migration, and health-policy recommendations. Her research gaze is also on the gendered and sexualized politics of nation building in Africa.

Roxana Cazan is an assistant professor of English at Saint Francis University, Pennsylvania. She teaches world literature and creative writing. Her scholarly articles have appeared in *Women Studies*

Quarterly and *Neophilologus*. Her poetry has been published in *Sojourn*, *The Portland Review*, *The Madison Review*, *Barnwood International*, and *Harpur Palate*.

Jocelyn O. Celero obtained her Ph.D. in International Studies at Waseda University-Graduate School of Asia-Pacific Studies in 2016. She earned her Master's degree in Global Studies at Sophia University for her thesis on Filipino mothers' transnational patterns of rearing Japanese-Filipino children in Japan. Prior to pursuing graduate studies in Japan, she earned a Master's degree in Asian Studies, majoring in Southeast Asia at the University of the Philippines-Asian Center in 2008.

Catherine Marsh Kennerley has taught Latin American Literature at the University of Puerto Rico, Río Piedras, for almost as long as she has been a mother. She is the author of *Negociaciones culturales* (2009).

Laila Malik is a Toronto-based writer, editor, researcher, and mother of two. She is a writer and editor with the Association for Women's Rights in Development, and her writing on gender, parenting, and globalization has been published on a variety of platforms, ranging from the academic to the poetic.

Gavaza Maluleke is working on Postdoctoral project at the University of Amsterdam as part of the Becoming Men: Masculinities in Urban Africa Research group researching various issues such as gendered violence and digital feminism in South Africa. Her research interests are in African studies, Feminism, Migration studies, Masculinities, Media Studies, Postcolonial studies and Rural development. She has a PhD from the Johannes Gutenburg University of Mainz.

Michelle Hughes Miller is an associate professor of women's and gender studies at the University of South Florida, USA. Her areas of research interest include legal constructions and intrusions on motherhood, and violence, victims and social justice. She has recently co-edited a volume on *Bad Mothers* for Demeter Press.

Elizabeth Cummins Muñoz is a writer and lecturer at Rice University. Her past research explores Mexican and U.S. Hispanic writers' engagement with history and gender. Her current work includes a collection of short stories and a project examining mothering identities among immigrant domestic care workers in the United States.

Abigail L. Palko is the director of the Maxine Platzer Lynn Women's Center at the University of Virginia. Her scholarship focuses on representations of mothering practices, with a particular interest in the ways Irish and Caribbean women writers negotiate new understandings of the figure of the Good Mother in their writing. Her book *Imagining Motherhood in Contemporary Irish and Caribbean Literature* is available from Palgrave Macmillan. Her work has appeared in a number of journals and Demeter Press publications.

Sucharita Sarkar is an associate professor in English at D.T.S.S College of Commerce, University of Mumbai. She is also pursuing her doctoral studies—on mothering narratives in contemporary India—at the University of Mumbai. Her research focuses on issues and intersections of gender, diaspora, media, identity, and culture studies.

Dorsía Smith Silva is an associate professor of English at the University of Puerto Rico, Río Piedras. She is the co-editor of *Caribbean without Borders: Caribbean Literature, Language and Culture* (2008), *Critical Perspectives on Caribbean Literature and Culture* (2010), and *Feminist and Critical Perspectives on Caribbean Mothering* (2013), and editor of *Latina/Chicana Mothering* (2011). She is currently co-editing *Mothers and Daughters* (2017) and *Travellin' Mama* (2018).

Aimee Tiu Wu, EdD, is an adult educator and mother of three toddlers. She earned her doctorate from Teachers College Columbia University, with specialization in adult learning and leadership through the AEGIS program, and a master's degree in TESOL from New York University.

Crystal M. Whetstone is in comparative and international politics with an emphasis on women and politics. Her dissertation explores a gender-specific form of women's political participation known as political motherhood. Whetstone is a political science PhD candidate at the University of Cincinnati. She received her MA in international and comparative politics from Wright State University.